SWEET DREAMS ARE MADE OF THIS

SWEET DREAMS ARE MADE OF THIS

A LIFE IN MUSIC

DAVE STEWART

 NEW AMERICAN LIBRARY

NEW AMERICAN LIBRARY
Published by New American Library,
an imprint of Penguin Random House LLC
375 Hudson Street, New York, New York 10014

This book is an original publication of New American Library.

First Printing, February 2016

For more information about Penguin Random House, visit penguin.com.

LIBRARY OF CONGRESS CATALOGING-IN-PUBLICATION DATA:
Names: Stewart, David A. (David Allan), 1952–
Title: Sweet dreams are made of this: a life in music/Dave Stewart.
Description: New York: New American Library, 2016.
Identifiers: LCCN 2015034916 | ISBN 9780451477682
Subjects: LCSH: Stewart, David A. (David Allan), 1952– | Rock musicians—England—Biography. | Eurythmics
(Musical group) | LCGFT: Biographies.
Classification: LCC ML410.S84 A3 2016 | DDC 782.42166092—dc23
LC record available at https://protect-us.mimecast.com/s/LL2mBEFx8G2SY

Printed in the United States of America
10 9 8 7 6 5 4 3 2 1

Designed by Laura K. Corless

Penguin
Random
House

This book is dedicated
to
ANOUSHKA

CONTENTS

FOREWORD BY MICK JAGGER

When you meet Dave Stewart and have any kind of rapport, small talk is swiftly bypassed. You are immediately thrust into an exchange of ideas, information, plans and projections. When we first met in 1983, we decided to record and write together. We also decided to buy an apartment in Paris, a house in Morocco and a loft in New York City from which we would launch a film company. And this was within a few hours of knowing each other.

Dave is an amazing enthusiast and seems to know as much about technology and business as he does recording and songwriting. He is, I suppose, some sort of creative genius, eccentric and endearing, and he has more e-mails in his in-box than anyone on the planet. He has also, on occasion, been spotted wearing a very long yellow overcoat and carrying a sword.

Dave does things his own way and is never one to follow rules or do things because "that's how they're done." He's created so many unique sounds and initiated musical trends because he's not afraid to try new things and experiment. And yet, even with this crazy, out-there kind of approach, he's also very disciplined. We've been longtime friends and collaborators, and he always makes me finish what I've started, which is not always what I do when I'm left on my own. In thirty years of knowing each other, we've shared a love of beautiful women, blues music, films, storytelling and the Caribbean. But what we love doing most is writing songs.

Dave and I are quite similar, both very focused and precise. We never have to explain a lot to each other about what's happening around us because we both read the temperature of the room as soon as we walk in. We also rarely stop laughing. We concentrate on very short bursts of work, and we would put down everything on old tape recorders, Pro Tools or Dictaphones or whatever recording setup we had at the time. Even though it's then improved and polished and worked on with other musicians, we often find that we like our original demo recording the best.

Dave's main criterion with all his work is that it has to be fun. There's no point getting into an angst-ridden anxiety attack over a song that's not working. Dave will simply advise you to chuck it like it never happened and then move on to the next song. On the other hand, things can lodge in the recesses of Dave's memory for years—a line, a phrase, a riff—and he will suddenly present them to you years later on some sophisticated digital device and transport you back to the exact moment you created it. Just when you think you remember things better than Dave, he will produce evidence to the contrary on film, photographs or voice memo. It's infuriating.

One of our favorite collaborations was SuperHeavy, our pop-up band, which included Joss Stone, A. R. Rahman and Damian Marley, in which we really combined many different musical styles and each of us brought our own unique sound to the table. It started with me receiving a phone call from Dave in Jamaica: "Hey, I've got a really great idea." Once we were in the studio he kept us on track during our marathon sessions, when we put down twenty-nine songs in ten days. All of the songs were composed on the spur of the moment, someone would start playing, someone would start singing, all of us completely extemporizing, and the song was recorded in one or two takes.

I love Dave's constant creative search and his passion for making music; I love the fact that he's constantly pushing the boundaries of what we think is possible. I love the support and belief he has for the people he collaborates with whether they are superstars or complete unknowns. He creates a fertile environment in which it's almost impossible not to be creative and innovative. This environment includes a compulsory martini at seven thirty in the evening, although by ten thirty, after two or three martinis, no one has gone home and everyone in the control room is dancing.

It's an honor to work with Dave and call him a friend. If you ever get a phone call and hear a low, soft voice with a northeastern English accent tell you, "Hey, I've got a great idea," take the call. It may not change your life, but it will make it much more fun.

—Mick Jagger

SWEET DREAMS ARE MADE OF THIS

INTRODUCTION

Writing songs with other people is like falling in love over and over again. It's a fast track into somebody's soul—you can feel their heart beating against yours. When I play guitar and they start to sing, even when we are just improvising, there's something else that starts to happen that no one can explain. We try to follow whatever that something is and understand what it is telling us to do. It's like when you were a child and you ran through a forest with a friend and you came across a hidden stream where you could bathe or quench your thirst—except this race is in your mind, and when words start to fall out of the improvisation, they are like fireflies lighting the way: they guide us back through the woods till we see the village in the distance. We are soon inside a safe place, a familiar place where melody lives with her best friend, rhythm. We go join them, and let our minds meld in the warm glow of creativity.

I've had the chance to experience this wonderful state of *being in the moment* with some of the greatest artists on the planet. To sit in a room, on a hill or in a taxi next to Mick Jagger singing as if he's onstage is overwhelming to say the least. To be in a room as small as a closet alone with Aretha Franklin as she plays the piano and cries real tears as she's singing "The Way We Were" before a recording session starts makes me wonder how I even got here. Or listening to Stevie Nicks reciting a poem about the Kennedys she wrote after a strange dream. Watching Tom Petty sit on the edge of his bed with a pen and paper and a Rickenbacker twelve-string guitar and hear his mind ticking like a time bomb as he crafts the next great anthem. Looking out my window to see Bob Dylan and George Harrison strumming guitars and laughing under a tree in my garden while immaculately dressed Bryan Ferry sits at a typewriter on my terrace in the south of France as the sun goes down. My dearest friend and closest collaborator, Annie Lennox, playing an old harmonium and singing me the most beautiful song while I sit on her bed in a tiny bedsit in Camden Town, thinking we would be together forever. These moments all seem as surreal and dreamlike to me as I'm sure they do to you. And yet these are the moments that define me. That have shaped me into the man and the musician that I am today.

I did step through the looking glass somewhere, sometime way back. My life has been an incredible series of relationships and moments. I've pushed myself in so many ways and learned so much about innovation, intuition, courage and the ability to see what others don't see.

Looking back during the writing of this book has been a lot of fun although it's sometimes difficult to remember the times that I'd rather forget. I'm not a reflective or introverted person by nature. I have a frenetic energy that propels me to engage, meet new people and push the boundaries. I've written this book to try to figure out myself how I got here or there or everywhere all at the same time. And like everything else I've done in my life and career so far, it's been a surprising, uplifting and meaningful process.

CHAPTER:1

GIRLS ARE DIFFERENT

The first thing I remember was a very large bright orange duck's beak, then a very loud quack. I hope that's not the last thing I see and hear on the way out!

I really don't remember if I saw a photo of me in a stroller, then later in life heard a duck quacking and put two and two together, or whether it was me in real time holding out bread crusts by the edge of a pond and a duck jumping up to grab it, quacking with delight. But the reader must understand a lot of the time I may not have been there, so to speak, even though I do have photos to prove it.

I was born and lived on Barnard Street, Sunderland, in the industrial northeast of England. When I was old enough I walked five days a week to Barnes Infant School; it seemed so far, though, in fairness, it was only about three streets away. But I did have to cross a main road, Cleveland Road, and I was only five years old! I remember so many red bricks you could write on with white chalk, and the smell of bubbling road tar you could poke holes in, which was so visceral and pleasing that I still miss it today.

When I think back I never can visualize it being cold or raining, which is insane, as Sunderland is freezing most of the time, with wind howling in from the North Sea. In fact, most of the rain is horizontal, and I do remember my little legs feeling like they had been shot at by a thousand peashooters by the time I arrived at school.

Mostly I remember my childhood being in sunshine, and the slow walk to school was a magical experience full of adventure, delight and sheer dread. Now, Cleveland Road in 1957 must have had only one car pass along every ten minutes, but it seemed very busy to me, and judging when to cross took a lot of calculation—the trajectory of the car driving uphill through space as a function of time, the slant range and inclination angle, and me crossing horizontally with one eye on the candy store and one on the car, mouth watering and dreaming of flying saucers (sherbet-filled wafers) and Spanish gold (sweet tobacco).

These were tough decisions even back then—how could I hold back from temptation when danger was approaching? So, unbeknownst to my parents, I nearly got flattened on a number of occasions and just made it to the sweet shop by the skin of my teeth!

I didn't know it at the time, but the teenage population was gripped by hysteria when Bill Haley and His Comets arrived from America. Skiffle was all the rage then, a kind of bluesy folk music played mostly on homemade instruments. It was the first Do It Yourself boom, as we call home improvement in England. Tommy Steele was our first teenage rock star. Joan Collins was a starlet. Elvis was just about to join the US Army and the British prime minister Anthony Eden resigned over the Suez crisis.

At one time, Sunderland was one of the biggest shipbuilding towns in the world. The city motto was *"Nil Desperandum Auspice Deo."* Which, loosely translated, means, "Never Despair, Trust in God," and my dad, John James Stewart, or Jack as everyone would call him, had that never-give-up mentality. In fact, he wasn't a religious man, but he was a very moral person and hated any sort of injustice.

My father came from the backstreets, from a working-class family. He and his brother, Dick, loved football with a passion, as did I. When they were kids, they would run around barefoot on the cobblestone streets, playing all day long. But footballs were far too expensive to buy, so they used to make one from a pig's bladder they would get at the butcher shop. They would blow it up like a balloon, tie it off and, when it dried, they would have something like a misshapen football.

My dad was an errand boy for a small accounting firm called Alan J. Gray and Son. Any job was hard to get back then, especially if you had little money, because you had to have the right clothes and a proper pair of shoes. His father saved money for about three years to buy my dad a bicycle so he could ride to work and back, but on his very first day of work, somebody stole it. He walked all the way home, crying, knowing how much his dad had worked and saved to get him that bicycle. When World War II broke out, my dad enlisted as a wireless operator in the Royal Air Force. His job was to send Morse code from the back of the plane in the air or on the ground. Morse code was vital during the war and extensively used by warplanes, especially by long-range patrol planes that were sent out to scout for enemy warships, and cargo and troop ships. Years later he built a Morse code tablet in the garage at our home, and I remember him showing my brother, John, and me how to use it and how to decipher a message.

My mom, Sadie, was born to a family of capable, headstrong women, including her twin sister, Louise; elder sister, Emily; and younger sister, Eleanor. My mom's dad died when she was only nine, and my grandmother had to look after four girls on her own, while running a pub called the Travellers Rest in Sunderland.

Mom went to work for the same firm where my dad worked. The owner encouraged the office girls to write to the boys abroad in the army or the RAF to cheer them up during their long stints away from home, so my parents started writing while my dad was stationed in India for four years.

When you're a boy growing up, you look up to your father. Jack was a perfect father figure, all man yet with a gentle side. I've met a lot of great people over the years, but very few who measured up to my dad.

Seaburn was Jack's favorite place on Earth. It is a breathtaking beach in Sunderland and it holds so many memories for me too. One special spot is called the Cat and Dog Steps. I'm not sure how it got its name; one theory is when the sea is really rough, it pounds against the seawall and it rains down on you like cats and dogs.

Sometimes we'd go to Notarianni's Ice Cream Parlour, where I would get a cornet with two scoops of real Italian homemade ice cream and a Cadbury Flake stuck in it. Magical! As I licked this frozen masterpiece, arms and face covered with scratches and bruises from football, with muddy knees and wet shorts, walking hand in hand with my dad and still managing to dribble a ball, I was as blissed out as any kid could be.

I loved to hear my dad laugh, and he laughed at the silliest things, like an umbrella blowing inside out. He laughed even louder when it was a truly uproarious moment—like when our dog, Solo, a black Labrador (named after Napoleon Solo from *The Man from U.N.C.L.E.*), decided to stand up from under my mom's legs, while she was in the front passenger seat of our car, as we stopped at a traffic light. Pedestrians stood with their mouths open, arms crossed, staring at our tiny Morris Minor car with my mum's feet on the dashboard, her dress and slip up to her waist and her bloomers on show. For an encore Solo stuck his head out from between her legs!

My father's hobby was carpentry; he made a workshop in the shed out back. This was where he made most of the furniture in our house. Everything we slept on, sat on and ate on was made in that tiny shed. I, however, was banned not once but twice from the shed. Once for setting fire to the wood shavings and nearly burning the place down, and the second time for almost killing the cat by getting its fur tangled up in Dad's electric drill.

One time my dad spent months and months working on something, and he wouldn't say what it was. I had noticed him on a ladder in the living room and the kitchen with small wooden boxes and wires, but I wasn't exactly sure what was happening. It was a closely guarded secret, and many months elapsed before we found out what he was working on.

On the day he was done, the house exploded with MUSIC—"Oh, What a Beautiful Mornin'," "I Whistle a Happy Tune," and songs from *South Pacific* like "There Is Nothing like a Dame" and "Bloody Mary." Show tunes. He had built a sound system for the house! He must have saved up and bought every Rodgers and Hammerstein musical sound track album he could find just for this moment.

From then on, every morning we would hear *South Pacific* and *The King and I, Oklahoma!, Flower Drum Song*, et cetera. Sides A and B of these amazing vinyl albums, playing one after the other, until I knew every song off each one by heart.

The neighbors would watch six-year-old Dave walking down those redbrick tar-bubble streets singing "There Is Nothing like a Dame" at the top of his lungs. Years later, even at the height of pop stardom, I'd catch myself in the shower or at an airport bursting into "Getting to Know You" from *The King and I* or "I Enjoy Being a Girl" from *Flower Drum Song*!

My father had a great voice and was always singing around the house to Perry Como, Nat King Cole and Frank Sinatra, the real crooners. Something very touching happened when he was about seventy—he admitted to me for the first time he had actually always wanted to be a singer. His love for music must have had an influence on me even if I didn't know it at the time.

I was surprised to learn that my dad harbored this secret desire, but in fact he was a multifaceted guy. He was surprisingly ahead of the health food craze. When he was posted to India during the Second World War, not only did he learn yoga, but he also became extremely interested in nutrition. So, after the war, in a place and time where the staple diet was pies and peas, fish and chips, canned vegetables,

Swiss rolls and Jaffa cakes, all washed down with fizzy drinks and beer, he was eating brown rice, yogurt, grains and nuts. In Sunderland! He was immensely proud that his weight, and waistline, stayed the same for sixty years.

My parents were born within a few miles of each other, but, as mentioned, they became friends by writing to each other during the war. My mom's twin sister, Louise, also had a pen pal in the services, and when the men came home, it was decided there would be a double wedding, fit for twins. All four of them were married on the same day and in the same church, and they lived together in the same house.

This, of course, was big news in the local newspaper, the *Sunderland Echo*. It's bizarre. The more I look back at my family's history, the more everything seems slightly odd or weird or strange.

In 1962, my father paid about four thousand pounds (a fortune in those days) for a larger house in Ettrick Grove. I always thought Grove sounded much posher than Street. The school I was about to attend was at the back of the house; the front of the house was attached to a row of shops that included an excellent chippy (fish-and-chip shop), a baker and pie shop, a chemist and a newsagent, which my grandmother owned.

Compared to what I was used to, this was a metropolis. I was always hyperactive, but now with all this stimulation around, I went into overdrive. I was so busy wanting to do everything at once, climbing trees (this house had a garden with beautiful apple trees) and looking for birds' nests in Barnes Park. One time, I found a little nest with tiny birds in it that I thought had been abandoned by the mother. I knocked on the kitchen window, my mum opened it, and I just pushed these helpless chicks and the nest in to my mum, who was at the sink washing up.

I shouted, "Worms three times a day!" and ran off.

My mom had to cope with all my eccentricities and obsessions, which could be anything from polishing old pennies to learning to pole vault, which I actually chose as a sport at school. I became so obsessed with it that I would use a giant eight-foot-long bamboo pole (from a carpet shop) to practice at home. I was also fencing imaginary foes with a homemade foil one minute, or trying to write Zorro on the wall with chalk on the tip of my sword, or orchestrating large-scale battle scenes between pirate figures and plastic knights in armor that came free with breakfast cereal.

I took everything deadly seriously, as if it was the only thing that mattered; yet there were maybe twenty different self-assigned tasks happening all in a day.

My dad had played football, and we were raised with the game. Although average in height, he was a big man in my mind, and he knew all about football, attending almost every game our home team, Sunderland A.F.C., played. My dad's brother, Dick, worked for Sunderland at the ticket gate on the turnstile, and that's how my dad always had a ticket to the match. It's like having season tickets to see the Lakers. And he took me many times when I was very young, and I absolutely loved it. Nothing compared to the excitement of that football ground until the first time Eurythmics played a stadium and we heard that same roar of approbation.

I wanted to impress my dad by being a good footballer too. He encouraged me to play, and he soon became just as passionate about my games as he was about the pros. He'd get all excited and animated if we scored or won, or he'd get equally frustrated if we were losing or missed an opportunity, shouting from the sides, "It's an open goal!"

I had so much energy, I didn't know how to contain it, and neither did my parents or anyone around. The only thing that would calm me down was football. I would be so manic that I'd play football for eight hours straight. Football helped me focus, and soon nothing was more important. Everything else faded into the background, like slowly turning the macro lens on a camera and suddenly Jiminy Cricket is standing there, crystal clear, and he taps on the lens with his umbrella handle and says, "You, my son, are a footballer!" From that moment on, it was all I cared about. I was just mad for it. I knew that one day I would play for Sunderland; it was only a matter of time.

I wasn't the only kid who was mad about football, of course. This was the northeast of England. Every kid was football mad. We loved watching it, playing it, talking about it, thinking about it. It was my first and only true passion before music took over. But that wasn't for two or three more years. Everybody played football in the street. You would open your door and make sure there was no car coming to knock you down, and then we were off banging balls against walls, and dribbling around lampposts, and in our ears, we heard the sound of sixty thousand rabid fans. It was good fun and it felt good, too. There was fresh air, no pollution, and we'd run around playing football until we were absolutely knackered. I never had any trouble falling asleep. I'd be so exhausted, I'd fall asleep with half my clothes on. I went to sleep with my football boots on the end of my bed so I could look at them as I dozed off.

When we played a real game on a real pitch, I would carry my boots home, looped around my neck on their long laces, scrape the mud off and then give them a good coating of Kiwi black boot polish—potent stuff. I'd sit in our kitchen, hunched over those boots, polishing them compulsively. On reflection I think it might have been the very first time I got high.

Football in England is always musical. Unlike sporting events in America, the crowds sing through the whole game—team songs and chants, hysterically funny as well as extremely offensive. Sometimes they sing pop or rock songs like "We Are the Champions" and "Start Me Up." During the 1966 World Cup final (when England beat West Germany), the England fans sang "Sunny Afternoon" by the Kinks, which was the current number one. And today it's a blast to hear a crowd of raucous voices singing "Sweet Dreams (Are Made of This)."

My first hero was not Superman or 007 or Steve McQueen; it was a slender Irish footballer called George Best, who became as famous as any sixties pop icon and who was photographed as frequently as any McCartney, Jagger, Shrimpton or Twiggy. He was the equivalent of gridiron legend Joe Namath. George was cut from the same cloth—he caroused, he drank and he bedded beautiful women and owned a nightclub called Slack Alice—but when he went on the field, he was brilliant and fearless.

As a preadolescent I started to get other interests besides kicking the ball in a street, or watching professionals at Roker Park or on television. But there didn't seem to be much culture readily available in Sunderland and the surrounding area. At that time you had to go looking for it. There were hardly any theater, art exhibitions or music going on. The one main theater, the Sunderland Empire (which was a bastion for a music hall, showing plays and pantomimes with jugglers, singers, ventriloquists and old-school comics), had long been being replaced by packaged rock-and-roll shows, featuring singers like Dickie Pride and Vince Eager and the best of them all, Marty Wilde and Billy Fury.

By the time I was aware of pop music, the Beatles performed at Sunderland Empire on February 9, 1963. They were on the bottom of the bill of the Helen Shapiro tour. I knew about it because my brother, John, came home from the show, saying he was practically deaf from the girls screaming at John, Paul, George and Ringo.

Despite their prominent role in my life later, both personally and professionally, I had no interest in girls to this point, although I did get strangely aroused when I first saw Emma Peel in a black leather catsuit on the television series *The Avengers*. To be honest, I've had a thing about black leather catsuits ever since.

Now the Sunderland Empire was beginning to sound like a very magical place. My brother, John, who was older than me, couldn't wait to tell me about the Beatles, which was probably the first time in my young life that he wanted to tell me anything. It was understandable. My brother and his friends were four years older than me; they talked about girls, smoked cigarettes and wore long trousers. John just found me to be a nuisance and was always trying to get rid of me—tying me to the rugby post in the school field and, on many occasions, jumping on a moving bus, leaving me crying on the pavement. The most extreme thing he did was lock me in a rabbit hutch in our yard for five hours, with the rabbit. My parents had no idea and sent for the police.

John and I started to fight more and more. It got pretty bad, and one time I hid behind the kitchen door with a huge carving knife, waiting for him to come home from school. When he sauntered in the kitchen, I leapt out from behind the door with the knife at his throat, spun him around and held him up against the wall and said, "If you're ever mean to me again, I will fucking kill you." Things got a bit better after that. He was a sweet boy really, but brothers four years apart at this particular age can be a disaster.

With John finally sharing his world of music and girls, it makes sense that this was the first time I really thought about girls myself. When I was ten or eleven years old, I went on a school trip to London, and we stayed for a week in a bed-and-breakfast place in Paddington, with about eight kids per room. Somewhere in the middle of the week, we took a boat trip on the Thames. The sun was going down, and I can remember looking at this girl, with her long hair blowing gently and the sun on her face as she smiled, looking at London go by as we floated down the Thames.

I remember thinking, *Hmmm . . . oh yeah. Girls are different.* It just sort of dawned on me then.

Not long after that, I was at the fairground on the Seaburn beachfront, and I saw the fair-haired beauty with a friend getting on the Waltzer (a terrible spinning circular seat that makes you feel a bit like the cat must have felt on the end of my dad's electric drill). I realized one of them was the same girl from the boat trip. Immediately my heart started beating, and with a dry mouth and shaky knees, I jumped in the seat with her and her friend, just as the bar came down and the thing started moving.

Suddenly this guy who looked like a young Elvis, with slicked-back black hair, tattoos and tight jeans, jumped on our Waltzer from behind, to collect our money—actually my money, as the girls seemed to ride free. He gave the girls a wink and a handsome smile, then, with one strong arm, spun our seat in the opposite direction to the whole ride.

At first I thought that was fine, as if body A exerts a force F on body B, and then body B exerts an equal and opposite force F back on body A, so in theory we'd just sit still—which we did for about two seconds (seeming like eternity) with Ray Charles's "I Can't Stop Loving You" blasting out of the PA system. I was in love for the first time.

Then Newton's third law kicked in, and we hurtled off at alarming speed, in what seemed like every direction at once. I remember smiling at this beautiful apparition, perhaps still fantasizing she was my girlfriend, then slowly gritting my teeth, realizing my brain was becoming disengaged from my body and my stomach had somehow appeared in my mouth. Without announcement a mixture of candy floss, toffee apple and what appeared to be pink goo escaped from my mouth and began floating (as if in zero gravity) slowly toward my true love's chest.

I clung to the bar in horror as she screamed a silent scream and her friend glared at me like I'd just ruined their entire plan—which was obviously to carry on flirting with the Gypsy-tattooed Elvis boy. When the thing eventually stopped, I staggered off and never looked back. This was clearly an omen for many relationships to come!

There was, however, one young girl who was completely enamored of me. She lived with her parents in the pie shop next door to us. I wasn't aware of her feelings until the day she left an ostrich egg on my front doorstep. After fifty years I still haven't worked out why or even where she got it from. I kept the egg tucked in the bottom of my bed, trying to incubate it, until my mother changed the sheets and was as startled as I had been when I discovered it in the first place.

This was the first of many peculiar approaches the girl next door made to me in the hope of capturing my attention or, presumably, my heart.

The most bizarre happened a month later, when she invited me to her house and took me through the pie shop and into the back garden, which was not the most romantic place for a first kiss, as the grass was stained with the blood and entrails of carcasses that were delivered on most days of the week.

She had something special to show me. My adolescent heart beat faster, and I thought she meant her breasts, but no, what she had was a cow's eye with a firecracker stuck in it. She smiled, put the eye on the grass, lit the firecracker with a match, stood back and put her small hand in mine. There was an explosion, and a moment later, my face was covered in goo as the cow's eye splattered all over me. It didn't stop her kissing me and whispering the immortal words, "Now do you love me?"

CHAPTER:2

MAGIC IN THE BLUES

There's an ancient monastery named in honor of St. Peter at Monkwearmouth, an area of Sunderland just north of the mouth of the river Wear. The legendary Saint Bede (aka the Venerable Bede) lived and worked there, and it's there in the year 731 that he completed the famous history text *Historia Ecclesiastica Gentis Anglorum (The Ecclesiastical History of the English People)*. For this one epic work, he became known as "the Father of English History." Our local grammar school, which I attended, was named in his honor: the Bede Grammar School for Boys.

Bede Grammar School was a very old-fashioned school when I started; it still had teachers with mortarboards and cloaks (think Harry Potter). But during the second year I was there (1964), the school system changed from the old-fashioned "selective" system to the modern "comprehensive" system, which meant it accepted kids of every kind of performance and background. This was good in some ways and bad in others. It afforded more students a good education, but we suddenly had overcrowded classes: forty or fifty kids all crammed into one room. And suddenly having kids of different backgrounds thrown together caused stress on all sides for the pupils and the teachers.

When I was ten, my grandmother gave me a delightful Christmas gift: a tiny, portable reel-to-reel, battery-operated toy tape recorder. Before I ever considered recording music, I used it to record people talking in the street, and I delighted at playing the tapes back. It was genuinely amazing to me, because in mere seconds, with this machine, I could capture reality and experience it over. I remember just being astounded by this, thinking, *Wow, just five minutes ago in the street, I heard this, and now they are talking in my room.* Of course, these days we take portable recording like this for granted. But to me it was a little miracle.

All my football dreams came to a sudden end one winter's afternoon on a muddy pitch near Seaburn. I was taking a corner kick when an opposing defender skidded along the ground and smashed his locked leg directly into my left kneecap. I hit the ground in a wave of sheer agony and was swiftly rushed off to the hospital.

I woke up after knee surgery to be told by the doctor that I would be on crutches for six months. "But don't worry, lad. You should be playing football again in a year or so." At twelve and a half years old, a year was a lifetime. I was devastated.

It wrecked me. The doctor's words swirled around until they stood up like prison bars in the front of my mind. It felt like my life had ended right then, because without football, all I had left was school. And I hated school. School terrified me because of the boys who bullied me and made my life misery from the ages of twelve to fourteen.

I was an easy target. I was a little strange, I was small, and now I had a limp. Other kids were victims too. The bullying was relentless and constant: taunting, verbal abuse, threatening phone calls, handwritten notes, excluding me, laughing about me in a group. Some kids would even slip razor blades inside of soap bars in the school bathrooms in the hope that someone would get their fingers slashed. Bullies made me afraid every day. It's something that has affected me for my whole life.

Not even weekly music lessons gave me a reprieve—in fact, quite the opposite. Music wasn't on my radar yet, and my teacher didn't help guide me into it. He always seemed angry or depressed. Instead of teaching us anything, he would put on a classical record and tell us to write what we thought it was about. That was the lesson!

During one such lesson, he noticed I was not writing, and assuming I was either bored or asleep, he picked up a brand-new red hardback hymnbook and in frustration threw it at me with such force that I ended up back in the hospital, this time getting stitches in my head. Right after the book made contact with my skull, I sat at my desk, in dazed disbelief. The teacher spun back to the blackboard, and the squeaking of the chalk created an unpleasant dissonance, that (mixed with the classical music) sounded like a horror film sound track. As he started to write "Wolfgang Amadeus, 27 January 1756," blood began trickling down my face. It was not exactly the greatest introduction to Mozart, but it made an impact I will never forget.

Sadly, he wasn't my only crazy teacher. Back then corporal punishment was still acceptable. A teacher named Mr. Jolly used to give us what he would call a "Jolly Knock," which sounds funny but was anything but. He'd drive his knuckle down really fast and hard on the top of your head. It was quite dangerous and extremely painful.

Once, Mr. Jolly took a few boys on a nature trek that included staying at his cottage on a remote stretch of the river Wear—cue horror film sound track again as the four of us followed him along the moors.

He was wearing a plastic mac against the rain, and the wind was blowing through his gray hair. We were all quite cold, wet and miserable. Mr. Jolly had a long stick in his hand and turned around with this weird, mad expression (a bit like Jack Nicholson in *The Shining*) and said, "Do you realize I could kill you all now?"

At the time, we were just too astonished to take him seriously, but looking back I realized it wasn't just a little weird; it was disturbing and frightening. "I could kill you all right now" . . . and his name was Mr. Jolly!

Or was it just me?

It seems a lack of supervision or perhaps an innate and unquestioning trust in school or local figures was common back then, unlike the more involved and wary parenting of today. When I joined the Boy Scouts, our first camping trip turned into another horror movie. When we arrived, our faces pressed against the bus window, we saw Farmer Joe for the first time. He was in the process of castrating a bull and held up his bloodstained pincers in welcome. Why we didn't all flee for the hills at that moment, I'll never know.

After setting up our tents in Joe's field, we were told we would be taking several "proficiency tests" to earn our badges, including one we had never heard of, "the hygiene badge." This test was administered by Farmer Joe himself and took place in his bathroom. We compared notes later that night in our sleeping bags and found the same thing had happened to all of us: Farmer Joe had washed all our willies and told us we had passed.

Three months later I came home from school to find two local policemen, or bobbies as we called them, talking intently to my mum. They wanted to know if I'd taken a hygiene test on the camping trip. I proudly told them, "Yes!" and that I'd passed! My mother burst into tears. Farmer Joe was soon in custody. Regrettably, as far as I know, Mr. Jolly never was.

My life wasn't all death threats and sexual misconduct. One good thing happened to me when I was in the hospital after my football injury. My brother, John, brought me a tiny Spanish guitar that belonged to my grandmother, and a leather jacket to look like a Levi's jacket I'd had specially made with money my grandmother gave me. I didn't know anything about guitars, but I was on the edge of thirteen, drowning in hospital boredom. So I picked it up and somehow, within half an hour, I realized I could play it! I didn't know any chords, but I found I could play any melody. The ability to locate the right strings and melodies was just there, instinctively. I could play.

Young nurses who heard me playing popped their heads around the door. They would stop for a listen and say, "Wow, you can play the guitar, and you have a leather jacket!" I knew I was never going to give it up.

By the time I was out of the hospital and back in the class, I was really not thinking about football anymore, because I couldn't play anyway with my injured leg. Now I was becoming obsessed with music. I had started becoming aware of fashion and music a few months earlier, but because I was so preoccupied with football, I just noticed these things out of the corner of my eye. Now they were becoming the full picture. I was listening to the radio at home and really excited by it; there was an explosion of stuff happening.

Even at my young age, in my tiny corner of the universe, I knew that (to quote Thunderclap Newman) there was *something in the air.* I turned thirteen in 1965, which was a remarkable year in many other ways: Winston Churchill died and the notorious British gangsters the Kray twins were arrested. Bob Dylan toured the UK and invented the pop video with "Subterranean Homesick Blues." The Beatles received their MBE medals, awarded by the Queen for significant achievement or outstanding service to the community. It was a groundbreaking time in music, inspired by social changes, politics and technological breakthroughs. And I'm in our kitchen with the radio on listening to the UK Top Ten countdown and can you believe what it was?

1. "I Got You Babe"—Sonny and Cher
2. "Help!"—The Beatles

3. "(I Can't Get No) Satisfaction"—The Rolling Stones
4. "All I Really Want to Do"—The Byrds
5. "A Walk in the Black Forest"—Horst Jankowski
6. "Zorba's Dance"—Marcello Minerbi
7. "Everybody's Gone to the Moon"—Jonathan King
8. "Make It Easy on Yourself"—Walker Brothers
9. "Like a Rolling Stone"—Bob Dylan
10. "See My Friends"—The Kinks

The Beatles, the Rolling Stones, the Kinks and Bob Dylan—enough to blow anyone's mind, especially a thirteen-year-old who had just picked up a guitar and started to play.

At this same time, I started to realize my brother was really interesting. In fact he was actually kind of cool. He had a great vinyl record collection, and as he was getting ready to go off to university in Liverpool, I realized this would all be mine—all those wonderful record sleeves and their magnificent artwork and liner notes (some of them took as long to read as the album did to listen to). At the same time, my cousin Ian came into play in my life and fueled my interest in this new sixties world of popular culture, music and fashion. He was eight years older than me, so already twenty-one when I was just thirteen. Continuing the weirdness that seems to be in the DNA of the Stewart family, at the age of fifteen Ian started to speak with a deliberate Memphis accent, more Elvis than Elvis, which was peculiar to hear in the northeast of England. For a kid in Sunderland to start speaking with a Memphis accent didn't go down well at all. Local kids would pick on him, taunt him, harass him. He left home at eighteen and ran off to join the United States Air Force. When he was discharged from the armed services, he moved and settled in—guess where—Memphis!

I always wondered, now that his dream was realized, if he'd reverted and gone back to speaking in a Sunderland accent. But since meeting him down in Memphis, I can guarantee that twang is thicker than ever!

Ian sent us a box, a magic box. It contained two pairs of Levi's corduroy jeans, the likes of which my brother, John, and I had never seen before. And he sent some albums, music I'd never heard: Memphis blues, Delta blues. My brother then found other similar artists like Mississippi John Hurt and one day came home with the amazing Robert Johnson album *King of the Delta Blues Singers*.

These were the records that changed my life. Even today, when I come home after a long day, I fix a drink and pick up my guitar, and my fingers just seem to automatically play the blues. Of course, as I live in a nice house in Southern California and not a tar paper shack in the Delta, I feel obliged to change the lyrics to something like "Woke up this morning, both my cars were gone." That music was also very different from the pop music we heard on the radio in Great Britain. Even the sounds of their voices were strange—the nasal notes of Robert Johnson and the whiny sound of a slide guitar.

Then my brother bought me an album for Christmas by the guitarist Stefan Grossman, *How to Play Blues Guitar*, which came with a free bottleneck slide. It looked like a wine bottle chopped off. They actually gave you instructions on how to make one, which consisted of wrapping string tightly around the neck of a bottle and pulling it back and forth until it got hot, then tapping it while putting it under cold water. It would make a clean break.

My favorite album at that time was Stefan Grossman's *Aunt Molly's Murray Farm*. I learned how to play all of side one and my favorite song was "Delia."

I would happily have lost myself in music but real life, then as always, intruded when I turned fourteen and my mother left home. I had never heard my parents arguing, never heard threats or raised voices. I was completely unaware of what was happening. She actually went through a kind of nervous breakdown and was checked into a hospital.

During this entire time, I was oblivious to the fact that my parents were breaking up. Never did they sit me down and tell me the truth. I was going through puberty during this time, and I was so confused about the world in general that I didn't catch on. Nowadays parents would explain to their children what was happening, but mine never did.

Instead, everything got really quiet. My brother was away at university, so it was just my father and me, alone.

I remember a really empty feeling then, because my dad's a quiet man and my mum was very busy. She'd be baking homemade bread, cooking meals, making art and thinking up activities for us. One day she would say, "Oh, today we're having an art competition!" And she would get everybody on the street to draw a picture or painting. She stuck them all on a wall, as if it were a gallery, and all these people were in our home looking at the artwork. She was like me in that respect. She liked to create happenings. She was fun, and it was exciting to be a part of her world.

So you can imagine when a personality like that is gone, it is a big change. Now there was just silence and sadness and of course the blues, which again was my consolation.

Years later I asked my mother why she left. She told me, "I wasn't strong enough to stay." It was a backward quote. She wanted to use her intellect more and needed to be among like-minded people interested in all of the things she had become interested in, such as literature, poetry, philosophy and all. She thought she would have gone bonkers if she stayed in Sunderland as a housewife.

My dad was very nice, a really good father and everything. All he wanted to do after the war, really, like a lot of veterans, was raise a family, work hard, get an income, get a nice little place to live, have a holiday and have nice food.

Dad was a man of few words, and just in small sentences he'd let me know what he was going through. He said, "I don't understand what's happening." It was like the rug had been pulled out from under his feet and he was just completely baffled.

Maybe he thought it would wear off and she was going to come back. But it didn't, and she never came back. The truth was, she felt stifled and suffocated, or maybe she was becoming increasingly aware of the social transformation and the seismic cultural shifts that were taking place in the sixties. My dad and people like him were rooted in the fifties and its clothes, its conformity and class boundaries. It's obvious to me in later years that what my mother was doing was breaking those boundaries. Her horizons tripled and quadrupled.

In the end she became a teacher for children with special needs, such as autism. She loved teaching these kids with a real passion. She was a free spirit, an original and, to the children she taught, an inspiration.

When my mother left, my father threw himself into his work as an accountant. He was still a loving father, but he had no idea how to look after me, discipline me or even talk to me, and with my brother, John, away at university, I became increasingly independent and wayward.

In a way, it made me very resilient. I realized then that you've got to do things in life yourself.

Now that I was playing guitar, I was channeling even more of my feelings and energy into music. It's an amazing thing when you're on your own to be able to play an instrument; it provides solace. The bedroom isn't lonely when it becomes a place where the imagination soars. My bedroom was a stage, a TV show, a recording studio. Anything I wanted it to be. I stood with my guitar and looked in the mirror, and I could visualize myself as the next big folksinger.

What's interesting is that I didn't picture myself in a group; I saw myself as a troubadour, a Leonard Cohen, Ralph McTell, Donovan, Bob Dylan. And the girls weren't screaming in my daydream; they were listening (with rapt attention) to my eloquent words. The only trouble was that I hadn't written any songs yet. It would be several years before I did that.

At some point I realized my guitar was almost impossible to play, as the strings were so far from the neck that I could hardly press them down. Each night I would soak my fingertips in vinegar, as I'd been told it made them tougher. One day one of my brother's friends told me my musical aspirations would be greatly enhanced if I had a guitar that was actually playable. I swapped guitars and borrowed some and went through several secondhand ones. Then one day I had an Eko acoustic. I can't remember where it came from. I do remember playing Bob Dylan's "Chimes of Freedom" over and over again, memorizing the words and how to play the chords without looking at my fingers. Before my brother left for university, we spent hours playing Dylan songs on the vinyl turntable, having to constantly stop and start, trying to scribble the words down.

There was nowhere to see pop or rock groups when you were fourteen, but we did have church youth clubs, and I heard that a band was going to play at St. Gabriel's Church Hall. I was eager to see one, and a friend from school agreed to go with me.

This was my first time seeing a band live, and my first introduction to prescription meds. My friend's mum was a doctor, and when he came round to my house to go to see the band, he said he had something that would guarantee we had a good time. He pulled some tablets out of his pocket and said, "Take two of these." Then we shared a bottle of Bulmers Cider (which contains alcohol), drank it down quickly, jumped up and down for a minute and then set out wildly climbing over the fence and crossing over Barnes Park to St. Gabriel's Church Hall.

I don't remember much apart from being in the vicar's bathroom, and he was stitching my crushed velvet trousers, which were all ripped on the bottom. The next thing I remember was waking up during the movie *Alfie* at the Odeon cinema. I never got to see the band and I felt like you could have punched me in the face and I wouldn't have cared. I staggered home somehow and went to sleep for about eighteen hours straight. What I had eagerly taken was two Mandrax tablets, or Quaa-

ludes as they are called in the U.S. Not an advisable night out for anyone reading this!

David Gibson lived two doors down from me and was the same age
as my brother. He liked playing the guitar too, which he had learned
from his father, Len Gibson, and he had a twelve-string. I liked David,
and I would nip around to his house to play whenever I saw he was in.

Len spent the war in the notorious Bantu POW camp. Prisoners
were routinely tortured and forced into slave labor and were used to
build the Burmese Railroad and the even more infamous Mergui Road,
hacked by hand, yard by painful yard, out of jungle and rock face.
Only a few survived, and Len was one of them.

During captivity, Len spotted an old wooden crate outside the
Japanese cookhouse and surreptitiously spirited it away one night. His
instrument-making skills came to the forefront as he dismantled the
box to fashion a crude guitar. For strings, he pilfered some telegraph
wires that he knew were steel encased in copper. He painstakingly
wound the copper around the steel to make the bass strings, and
stretched the wire itself for the upper strings. The key from a bully
beef tin was used to dig out holes for tuning pegs. The guitar made,
Len had only one problem: he didn't know how to play guitar! But he
knew a bit of banjo.

He said to me one day, "You like the guitar, son, don't you?"

I said, "Yeah."

He said, "Look." And he played his guitar for me and sang. I was
amazed, as he sounded like those Memphis Blues records; then I realized it was the tuning of the guitar, and I loved it. Years later, while
making a movie about the blues, I realized they had made an instrument just like Len had done out of scraps of wood and wire too.

So, for a long time, I played in these very weird tunings like he did.
That is, until another one of my brother's friends, John Graham,
showed me the normal tuning for the first time and how you made
the chords, all of which seemed very weird at first to me, but gradually

I adjusted to it. I learned how to fingerpick by imitating Mississippi John Hurt. I would play exactly what he played, like a sponge, soaking up everything I could.

I'd spend hours, daily, playing and learning. I was fourteen years old and didn't have many friends, but around that time I met this guy who became a great friend, Richard Allison. He had an old guitar and knew how to bend the notes like the blues. Like Eric Clapton or Buddy Guy, he was like nobody I'd ever heard play in Sunderland. I was fascinated by Richard's playing.

So that was the music that I learned to play first, blues and folk. I tried to learn all the songs from Bob Dylan's first album. I wasn't really into the Beatles and pop then, even though they were constantly on the radio. But after my musical awakening, I began to hear music differently. I was hearing music as a musician does, and I'd realize, "Oh . . . the Beatles are playing in E minor."

I was at the stage where I knew I had to play somewhere other than the kitchen, or my bedroom, but I didn't know how to start. I was looking through our local newspaper, the *Sunderland Echo*, and saw the mention of a few pubs in town. The Londonderry was the name of one, and there were others called the Dun Cow and the Rose and Crown. They had rooms upstairs or in the back, where people sang folk songs. I had to get in there!

I was fifteen by now, but I looked about three years younger, so they wouldn't let me in. Determined, I sat right on the pavement outside the pub door, and I would strum and fingerpick. Eventually they realized I could really play, and they let me in and even gave me a beer. I was known as "that little kid Dave with the big guitar," and I was also nicknamed the Wasp by Dave Docherty, who owned the only clothes boutique on Wearside. As soon as I had money, I went in there and ordered another bespoke leather jacket.

I was in heaven being part of the funky folk club scene in Sunderland, but in my imagination it was Greenwich Village. There was alcohol there, along with cigarette smoke and older women in black stockings and hooped earrings. I was a musician. I soon realized that with the guitar I needn't be alone. I could play with other people. It was an epiphany to me. It was like I was taking Doctor Who's TARDIS and traveling into another world. Of course, the folk scene was insular and indigenous to the northeast: big, hairy middle-aged men sang about coal mines, being on the dole, fishing disasters and big fat lasses called Cushie Butterfield:

She's a big lass and a bonnie lass
And she likes her beer
And they call her Cushie Butterfield
And I wish she was here

One of my favorite local songs, one that I learned by heart and can still recite today, was called "The Day We Went to the Coast":

No sooner had we got there we sit worsels all doon
The bairnies rush to buy ice cream, cryin', "Lend us half a croon."
I licked me chops me tongue was dry I said that's just the job
But I got more ice cream all ower me claes
Than ever went in me gob!

Like most things I try, if I like it, I dive in all the way. So soon after I began playing onstage, I ran off with the band Amazing Blondel, though they didn't know it. The band played progressive folk, based on medieval music played on lutes and recorders. They had long romantic hair, wore suede boots with fringes and looked quite like minstrels from another time—Elizabethan rock stars, if you will. I loved them. They were from Lincolnshire and sang songs about Lincoln Cathedral and Saxon ladies.

When they played in Sunderland, I climbed in their van and hid.

They went about one hundred and fifty miles back to their hometown, Scunthorpe, before they realized I was there. It was about six in the morning, and the roadies were unpacking the gear and found me and said, "What the fuck?" Then they asked for my dad's number and rang him. They said, "Your son stowed away in our van. What do we do with this kid?"

I got on the phone and said, "Dad, I really want to be on the road. Can I stay here? Can I? They'll teach me how to do stuff."

It was summer holiday, so I didn't have school, and he said okay. So they went for it and said, "All right, kid. You can stay for a bit."

This was a dream for me. I was on the road with a real band! For the first time ever—this thing that would become my life for the next many decades—I sensed it was the path I should walk, and I never turned back. I didn't even mind that I had to sleep in a dog basket. They had a Great Dane, and they kicked him out so I could have the bed. (I felt a tad guilty, as he was a sweet dog, and I was happy to share.)

They let me go on gigs and showed me everything—how to plug in and mic up an amp, just like a roadie. After a little while, they even let me open for them with two songs before they came on. We became friends, and I stayed on the road with them for what seemed like ages, though it was probably only two weeks. Then they took me home to Sunderland and met my dad.

So that was the start. I loved being with a band. It was my first taste of that. They were a little eccentric, sure, but good eccentric, which appealed to me. I started then to go on private train adventures of my own design. Every Saturday I would go to Sunderland train station and ask how far I could get for a shilling or half a crown, the equivalent of twelve and a half pence. I'd have my guitar on my back wrapped like a baby in a small blanket inside a soft guitar case. When Dave Gibson went off to college in York, I would catch the train there to see him. One time in the middle of winter I arrived at his bedsit unannounced, but he had gone away for the weekend, so I slept freezing with the tiny guitar blanket in the hallway.

Years later I wrote all about this time, the time of my mum leaving home and my embarking on all these adventures, in a song I called "Magic in the Blues" from my album *The Blackbird Diaries*.

I was feeling empty-hearted
Colder than a stone
Walked around the house all day
Looking for a home
Lay down on my brother's bed
Tried on my father's shoes
Picked up my mother's wedding ring
The one she tried to lose
When she went looking for some clues
To find Magic in the Blues

At this time, Brian Harrison, a substitute teacher fresh out of college, came into my life. He played the guitar, knew all about harmonies and had already played many gigs in folk clubs while he was at college. He had also made friends with some established folk duos like the Dransfields (Robin and Barry) and the Fureys (Eddie and Finbar) from Ireland. Both duos played traditional folk music and were powerfully great singers and multi-instrumentalists. Brian became my entry into a world I'd been dying to reach. He not only knew how to do that; he suggested we could also be a duo like the others.

Brian became my teacher, and I was an extremely willing pupil. For me, this was the very opposite of a boring school lesson about algebra, or how tadpoles turn into frogs along with a Jolly Knock. After all, "it takes more than logic to turn a caterpillar into a butterfly," as my stepfather was to tell me years later. Brian was a catalyst for me, about to introduce me to the world of being a folk singer—a troubadour—and I was so ready to learn.

At first we played guitars and sang in my dad's kitchen, as it had a tiled floor. Acoustic guitars sounded so bright and great there, and there was never anyone home, so we could happily practice for hours. I learned to sing harmony parts and became quite accurate with my fingerpicking and strumming techniques. The songs we decided to play together were the more melancholy-type Scottish or Irish numbers and a few Northumbrian songs. Songs like "Dirty Old Town," written by Ewan MacColl, and "The Galway Shawl," an Irish song we learned from the Fureys. We learned old English folk songs that bands like Steeleye Span were playing. There was one called "A Blacksmith Courted Me," which we later recorded.

I was excited about a new band called the Incredible String Band, so we learned a song of theirs called "Painting Box." We also played instrumentals that John Renbourn had composed. When Brian left, I would continue playing for hours until I could play "Angie," a beautiful instrumental performed by folk singer Bert Jansch. I played until I literally had huge indented string marks on my fingertips because I wanted it to sound just like him.

Soon we had a whole set of songs we could sing and play, and before I knew it, a new duo was born. I was now half of Stewart & Harrison, and we were playing gigs and driving to them in Brian's car, sometimes as far as fifty miles away. It was amazing; we would park and get out, and everyone around was speaking in a different accent.

Eddie and Finbar Furey arrived in Sunderland in 1968 to perform, and Brian invited them for a drink after the show. I'd heard so much about them from Brian, I was thrilled to meet them and hear their stories. We stayed up most of the night, drinking whiskey, singing, playing and laughing. I was fifteen years old and had already had a few adventures myself, but this was different. It was like two wizards had arrived. When Eddie took his boots off, and all this money fell on the floor, literally hundreds of pound notes, I was in absolute awe! From the first minute I heard the two of them, I was enamored. They were an amazing roving Gypsy storytelling full-on folk duo. Finbar was already an All-Ireland Uilleann Pipe and Whistle Champion, and a singer-songwriter, as well as a five-string banjo and guitar player. And Eddie sang and played guitar, and he had the sweetest voice. I could listen to him talk and sing for hours.

I ran away with the Fureys for a bit, up to Peebles, in Scotland. We were living in an abandoned railway shed, Eddie and Finbar Furey and me. I remember one night we were in a pub drinking whiskey, and these guys were serious drinkers. A fight started to brew up, I think, because they were Irish and loud in a Scottish pub. I didn't know what was going on, and suddenly I heard them yelling to me, "Go on, kid! Get under the table!"

I ducked under the table as the fight unfolded around me. After a few minutes, someone grabbed me out from the table, and we dashed back to the railway shack. They were yelling, "Hurry up! We've got to board up the doors!" We ran into the shack and frantically began to bang in nails for protection to stop some guys who were going to come and beat the shit out of us. It was terrifying but exciting! I went back to Sunderland with my eyes wide-open.

All the people around me were much older. They were adults, and I was just a kid. My head was exploding with the idea of being part of a rambling Gypsy-type folk singing duo, and I knew I had to make something like this happen for the rest of my life.

Enter Dick Bradshaw. A teacher from Bede, he had fingers stained brown from nicotine and longer hair than any of the students. He played great jazz and blues on an upright piano, and we became close friends. He talked to me like a grown-up.

One day he told me he wrote songs, which was something that had never even occurred to me. So I asked him: "Could I write a song?" He assured me I could, and he played me some of his, sitting at the piano and banging out the chords.

It led to the very first recording I ever made—the first of many thousands by now. It was with Brian as our duo of Stewart & Harrison. We went into a tiny recording studio, which we rented for just a few hours. It had egg boxes stapled to the wall, used as sound baffling, and was owned by a chap called Ken McKenzie, who to me seemed like a wizard at the controls. It was two-track, which means we couldn't overdub anything; we had to play together live and capture it all at once.

We sang two songs that Dick wrote, "Girl" and "Green, She Said." We also recorded one traditional song, "A Blacksmith Courted Me," and my very own first composition, "Deep December," cowritten with a bohemian painter I befriended named Eric Scott, aka Eric the Artist.

Since we were playing at folk clubs, we decided to press our EP into vinyl to sell at our gigs. It was a huge moment for me when the boxes arrived from the factory with our EPs inside. It was hard to believe that we'd actually made a record. A dream come true. Looking back it was much like indie bands today, but at the time it was groundbreaking. Nobody I had ever met had made a real album! I was still at school when this package of our vinyl records arrived in the parcel post, looking exactly like records in a store. It was on Ken McKenzie's Multicord label, and there was the label: bright banana yellow, with MULTICORD in big black letters and then the songs

1. GIRL (Dick Bradshaw)

2. GREEN, SHE SAID (Dick Bradshaw)

our names in big letters too

STEWART & HARRISON
Produced by Ken McKenzie

And when we played the record—it was an incredible moment: to see those words spinning on the turntable, and then our voices came out! Was this all really possible?

———

was still shy of my sixteenth birthday when I moved in with Eric. He liked having music around while he was painting, and he even asked me to play at his art exhibit, going so far as to decorate my guitar for the occasion. I don't know why my dad allowed me to move out of the family home and in with a long-haired crazy artist. Sunderland didn't have a large artists' community; in fact, Eric was the only real artist living off of his paintings. I could hardly fathom such a thing. It was my first taste of a bohemian life. He lived quite poorly, but he was a great painter. This introduced me to a parallel world called being an artist that existed, but that I'd never seen before. I slept on the floor among the canvases and cans of paint, me and my guitar, and a tiny tartan blanket.

Eric slept in the next room with his girlfriend, Ann. They had the bed, but, after all, it was his place, and I was so young I didn't care.

Being an artist was a brilliant thing, but we had little to eat. We survived on McVitie's Jamaica Ginger Cake and very strong black coffee. That's all we would eat all day, unless Eric sold a painting, in which case we went to the pub and spent the money on beer and chips.

Homework wasn't a problem, as I'd decided never to go to school again. I was an artist now. Dig it!

My dad did try to get me to attend Monkwearmouth College for further education. I think I lasted a week. I just wanted to play.

Eric and I remained close friends forever. Whenever I moved, he would move, too. Sadly he passed away a few years ago. I sang at his memorial in the small village of Les Adrets in the south of France, where we both spent many a night talking, laughing and drinking cheap red wine until the small hours, very often with his beautiful son, Beau, who would fall asleep on his lap at the table.

Today I own twenty-seven of his paintings and drawings. I wish he was still alive to tell me where to hang them. I was always trying to hustle work for him. He painted an amazing portrait of George Harrison, and George bought it, as did Mick Jagger a painting of him as Ned Kelly. When I signed a deal with Rocket Records, I told Eric to bring some paintings to the office, and Elton John bought four without even looking at them!

Those halcyon days on Eric's floor were the most exciting times, and the exact moment at which I left the normal world behind forever. Which was okay by me, because I'd never felt part of the normal world anyway.

During my entire childhood, I'd never felt like I fit in. I really feel sorry for my parents because my behavior was really quite eccentric. I never knew why at the time. I didn't understand I was an artist. All I knew was that I didn't fit in anywhere. I felt completely alien. So I used to do things just to rile my parents. Looking back now, I see they were little living art projects.

Once, my dad came home and found me lying underwater in the tiny fishpond, breathing through a snorkel while brandishing my brother's harpoon gun and wearing his wet suit. It was a tiny pond, with just enough room for me to squeeze in. My dad looked at me for several moments, then just shook his head and went into the kitchen to put the kettle on.

Another time I put on a pair of wobbly homemade wooden skis my father had made and a pair of homemade goggles and stood there as if in motion, like a living sculpture in front of our home. People would walk by and gape and say, "He's fucking mad! What's he doing?"

Or once, before my mum left, she was at the kitchen sink doing dishes, and she saw me stumble past the window clutching my throat with blood gushing everywhere. It was ketchup, of course, but it didn't stop her from almost having a heart attack.

Some people would say all these actions were a cry for attention. And, of course, they were. My parents were splitting up. I didn't know that at the time, but I must have sensed something was dreadfully wrong, and everything was going to change. But by the time I was living on Eric's floor, I was beginning to feel like an adult, and my parents' problems weren't mine.

After we received Stewart & Harrison vinyl in the mail, all I could think about was how it would feel to hear one of our songs on the radio. I looked up radio stations, and I saw that Radio Durham was only about ten miles away. So I rang up Radio Durham, and a woman answered, and I said, "Hi. I'm Dave Stewart, and I play the guitar and sing." Then I put the phone down, and I sang this song that I had just written.

Now, in the real world, you would imagine she would think it was a prank call and hang up immediately, but she hung on and listened all the way through. I picked up the phone and I said, "So what do you think?"

She replied, "Well, that's very sweet, pet, but I'm just the receptionist."

I said, "Oh, okay. Can you tell them Dave Stewart called, and I want to be on the radio and that was a song I wrote?"

About a week later, I was home with my dad, watching TV, when the phone rang. He jumped! The phone never rang, and it had a big, loud ring almost like a fire bell. He answered, and came back in the room, looking confused, and said, "It's Radio Durham on the phone for you."

I of course was expecting the call! A man's voice said, "How old are you, son?" I told them I was fifteen.

He said, "The girl said you played a song for her; she said you wrote the song."

I said, "Yeah."

He replied, "Well, we'd like you to come in to chat and bring your guitar." He said it was for a local interest story.

I said, "Okay!" and hung up. Then I thought, *Jesus, how am I going to get there?*

It was twelve miles outside of town. So I got a bus to Durham with my guitar. And for the first time ever, I played on the radio. They interviewed me, and I sang a song, and they recorded it. Then I told them I was in a duo and gave them our EP. They were a bit taken aback but said they would play it.

I listened to Radio Durham twenty-four hours a day for about a week until one day the deejay said, "Here's a local duo from Sunderland." Suddenly, remarkably, the guitar opening of "Green, She Said" came tumbling out of the speaker. It sounded amazing. Luckily Brian had just come round to rehearse and was gobsmacked. I think I went up in his estimation a few notches!

A couple weeks later, a check came through the post, from the BBC, for five pounds, because I had played on the radio. Wow! I was stunned. Not only did they let you play on their radio station; they paid you for it, too. Holy shit! I was on my way. After that, Brian and I got invited to do a TV show in Newcastle.

During the next eighteen months, the two of us continued to play, still under the name Stewart & Harrison, and I began to share a flat with a guy called Eddie, whom I had met when he came to have guitar lessons. I'd advertised in the local paper, a tiny one-inch ad saying, "Guitar lessons given, any style," to try to make some money.

People were shocked when they turned up and met this kid with long hair who looked about fourteen years old. But soon I had a few regulars, including a sweet young woman called Pauline, and a guy named Eddie who had a business erecting TV aerials.

The flat we rented happened to be at the end of the street that connected to an all-girls school, and word got out that these two guys had an apartment, which was unusual in Sunderland at such a young age. Soon it became party central. I was growing up fast, smoking hash and experimenting with LSD. Girls were climbing in through the windows in their school uniforms and joining in the activities.

Sometimes Eddie and I would wake up and a couple of sixteen-year-old schoolgirls were having their breakfast and making ours; they used to climb in through the ground-floor window without waking us up and help themselves. This soon turned into more than breakfast and I became very attached to a few of them. They became our friends, and in return we, or rather I, introduced them to drugs.

For one pound sterling (we called it a quid deal), you could get black hash from Pakistan, or light brown hash from Morocco, rarely grass or weed. I was smoking whatever I could get my hands on and sharing it with the girls and other people who would call around, as our flat became notorious in the town. So often there were a number of people just lying around the place getting really zonked.

Then LSD, or acid as we called it, entered the picture. It came in different varieties. First we had purple microdot, and then windowpane, and we'd experiment with various kinds and stay up tripping all night.

Sunderland started to become a very different place. Hints of London were appearing, drugs were getting easier to acquire and colorful characters started to open up shops. I bought a pair of purple suede boots from Alan Hogg, or "Hoggy," as we called him, who had a trendy shoe shop, and a fringed waistcoat from West One, Dave Docherty's boutique, which was rammed with not only groovy clothes but gorgeous teenage girls.

The music scene in Sunderland was becoming very exciting too, largely thanks to a few local promoters. One in particular, Geoff Docherty, started working at the Bay Hotel as a doorman for two pounds a night and a free drink but soon realized his calling after listening to DJ John Peel on the radio. He saved his two pounds a night and booked a band called Family to come up from London and appear at the Bay Hotel for one hundred fifty pounds, all his savings. It was a huge success, packed with eight hundred kids going crazy, and a new era was born. Next came the band Free with Paul Rodgers, Paul Kossoff, Simon Kirke and Andy Fraser. They came up north and played at the Bay to absolute crowd hysteria. No one had seen these bands other than in photos, or heard them other than on the radio.

I read in the *Melody Maker* weekly newspaper that Eric Clapton, Steve Winwood and Ginger Baker had formed a supergroup called Blind Faith. I was watching TV, and Jimi Hendrix appeared on this music-and-sketch show called *Happening for Lulu*. He was supposed to perform "Hey Joe," but halfway through the song he led his band, the Experience, into an unrehearsed rendition of "Sunshine of Your Love" in tribute to Cream, who had just disbanded. It was total beautiful chaos, but Hendrix looked gleeful as he shouted, "We're being thrown off the air," as the producers cut the broadcast.

We saw on the TV news that the Beatles had performed an impromptu concert on the roof of the Apple headquarters in Savile Row in London, triggering total mayhem down below on the streets as people realized it was them. I was seventeen years old and soaking all this in; this was the world I wanted to live in, not boring old BBC newscasters telling us the Queen had bought a refrigerator today. I felt alive, like I was plugged into an electric socket and my head was buzzing with possibilities.

Then Tyrannosaurus Rex came up to play live. Marc Bolan was the sexiest guy I'd ever seen. He just stood there onstage with curly locks and an iridescent glow, singing "Debora." Girls were going bonkers, and I thought this must have been a bit like what my brother experienced at the Beatles' concert. I was mesmerized. After they played, somehow I managed to get to meet Marc Bolan and his partner, Steve Peregrin Took, as I was taken in along with a gaggle of girls. Marc was the sweetest guy I'd ever met, up to then. We all went down to the beach, and he carried on singing and playing guitar. None of us could believe it was happening.

I was suddenly part of a scene and, without realizing it, becoming a bit of a ringleader. I wasn't an adult yet, but I'd traveled around, and now had a few escapades. I knew a lot of things that kids still at school didn't know or hadn't experienced yet. And I was living away from home and could do whatever I wanted!

A typical night at the flat I shared with Eddie would begin as a small gathering, just two or three of us smoking hash and playing guitars. Then girls would arrive. On one particular night, during a very strong acid trip, a lovely lass named Pam, who was fifteen years old and Eddie's girlfriend, suddenly became my girlfriend in the middle of a very strong hallucinogenic moment. Eddie was also with us tripping at the time, yet there was no animosity when Pam lay down with me; it was just the way it was. Things were different back then!

Soon Pam and I became inseparable, and even though she was just turning sixteen, she moved in with me, and we began living together like a married couple. In fact, she was soon to become my first wife.

CHAPTER: 3

THE SMOKE

A t one point during this psychedelic love-in period, I met Steve Sproxton and Kai Olsson, who were playing together as a duo. I think they must have heard about the flat, and they were curious as to what was going on. I heard them play and sing together, and they sounded great, so I said to Brian, "Why don't we join up with these guys? With all of our harmonies and guitars, combined with their harmonies and guitars, it could be like an English Crosby, Stills, Nash and Young!" (Although Graham Nash was British, we still saw and heard them as an exotic American band with a California sound.)

We tried it out, and it worked. We started playing together and rehearsing like crazy. At first we couldn't think of a name, so we just put our first initials of our first names together—Brian, Steve, Kai, Dave—and played some concerts as BSKD, which was a terrible name, but we didn't care; we were experimenting. For a short period Kai and Steve moved in with Eddie and me, and it was madness, as we had one bedroom with four single beds in a row and we all had girlfriends—awkward, to say the least. Somehow we made it work.

Then Brian suggested we get a large house and all have a room each and share the rent. So we moved into a huge old Victorian house within walking distance of the town center. Pam and I took the front room overlooking the street.

What happened next was relatively fast. We sent a demo tape to London, and it got into the hands of Lionel Conway, who ran Island Music publishing for the founder, Chris Blackwell. There was a lot of interest, and we were invited down to London for a meeting.

But before that, Kai's brother, Nigel Olsson (who was drumming with Elton John at the time), told us that he was coming to hear us play in the big house we all shared and that he was going to bring Mickey Grabham, the amazing guitarist from the band Cochise, so we were a little anxious.

By this time, we had started getting high quite often, smoking hash around the house. Nigel brought Mickey over around six p.m., and he brought a huge bag of the most astoundingly strong grass from Jamaica, which we were not used to. We were all crammed in Kai's tiny bedroom, which was now blanketed with a London fog of lethal dope so strong that it wiped us out. We wanted to play for them, but we just couldn't! We tried to tune up for about an hour and couldn't even manage that. We couldn't tell if we were anywhere near being in tune, we were so stoned.

It was insanely embarrassing.

Luckily they were as stoned and zoned out themselves that when they went back to London, they told everyone we were great!

I was eighteen years old in 1971, when Lionel Conway got our demos to Elton John's record company, Rocket Records. They loved us! They thought we had good songs and strong harmonies and we all could play. And it's true: when we weren't too stoned, we could really play. So we got signed. Suddenly we had a record deal with Elton John's Rocket Records, and we had a publishing deal for our song-writing, though none of us knew what that meant, really, except Brian, who suddenly had all this responsibility with three kids running around with money, guitars and weed. This was all heaven on Earth to me, and so was the move to London.

We signed with Rocket Records for recording and Chris Blackwell's Island Music for our music publishing. Chris's company also controlled Blue Mountain Music, Witchseason Music and many more. His roster of writers and artists became familiar faces to me in his offices on Oxford Street, which were situated above a groovy boutique called 2001: Cat Stevens, Nick Drake, John Martyn, Mott the Hoople, Traffic, Stevie Winwood and Bob Marley. I spoke to Bob on one occasion. It was interesting because he seemed to understand my northeast accent better than the Londoners did.

Island Music was the source of such great dope. I remember one payday, we were all sitting around in Island's offices, getting stoned on the same Jamaican weed that Nigel had that we were getting used to, and Ian Hunter, from Mott the Hoople, got passed the last embers of a joint. He took a long drag and coughed, spluttered and said, "Fuckin' hell, that's a bloody Lung Dancer!" Meaning it nearly burned his lungs. We were laughing hysterically, and then someone said, "Longdancer, that's not a bad name!" We had been searching for the right name for months. So our band had the perfect name—Longdancer—thanks entirely to the thick Shropshire accent of Sir Ian Hunter.

The Smoke was the name used for London by people up north at that time. Our local musicians, shop owners and artists were always saying, "Are you going back down to the Smoke?" And now we were moving there. We were a young and excited bunch of kids diving headfirst into the music business. The sixties were over and we entered what was to be a year full of bad news. Janis Joplin died of a drug overdose. Jim Morrison died supposedly of heroin and alcohol. Jimi Hendrix choked on his own vomit.

On April 10, 1970, the day we arrived in London, Paul McCartney announced he'd quit the Beatles, and that band was no more. That was the news we heard as we entered London with our guitars, sleeping bags, purple boots and heads full of dreams.

What happened next was that we went bonkers. It was like arriving in Neverland, and in fact, J. M. Barrie must have predicted rock and roll, as the Peter Pan effect does seem to exist in the minds of rock stars. The music business also has its own Pinocchio's Pleasure Island, a cursed amusement park that Hunter Thompson described as "a cruel and shallow money trench, a long plastic hallway where thieves and pimps run free, and good men die like dogs," adding, "There's also a negative side."

None of this concerned us one bit. We were in London, and we were getting paid to go in real recording studios and make music! We could walk down Chelsea's King's Road or go to Kensington Market and buy velvet trousers from heavenly, beautiful girls wearing floppy hats, patchouli oil and not much else.

For the first week I was with my mum again. I slept on her floor. By now she was living in Hampstead and sharing a house with a married couple and their three children. The mother met my mum and told her husband she'd met this vibrant and exciting woman named Sadie while doing further studies in London. Julian, the father, who was a Zen Buddhist, knew Sadie was coming to tea one day, so to make an impression on her, he marched up and down Rosslyn Hill with a sign, warning everyone about the ice caps melting, and saying, "We are all in great danger! For more information, ring this number!" He gave out a phone number very clearly with much volume.

My mum went strolling by, then stopped, turned around and said to him, "Excuse me. There must be some mistake; that's my telephone number!"

Julian said, "Sadie, I've been dying to meet you!"

Years later Julian and his wife got divorced, and he married my mum. My dad turned up and gave Sadie away, in place of her deceased father. I always thought that my dad showed amazing strength and respect by doing that.

Next I moved onto the floor of a Swedish lady, Ann Zadik, who worked at Island Music. But soon I wanted Pam to join me, so the band found a small house in Bourne Road, Tottenham, North London, for us all to share.

I was eighteen years old. We were very young to be in London trying to understand everything, including finances. I don't remember having a checkbook, and of course we weren't eligible for a Diners Club card, which was the only credit card available in those days. We would be paid on a Friday by a guy called Steve, the accountant from Island Music.

Steve had long straight blond hair and dark glasses, and he was stoned all the time. He was a really nice guy, though, and he would pay us in cash, weed, hash or maybe some speed or cocaine. It was a tough decision as he laid out the weekly payroll on his desk: a square silver packet of Moroccan dope, a bag of the finest weed or maybe even a Thai stick (extremely potent grass from Thailand rolled around a tiny piece of bamboo), and occasionally a small, thin rectangle of folded paper that you knew could keep you awake for days, which is why we called it marching powder. We had to enter one by one and decide whether to have enough cash to eat for half the week or the whole week.

Being around Elton John was always fun; he was super flamboyant, always immaculately dressed. It really was like signing a record deal with the Mad Hatter. We were amazed at the amount of everything around him: the vast profusion of shoes, sunglasses, hats, cologne and much more. Everyone at Rocket Records always smelled amazing and wore beautiful watches. Elton was remarkably generous to everybody, always handing out piles of gifts the second he walked through the door. It was like walking into a very expensive private store, not a record label.

Rocket was based at 101 Wardour Street in the heart of Soho, only a few minutes' walk from the Island Music offices, so we went back and forth between the two. Longdancer was one of the first signings to Rocket Records, and we soon discovered a whole new meaning to the phrase "over-the-top."

By then, Elton already had four hit albums, back when a hit meant selling millions of vinyl albums: *Empty Sky*, *Elton John*, *Tumbleweed Connection*, and *Madman Across the Water*. We were huge fans like everyone else, and I still am. At the time *Madman* was the newest album, and we all adored it. It was never off our stereo. We got to hear his next album, *Honky Château*, before anyone else. He was an amazingly inspirational songwriter and performer. And also one of the sharpest wits I've ever encountered. He would always have us in hysterics by mimicking everyone from the Queen to Winston Churchill, and he could switch between the two in a nanosecond.

We were given a whole heap of money, advances from our label and from our publisher, and we went completely out of control. A couple of people from the publishing company came to visit us in our little Tottenham house, and just like before, we were stoned out of our heads and were just lying on the floor. There were many visiting friends lying around too. We had bought a pound of hash, not a sterling pound this time, but a pound in weight—a slab the size of a coffee table book. Not only that, but I had decided to buy mescaline in bulk, hundreds of capsules filled with blue powder that contained the very potent chemical trimethoxyphenethylamine, which is found in peyote.

(In 1955, English politician Christopher Mayhew took part in an experiment for the BBC's *Panorama*, in which he ingested four hundred milligrams of mescaline under the supervision of psychiatrist Humphry Osmond. Though the recording was deemed too controversial and ultimately omitted from the show, Mayhew praised the experience, calling it "the most interesting thing I ever did.")

So when our benefactors arrived to hear some of our new songs, we of course couldn't even talk. We were completely wasted. They were a little shocked, to say the least, as they were expecting to hear our new songs for the album. They could see we were spiraling off into the void, so they figured they had to get us back down to Earth and bring some kind of order into our lives. They booked a recording studio and brought in Iain Matthews from Fairport Convention (and later Matthews' Southern Comfort) to try to produce us. He gave up after about a week, as we were so inexperienced and were way too stoned to comprehend the recording process. How we ever made our first album—called *If It Was So Simple*—I'll never know.

But we did and it came out, and a ridiculously lavish release party was thrown for us. Elton hired an entire British Rail train and packed it with press, radio, TV, other artists and many hangers-on, who had heard this was going to be a blast. As soon as people got on the train, they were plied with champagne and hors d'oeuvres, and the party had already started when the train got on its way to Moreton-in-Marsh.

When we got there, everyone staggered off the train, and we were met by a magical band in colorful costumes, who paraded us off to the village hall for more food and drink, and a performance by Longdancer. The performance got so out of control that at one point I remember Muff Winwood onstage with us playing a folding chair with bleeding fingers! No expense was spared, and everyone left with handmade tapestry bags containing our album and beautifully designed T-shirts and little toy trains to remember the day. In fact most people can't remember much about it, but it did go down as one of the most extravagant record launches ever. Had they spent all that money on promotion to radio, we would have done a lot better possibly. But it was a great party.

Pam and I decided to get married. I've no idea why we made this decision, especially as I was only nineteen and she was two years younger. Marriage seemed such an old-fashioned thing to do. But off we went up to Sunderland and tied the knot at the local registry office. By now we'd befriended lots of eccentrics and interesting people. And my mum, by then, had started living with Julian.

Our friend Tim Daly, who had just come out of prison for setting fire to the Imperial War Museum, was fast asleep on the registry office steps when Pam and I arrived with my dad. Tim was clutching an enormous samurai sword as a gift. I think Pam would have preferred a blender. My father took in all the proceedings as if it was just another everyday occurrence in the life of the Stewarts.

After the wedding ceremony at the registry office, Pam and I invited a few friends back to our friends Brian and Pauline's house for a celebration. As the party kicked into overdrive, Dad simply shook his head, sighed and muttered, *"Bedlam. Sheer bedlam."*

And it was bedlam. Longdancer now had roadies, and these roadies had met the Grateful Dead when the Dead came to London to play the Strand Lyceum. The Dead had with them some California Sunshine, which was LSD produced by the famous supplier Owsley Stanley. The drug looked like little orange barrels. I had one in my hand, and I realized within ten minutes I could feel it through the pores of my skin. This stuff was extremely potent and meant to be diluted in a glass of water for about eight to ten people.

But we all took a barrel each, far more than was sensible or safe—especially for the four people who had never taken acid before.

I realized very quickly that this was way too strong, and the last thing you want is feeling responsible for other people when you are about to pass into another dimension. It was at this moment that my young bride got trapped in the toilet and became convinced the door was breathing. That worried me, but only for a moment because like everyone else I was staring at the wall or reading the carpet.

Not only was I reading the carpet. I was convinced there was an article about us all in it!

With everybody hallucinating, I decided we should all go outside, and I led everyone into a small field behind the houses. We felt a lot better under the sky, lying on the grass in a circle with our heads together. We did that for what could have been ten seconds or eight hours. Time became meaningless. Suddenly we realized that though we were eight people, we could all see and hear the same thing, as if we shared one consciousness. We had all sorts of visions—chariots in the sky and such. And we watched as we gradually came down to Earth, like seeing ourselves in a mirror. It was the most full-on hallucinating I've ever experienced.

Suddenly we saw an older man and a lady taking a dog for a walk. Now, they might not have been there, but we all saw them, and they looked back at us, surprised I would guess by how we were staring at them. They said, "Oh, hi. This is our little dog called Jack. He's a Jack Russell." We just took it all in totally silent with eyes wide-open.

The man said, "This dog can do any trick. Give him a knife and fork, and he'll eat his dinner!"

Of course, he was just joking, but it sounded very weird to us. So we wanted to go back to Brian and Pauline's house, but we couldn't find it. All of the houses on the estate looked the same. We felt a little panicked, eight people holding hands, freaking out, feeling like we were trapped in a maze. I knew I had to do something to help.

I suggested to Pam that we knock on a door, explain to whoever answered what had happened and ask them to help. By then, Pam was completely gone and didn't understand a word I was saying.

We knocked on a random door. Pam was wearing a daisy chain and a long velvet cloak, but somehow she'd lost her wedding dress and she was naked underneath. The poor guy opened the door and saw a helpless stoned boy and a seminaked girl standing there, with our eyes as huge as dustbin lids.

I said, "Excuse me. My wife and I [which sounded weird, as we looked about fourteen] just took a very strong hallucinogenic drug, and we may need to go to hospital. Can you help us?"

He was a big guy, a manual worker, by the look of him, but he could tell there was something wrong and asked us inside. In the living room, his wife was pressing shirts on an ironing board. The whole room was covered with flowered wallpaper and a patterned carpet, which is pretty intense when you are tripping. When the wife found out what we'd done, she said, "I've heard about LSD—doesn't that destroy your brain cells or something?"

Then, with true northeastern hospitality, she said, "How about I make you a cup of tea?" In England, we believe a cup of tea will cure anything and everything.

So the guy was looking at us strangely and trying to talk to us. Pam was sitting there, looking at the carpet, just completely out of her mind. I was thinking, *God, we'd better get out of here.*

The woman brought the tea, and Pam took the cup and just turned it over and poured the whole thing onto their carpet. I could see what she was doing, and it created these amazing patterns! But to these people, we just looked crazy. Needless to say, I hurriedly backed us out of their front door, thanking them profusely, only to find our friends still hiding behind the front wall, where we had left them, completely lost and bewildered.

After the wedding we returned to London, still shaken from our experience, only to be told our band was going to be opening for Elton on a couple of shows in the UK. Then we were off to Italy, where we would be supporting him on a few more shows in sports arenas. And so I was suddenly thrown into rehearsals, now a married man.

We were pretty hopeless on the road, totally inexperienced and undisciplined, but we had enormous fun. As well as being the support act, we enjoyed singing backing vocals during Elton's set—on epic songs like "Rocket Man" and "Daniel." The last night of the tour, we stayed at the Hilton Hotel in Rome, which at that time was very grand. Everyone was getting on great. Davey Johnstone, Elton's guitarist, and Dee Murray, the bass player, were really friendly, and we had Kiki Dee join us; she was a real sweetheart who was about to sign to Rocket.

One night after a show, we were all invited to Elton's enormous suite in the early hours. I was lying on top of the giant four-poster bed, reading American comics Elton acquired for me as a gift. The room was packed with a mixture of male ballet dancers, band members, Elton's manager, John Reid, and assorted men and stunning girls. The food, drink and drugs were flowing.

At one point I decided to go into the bathroom, and came out dancing with a towel around my head and wearing a robe—anything to get attention, among all these fashionistas and glitterati. This small, intense guy in the corner of the room was watching, and he had two beautiful girls with him. They asked me to join them, so I did, and he told me these actresses were in his new movie called *Diary of Forbidden Dreams*, which, from what I gathered, was about male erotic fantasies. He asked me if I would appear in it. Sounded good to a juvenile delinquent from Sunderland.

I thought the least I could do was inform my wife. So I called Pam from the party to say I might have to stay on in Italy for an extra week because this director had offered me a part in his movie. No, I couldn't tell her what the movie was about or even what the director's name was, which must have made her deeply suspicious. The fact that she was on the other end of the line using the communal phone in the empty hallway of our drafty house while I was swanning about in a debauched decadent party in Rome wasn't lost on her, I'm sure.

I waffled on about how important it was for me to branch out into another creative area. Pam listened patiently, then told me quite simply, "Get home now," and hung up.

Twenty-five years later, I was having dinner at the Hôtel Costes in Paris with my current wife, Anoushka, and this chap came up to our table, interrupted us, and said, "Hey, aren't you that kid from Elton's room in Rome?" We chatted for about five minutes about that evening. Anoushka was impressed, and as he walked away, she said, "Wow, you know Roman Polanski!" I, of course, said yeah, but in fact I had had no idea who he was then or back in 1973, and even less idea why he wanted me to be in his film!

Longdancer had made one album, and we'd been on tour and played in England and Italy for Elton John. We also did our own shows in Holland, France and other places. But the band basically disintegrated in Germany. We were in Hamburg when Kai had a meltdown. We were all getting on one another's nerves. It kind of all fell apart at the German record launch party, which was an absolute fiasco, with Kai walking along a parapet of a penthouse rooftop, threatening to jump in front of all the German press. I decided to retire to the bathroom and not be part of it. Instead, I lay in the tub. The door opened and several photographers snapped off pictures, so in terms of press coverage the event was a resounding success. And thankfully Kai didn't jump.

Later we went to perform for the media in a Hamburg club, but it was not so successful, as we repeated our stoned tuning-up performance that got us the record deal in the first place. Longdancer danced on valiantly as a band for a little while longer, but basically, by then, we were done. It was over.

Life in London resumed. Pamela was working as a nurse, while I was working on trying all sorts of different drugs, but mainly LSD. I was probably taking it every third day of the week. After a while, this behavior really got Pam down. I was a complete nutcase. I'd even written my own language down on paper so we could speak it to each other. It was just gobbledygook. In fact, I saw some of it years later and it was just a load of scribble marks on paper and didn't make any sense at all.

We were unlike a normal married couple at that time, as Pam was at work and I would be at home. The trouble was that I took too many drugs. She'd often come home and find me staring at the wall, or there'd be some other people around, all smoking Thai sticks. We were together still but becoming estranged. Pam was holding down a straight job, and I was anything but straight.

I started to sell records in a market at Camden Lock, one of the first people doing it. I used to go to a warehouse to get Trojan Records and imports like Neil Young, Joni Mitchell, stuff like that, all on sale or return. I would still listen to music but had stopped playing it completely. I had a record stall, the only one shrouded in marijuana smoke.

Then I got a stall in Swiss Cottage. One day, when the smoke cleared, I became aware of the guy running the stall next to me who was selling vegetables and fruit. He explained later that the veg was just the front; his main source of income was selling stolen jewelry, which he hid under the bruised parsnips. He was an interesting character, maybe ten or fifteen years older than me, and enamored by my weirdness. We were from completely different origins; he was from the East End of London and he had a criminal background. He'd even been to prison.

One morning he suggested we could go into business together and have an actual little record shop. It turned out to be the smallest record store in London. It was just inside the entrance to Kilburn tube station.

I came up with the name Small Mercies. I remember thinking then, for a moment, *I'll have a band called Small Mercies, and the record business will help finance it.*

Soon, though, I felt like I was in the retail business. I had to open up the shop in the morning, be there all day and close it up at night. It became very popular, selling our reggae dub records. We had several Jamaican customers, so once again the whole place was shrouded in a fog of marijuana smoke, which didn't go down well in a London Underground station, and even less with my partner, Ray, who was constantly avoiding the police.

The Jamaican customers and African musicians started to inspire me to play again. One very tall and handsome chap was from the band Osibisa, and he invited me to jam with them, so I picked up the guitar once more. That period working in the market where I stared at my Telecaster in the corner of the room was the longest period of my life when I didn't touch a guitar.

Osibisa means "crisscross rhythms that lead to happiness," and they did. I learned all these weird rhythmic ways of playing that later I would use on Eurythmics records. The members of Osibisa cooked amazing African food, and I delved into African and Caribbean culture, which expanded my horizons more than I could have imagined. It also gave me a whole new perspective on London.

The shop came to an abrupt halt, and so did I as the result of a massive car crash. It wasn't my fault. I was driving the little minivan that we used for moving vinyl albums around. This guy just came straight out of a side street and banged into me in his Ford Zodiac, which was as massive and as heavy as a Sherman tank. I don't remember much about the collision. All I recall is waking up in somebody's garden and the police were already there. When I first saw all those helmeted, blue-uniformed bobbies, my first thought was they had come for Ray.

I was taken to the hospital in an ambulance, and of all the places to take me, it was the Whittington in Highgate, where Pam worked. On my way there I realized that my bag was filled with ganja, so I opened my jeans under the blanket and shoved the dope down the front of my underwear. When I was in the treatment room, two nurses came in and started cutting off my jeans. I was pretending to be really delirious and shouting a lot, trying to stop them from uncovering my secret stash. The police were trying to calm me down, saying softly, "It's all right, son. It's all right. The girls are just doing their job."

At that moment, Pam walked in, one of the luckiest coincidences in my life. At first she thought I was shy about having my jeans removed, so she said, "It's all right. They've seen it all before."

I told the nurses and the cops that Pam was my wife and I'd like to spend some moments alone with her. Believing this might calm me down, they all left the room. I then pulled out all the ganja from my underwear.

She said, "Oh, bloody hell," and started to stuff it in her nurse's uniform pockets. I think that was the last straw with Pam. Here I was now bringing problems into her place of work.

After that, we started to drift apart. She had hit it off with another musician in our circle, Barry Dransfield, and I think I encouraged them to spend time together, even to the point of suggesting Pam sleep with Barry when we all stayed together in a country mansion. Barry was playing with his brother as the Dransfields and was becoming quite a well-known solo artist himself on the folk scene. I was happy for them to be together, if that's what they wanted, as I was beginning to think we may have married a wee bit too early.

But one evening the three of us almost died at the hands of Barry. We were drinking in the Queens Pub in Crouch End, which at the time was notorious for drug deals. It was a rowdy pub with live music and people dancing on the tables. Barry and I had already been banned from the Railway Tavern just up the street for causing a disturbance, so this time we were quietly sipping our beer and keeping a low profile. Being so docile could also be explained by the fact that we'd taken Secanol, a drug commonly used to calm you just before surgery.

At one point we decided to leave and go back to Barry's for a smoke, and I asked along my buddy Big Dave, a great saxophone player, but also a heroin and morphine fiend (well, any drug, actually).

As we were leaving, I saw Barry pop another Secanol. I told him he shouldn't be driving on that cocktail of beer and pills. He said he was fine and it was only up the road anyway. We all climbed into the Dransfields' Ford Transit van, Pam and me on the front bench seat, Big Dave in the back and Barry at the wheel.

Then all hell broke loose as Barry started the van up, put it into first gear and swerved into the road and immediately passed out at the wheel, with his foot jammed down on the accelerator. We took off with such force that Pam and I were thrown into the back with Big Dave as our seat snapped. Then we were tossed about like rag dolls as the van hurtled up Crouch End Broadway with Barry asleep, sprawled across the steering wheel. We were about to demolish the clock tower, but somehow I managed to push Barry away. I tried to steer standing up but couldn't move his foot, which was now jammed between the accelerator and the clutch. This seemed like the longest crash in history as we zoomed off up Crouch Hill with Pam screaming and Secanol pills bouncing loose around the van. Dave, meanwhile, was eating them all. He later used the excuse that he thought we would all get busted.

I managed to navigate past the Railway Tavern and swerved, turning into Hornsey Lane. We crunched and grinded to a halt, plowing right into several parked cars along the way. The three of us escaped out the back door of the van. Barry was slumped at the wheel when police cars descended on us from all directions. Pam and I looked like innocent bystanders who were trying to pull Barry from the wreckage. Trouble was, just as two burly policemen came to help, Barry opened one eye and said to me, "Dave, we can still get away."

I immediately looked confused and said, "He must be delirious, Officer," and stood aside to let them assist.

By now half the street was full of pajama-clad residents, and as the scene became more confusing, Pam, Dave and I slipped away unnoticed. By the time we got home, Pam was shaking and went to bed, while I tried to get Dave to do the same. Around three a.m., we heard an awful crash coming from the kitchen, only to find Dave upside down, covered in plates, saucers and cutlery, trying to open a tin of beans sideways with a screwdriver. He smiled and asked me—"Want some?"

Pam and I decided to move out of our flat and into a squat in London. It was all getting increasingly scary for her, and things were just too unstable. We didn't have any money, and London prices were exorbitant, so it was my idea to move into a squat to save money on rent.

Just before we moved, Pam announced she had some savings and was going to America to visit Ann Zadik, the girl from Island Music who'd moved to Laguna Beach and married an American. When Pam went there, she quickly realized how rough and tumble her life in London was compared to Laguna and the California lifestyle. She fell in love with the idea of moving there, especially as we had already started drifting apart.

While she was in the USA, which seemed to be for ages, she met somebody new, and so did I. Her name was Katy, and she inspired me to start writing songs again, the first in a long while. One of the songs I wrote was about her, and that night she stayed with me. In the morning—while getting in the car to drive her to work—I was nabbed by the police, who were waiting right outside my front door. I had some grass in my bag, and they arrested us. I explained that Katy knew nothing about it, so they let her go. I, however, was well and truly busted and had to go to the police station and later to the magistrates' court.

Pam returned, and although our relationship had obviously gone sideways, we moved in with the poet Tim Daly and his girlfriend, Pauline. They had a flat, and we had one room in it. Now we'd gone from sharing a house and having our own apartment to one room in somebody else's flat. It was totally claustrophobic.

Around this time I was approached by Transatlantic Records to see if I would work with a band of theirs called the Sadista Sisters. I had met Jude, the lead singer, along with Teresa D'Abreu and Linda Marlowe. At first they were a formidable lineup of nine women. I'd never seen or heard anything like them, because they weren't like any group I'd ever experienced. Not rock and roll, not soul, not folk. They were an underground feminist theater group that played music. Jude's style was kind of prepunk. The developing fringe theater at the time had little to offer women in terms of roles, or even as audience members; the Sadista Sisters was formed as a direct response to the male-dominated establishment theater of the early 1970s.

Jude had been a trapeze artist in California, worked in a Grotowski-based company called KISS in France and was a member of Steven Berkoff's first companies playing in Vienna and London's Roundhouse. In fact, Teresa and Jude had formed Sadista Sisters as a direct response to working with the brilliant but misogynistic Steven Berkoff. Jude was five months pregnant when she signed the album contract with Transatlantic Records. She didn't know she was pregnant and was horrified when she found out. They received a lot of great press when they played a season at Ronnie Scott's club. Jude's baby was practically born on the stage.

Jude was maybe five or six years older than me and had truly been through a lot. A few years before she'd been to America and landed a role in a movie, but the night before the first day of filming, her nightgown caught fire as she was making toast. When her roommate came home, he stood and watched, frozen, as he was tripping, and once had watched his father's house burn down. He didn't understand that this was really happening. Jude had third-degree burns and was told her arm was going to be amputated. But there was nobody there to sign a release from her family, so she had to have painful skin grafts.

As she told all of this (and the stories got stranger and stranger), she became more and more fascinating to me. I fell for Jude big-time. It was one of the first times I'd encountered a female artist who was extremely strong, sexually provocative and anarchic at the same time. She had a well-defined idea of what she was going to do and how to achieve it.

I went flying into this relationship. But I was stupidly naive to have jumped into a relationship with her, knowing she had a two-year-old daughter named Amy. I had no grasp of the responsibility that comes with having a child. But I was besotted, totally under her spell, sexually intoxicated. I had no idea about theater or why an all-girl feminist troupe would hire male musicians; evidently the label forced them into it.

I must admit I was confused most of the time, but it seemed crazy, edgy and stimulating, and after rehearsals Jude and I would have passionate sex anywhere and everywhere. I was crazy about her and willingly agreed to go on tour with the Sadista Sisters and the whole entourage.

The first tour we did was interesting, to say the least. After the extravagant Elton days of touring, this was hard-core hand-to-mouth survival. At first we stayed in what seemed like an army camp in the woods in Holland. I can't remember much apart from sleeping with Jude on the floor of a cabin every night, and it seemed very romantic in an impoverished-artist kind of way. When we eventually played shows they were haphazard and maybe the worst-organized tour I'd ever encountered. Because none of us had any money, we even took to busking in the street.

I invented myself as a new character who could remember anything, any date, any name, all at the click of my fingers. I became Memory Man, except the whole joke was that I couldn't remember anything. In Stuttgart I managed to get a slot before the striptease act came on, and the guys in the club were really mad because they were told I was Memory Man and they wanted strippers. I'd come on and always have a plant in the audience, who would say, "Who won the World Cup in 1962?" And, of course, I would not remember anything and slowly have a nervous breakdown onstage and get carried off. And that was my act.

(Years later I turned my adventures as Memory Man into a graphic novel called *Walk In*, the term used when the original soul leaves a person's body and another soul "walks in." It often occurs around an accident or trauma. I often wonder if this has happened to me and that somehow when I was at death's door, another spirit entered my body. One of those experiences happened, I'm sure, at the beginning of our next tour.)

Jude and I had slowly cut ourselves off from the rest of the band, and there was a lot of tension in the air. I decided to ask Eddie, my friend from Sunderland who had previously worked as a roadie with Longdancer, to come on the road and help us. Because Jude and I were together, the band was getting fractious, so we decided to have a separate car from them. I rented one and drove it from a seaport in Holland, where we picked up Eddie, all the way to Germany, where we switched drivers.

Eddie got in the driver's seat, and with one fatal turn of the wheel, he pulled the wrong way onto the Autobahn, headfirst into the oncoming traffic. It was late at night and cars were doing about eighty miles an hour. For a second everything went in slow motion. Then I screamed, "Wrong way." But it was too late. A car hit us full force, and we went spinning around. I don't remember much about it. I don't remember hearing any noise. I just remember glass shattering. I was so freaked-out, because baby Amy was in the back and got thrown out of the car. Amy miraculously survived without serious injury. Jude suffered serious internal bleeding, and I was bruised and banged up. It was a terrible crash. It was on the front page of the German national newspapers because it caused a pileup. It really was a miracle that no one died, but there were a lot of very badly injured people.

We had to go to a hospital in Wilhelmshaven, and we couldn't understand anything the doctors or nurses were saying and there was just one person there who could interpret English. It really was a nightmare. Then we were taken in an ambulance all the way to Hamburg. It obviously really messed up my relationship with Jude, because the first thing that happened, after embarking on this adventure together in our own car was, boom, a crash.

Then we got stranded in Hamburg because the label refused to help. We survived only because of Jude's longtime friend Heidi Gudrun, the Bahlsen biscuits heiress who lent us two thousand deutsche marks and let us stay in her flat in Berlin for two weeks. Gudrun had driven through East Berlin to pick up Amy because Jude was in the hospital alone with internal bleeding for a week, and couldn't sit up to nurse her. Gudrun also smuggled Amy through the Iron Curtain with no papers like in a John le Carré novel.

That was the end of my relationship with Jude. We didn't meet or talk after we returned to England. It all seemed like an amazing acid trip that had suddenly gone horribly wrong. I liked her so much and respected her as an artist and wanted us to get back together but I knew that dream was well and truly over.

It was 1975, and I was on my own for the first time since I was seventeen. There were strikes and power cuts. Margaret Thatcher replaced Edward Heath as prime minister. People drank Blue Nun wine at dinner parties and finished with Black Forest gâteau. Punk musicians were about to challenge all the millionaire rock stars who lived in stately homes. I would go walking up the street in Crouch End from my mother's miniature apartment. It was a tiny little room with a bright purple carpet and a section for the kitchen sink with large black-and-white tiles, which was not good for hallucinating at all.

One day, on one of my strolls, I ran into Paul Jacobs, a friend I hadn't seen for a while. I used to know him when he worked at Camden Market, where he also sold records. He was opening a shop called Spanish Moon after the song by Little Feat. He didn't explain it to me until later that he wasn't renting; it was a squat, the whole house. He just moved in and made it look like such a legitimate shop that people assumed it must be official, like a bona fide record store.

So when Paul saw me walking up the street, he knocked on the window and invited me in. He had a bottle of Jack Daniel's, so we had a nip or two while we explained to each other what had been going on since we last met. It was about six o'clock in the evening and he said, "Oh, you must come and meet this girl," because he knew I was a musician and crazier about music than anything else. He said, "I've just met her. And she can play and sing on a harmonium, an old harmonium. And she's really got a great voice."

And I said, "Yeah, okay, I'd like to meet her."

CHAPTER:4

FROM THE MIDDLE ROOM

Paul said that the girl's name was Annie, and that she worked in a restaurant called Pippin's. It was a health food restaurant—still a new concept then—on Hampstead High Street. Only posh Hampstead would have such a shop. There wasn't much wheatgrass or braised tofu in Sunderland.

So we drove there, but we didn't actually go in. We could see her through the window and we waited outside. I started steaming up the window from the outside with my breath, and I began drawing on the window's condensation. I wrote, in reverse so she could read, "Will you marry me?" I couldn't really see her that properly because it was this packed little place. As usual I looked quirky and odd, wearing Kellogg's Frosted Flakes "Tony the Tiger" sunglasses and cropped spiky hair. We could see the manager of the restaurant mouthing to Annie, "Do you know these people?"

Paul knew what time she was finished—seven o'clock—so we waited till she came out. When she did, she was a bit annoyed and worried she could lose her job. But we started talking, and we connected straightaway.

Paul wanted to go to a bar called the Speakeasy, so Annie and I went with him, and we carried on talking. We were in this place for about ten minutes when we both said, "Don't really like this place. Where should we go?"

We went back to her tiny bedsit room in Camden Town, with just enough room for a little bed and her old wooden harmonium, and started talking. Annie and I basically didn't stop talking for the next twenty years.

She had longish hair, not blond or dark, but brownish, and a secondhand fake fur coat she wore over an old-fashioned print dress. She looked very studentlike, and she really was—a student living on hardly anything. But she had incredibly stunning, piercing blue eyes and the most beautiful face I'd ever seen. I could tell she was very sensitively alert to everything, like a real artist.

She played a couple of her songs on her harmonium. One was called "Tower of Capricorn," and there was another one called "Song for Matt," about a boyfriend she'd had who had died rather tragically. She sang, "Matt I got your letter, on the thin blue paper/the kind that come from long distances . . ."

I was utterly knocked out by everything about her: her singing, the chords she was playing, her delicate words and her haunting beauty.

Her singing and her songs reminded me of Joni Mitchell. I'd been a big Joni fan, especially the album *Blue*. This reminded me a little bit of that, except the instrumentation was different, because Joni was playing dulcimers and guitars. But Annie was singing while playing this big old harmonium. Pam told me just before we parted that she knew I was going to be with someone more like a Joni Mitchell type, an artist who could sing and play. Annie was all this and more. I had found my soul mate, and I knew it with absolute certainty.

It was 1975. We stayed together that night and every single night after that for the next five years and to this day are still best friends.

I immediately thought, "Well, this girl is incredibly talented." And she kept saying, "I don't know if anybody will like these songs."

I said, "Are you joking? I'm telling you. You're a phenomenal song-writer."

From the first day, I told her she was an artist, and I think that meant a lot to her. Until then, she'd been torn about sticking in at the Royal Academy of Music. She had been studying flute and harpsichord, but she didn't like it because the place was very stiff, and everything was too competitive. Everyone there was practicing all the time, practicing to be the best violinist or the best flute player. And she was more excited about Joni Mitchell or Stevie Wonder, which was at odds with this formal, traditional, classically oriented world where she was studying.

She had no money and was starting to do tiny gigs with a friend, doing cover versions of Elton John songs and others to make some cash, in addition to working in this vegetarian restaurant. So when I said she was an artist, it was very affirming to her. And from the minute we met, I never saw her go to college again. And from that moment on, we were together. We didn't leave each other's side; we went everywhere together.

The next morning Annie told me she suffered from panic attacks, and she was feeling very anxious a lot of the time. I felt really bad for her, so I said, "Well, look, I tell you what. Why don't we go and chat to my mom, who lives in this tiny room in Crouch End?" She agreed and we took the double-decker bus. Halfway there, she was panicking, going, "I don't know. Don't really know you very well, and I don't know your mom, and I don't know why we're even on this bus."

I tried to reassure her by saying my mum had been through all this stuff and she knew about these kinds of things.

When we got there, Annie felt more relaxed, and my mom was very sweet, but she was packing to go on holiday for a few weeks. She said we could have the flat key and stay while she was gone.

So we moved in that night. But Annie didn't realize I was a drug addict, addicted to speed. That first night I went out to get some bread and milk and didn't come back. She was in my mom's flat on her own, not knowing really where she was or what was going on. I didn't come back until six o'clock in the morning, telling her excited stories about Piccadilly and some girl called Circles. I must have seemed really bonkers, but I was so used to this crazy lifestyle of staying up all night. I was being really honest. I would tell her everything. I was always meeting and talking to twenty different people in a day, and I think Annie slowly caught on; she knew something wasn't right. I felt very natural around Annie and she did around me, so I told her about my drug taking.

I was falling madly in love, and I told her so. We then decided we were going to live together. This must have been only three or four days into our relationship, but there was no denying it. But we couldn't live together in my mom's flat and we couldn't live in Annie's little room, which was only big enough to have the harmonium, a single bed, a tiny sink and a kettle. So we went to talk to Paul, who had the shop and the three floors above, which were part of the squat, and he was going to live up there. But there were other rooms in the house, and he had already said to Annie that she could have one of the rooms. So she went to see him and said, "Hey, do you mind if Dave and I both move in?" He thought about it for a second and agreed.

Of course, there was nothing in there. It was just a derelict empty house with no furniture and rubble everywhere. Nothing worked. You had to climb over bricks and debris to get to brush your teeth. When people talk about starting from scratch, it means from zero, right? Well, this, literally, was where we were: at zero. No money, no carpet, no bed, no nothing; just the idea that we would live together in this run-down house.

Normally when you meet somebody you fall in love with, you go through tentative stages. There was none of that with us. It was like I didn't know her one minute, and the next minute we were living together. We were never apart. It wasn't like we would see each other occasionally. We were together. Inseparable.

We lived there for at least two years. And eventually, we made it better and better. We got rid of the bricks. Luxury!

Paul was quite amazing, and he just seemed to understand that we got on like a house on fire, like two musicians in love. Paul was a really funny guy, a mensch really, but he was also kind of crazy. If we complained that it was freezing, he would simply say okay and chop up the kitchen cabinet and throw it on the fire. He was thinking that it was just a squat anyway. But Annie and I were trying to make it into a little home.

We went shopping in jumble sales and junkyards, looking for plates and cups for a few pennies, or a sofa that we bought for one pound. Annie was such fun to be around when it was just the two of us. We were always laughing and talking constantly, chatting about our lives and what had happened to us up to that point. After a month I knew everything about Annie and she knew everything about me. Every painful thing that we had experienced we found easy to talk about with each other, and we shared the same surreal sense of humor that sometimes only the two of us could get. We never played music together, didn't even talk about it that much.

One simple thing that Annie decided to do saved my life. Instead of being confrontational about my addiction to speed and cocaine, she just asked me one day how much I took. She had a little notebook, and she wanted to know how many lines of speed or coke I took over twenty-four hours, and she said she would write it down. Then she showed me and suggested that I try to cut down from, say, twenty times to nineteen, then to eighteen and so on.

She started making healthy food. At the time I had a twenty-four-inch waist and ate hardly anything, because you don't feel hungry when you are speeding away all the time. The combination of cutting down on drugs very slowly, tapering off them, mixed with eating small amounts of real homemade food and living with someone who loved me enough to care for me in such a delicate way helped me eventually quit drugs altogether. It wasn't easy, though, and it took a very long time to get totally clean. But she never left me during this period. While I was trying to detox, Annie would have to put up with dealers coming around the house at all hours, one time even being woken up in our bedroom by Blue, the Hell's Angel, trying to give me coke on the end of a flick knife while I was still asleep. Annie shouted for him to get out, and she has a very loud voice!

So our lives together were a mixture of very extreme situations with many oddball characters popping in and out, but then, when we were left alone, we were incredibly sweet to each other and loved to do simple things. It was an amazing time to be young and in love. There was a wild energy in the air. Margaret Thatcher had become the first female leader of the Conservative Party, white nationalist groups, such as the National Front, were becoming more outspoken, and there was racial conflict in the air. Bands like the Sex Pistols and Sham 69 formed, and people were out in the street drunk and shouting outside our window like there was a riot about to happen most nights.

In the record store below us, Paul was blasting out either punk or heavy reggae/dub music, and our floor was constantly shaking with the bass throbbing through the house. Sometimes it was so loud that we couldn't think straight, so we would have to go for a walk or go visit someone. We didn't really know many people as a couple, and for some reason we were quite shy about getting to know new people. But eventually we had a small circle of friends who were mainly people I knew, artists I'd met who Annie could relate to. As we rarely had any money, we stayed mainly within walking distance of the squat. The first time I took Annie to the Railway Tavern up the road, she was shocked, as the landlord immediately kicked us out, saying I was banned. The same thing happened when we walked down to the Queens, another pub in Crouch End. I had to explain that I had been dragged out and down to the police station from both places in the past for "causing a disturbance" along with Barry Dransfield. Annie took all of this rather well and just adapted to each situation as it came. I knew she always had my back and I had hers; our bond became stronger and stronger.

I decided to introduce Annie to my friend Peet Coombes. Peet was my good friend, and a great songwriter I hung out with a lot. Because

I'd fallen so madly in love, I hadn't even seen him for a month or two. One day he came around to visit us, and he brought his guitar. He played some new songs around the kitchen table, and they were all great. One was called "Just the Wind" and another "Dot." Annie joined in singing harmonies immediately, and it was as if they had sung together for years, their voices blended so well together. We discussed right then and there the idea of forming a band around the three of us, which would eventually become the Tourists.

Now we were three, and we were a band. Peet was very much the leader—the songwriter and lead singer. Annie played keyboards and sang harmonies mostly. A lot of the time we'd have the lead voice and harmony together all the way through. I played rhythm guitar and lead guitar.

I'd met a guy called Rob Gold a while back at Island Music, and he paid for us to record some demos for Logo Songs, a small publishing company he was now working with. I had no ambition whatsoever then about being a songwriter myself. I was always the fan of Peet's and now Annie's songs, so when it came to recording the demos, I didn't do much apart from being enthusiastic and playing guitar a bit on a couple of Peet's songs. Annie sang her songs and played harmonium or piano. The demos were good.

Rob was impressed, but not quite sure how this raggle-taggle bunch would fit together. We didn't really know yet either. At first we called ourselves the Catch, and we soon got signed to a publishing deal with Logo Songs and a record deal with Logo Records. I remember when we were sitting in their offices and they started talking about advances, paying us money for signing the contracts, and Annie said, "Oh no, you don't have to pay us."

I was standing on her foot under the table, as I'd had a publishing deal and a record deal before and knew they needed to give us an advance. Besides, we were completely penniless, broke and living in a squat at the time. Annie and I had no idea yet of the power that we were going to have as a duo in Eurythmics, so we were happy to have any kind of recognition, and a record deal was not an easy thing to get back then. I was happy for Peet to be the songwriter, as he was very talented, and Annie seemed fine about that too.

At first the label obviously thought Annie was a really great singer and a great-looking girl, so what was she doing with these two drug fiends? To make our record, they put us in the studio with session musicians. We'd never heard of having session musicians. I'd always had a band, and Peet had always had a band or played his own material. We were confused, as we played our own music the way we thought it should sound! Everything was taken out of our hands, and the session players played our music their way.

Unsurprisingly, the record didn't sound anything like how we wanted it to. It had lead vocals by Annie and harmonies by Peet. But that was where it stopped. It didn't resemble anything like the quirky sound the three of us made or even how Annie did as herself. But the production was all wrong; the session players made it sound dated and bland. We didn't understand why they were doing this, but we went along with it.

We stopped recording for a while, stunned at what had happened, but we had a tiny amount of money from the advance, so Annie and I bought the cheapest little Morris Minor van for about two hundred pounds. It was a real bone shaker. But we loved the freedom to be able to go anywhere anytime we wanted.

I have a hopeless sense of direction, but Annie's is so good I used to call her "Annie's Atlas," and she would navigate while I drove (badly, I must add) to Hampstead Heath or Camden Town or to visit our friends Willy and Karen up in North London. We even ventured outside London but were very aware the van could break down at any minute or we would run out of petrol and be stranded.

On one of these outings we drove through the East End of London and witnessed a terrible racist attack. It was brutal. The car in front of us slowed down and four men jumped out and proceeded to attack an innocent elderly Asian man, hitting him repeatedly with a hammer.

Annie and I stopped our car and got out to try to help the poor man, so we were the only witnesses. The police seemed racist in the way they were talking to him, blaming him as if it was his fault for walking along that particular street. We were furious as they took our statements. The next day the police said they needed to come and see us; they warned us that we could be in danger from an East End gang. That same night we had to play a gig in London, and a horrendous fight broke out by the back entrance. There were split heads, a few broken bones and blood everywhere.

With these two things happening on top of each other, we were so stressed out that we decided to go miles up north, camping with a tiny tent at a rock festival, of all places. There was social unrest brewing in the UK, and in 1976, it all came out: there were riots and Rock Against Racism concerts, punk music peaked and the country erupted to the sound track of the Damned, the Buzzcocks, Siouxsie and the Banshees, the Slits, Subway Sect and the Vibrators.

It was then we realized we had to have players we got along with before we recorded anything else, and we went searching for musicians to make a band sound.

We held some auditions, which was how we met Jim Toomey, the drummer. He lived with a guy who was really good at recording and made some great demos of us. Then we got the great bass player Andy Brown in the band, and the Tourists were born.

We played our first gigs and quickly got loads of attention. We got an agent and played all over London, all the places that were happening: the Hope and Anchor in Islington, the Electric Ballroom in Camden Town, the Marquee Club in Soho. Our gigs went from fifty people to a hundred, two hundred, then four hundred. We were heading on an upward trajectory fast. Andy thought it was too risky financially to play with us, as he could make money playing with a few different people, so he left and we found a new bass player, Eddie Chin.

We announced to Logo Records we were now called the Tourists, and we made our self-titled first album. We released a song called

"Blind Among the Flowers" as the first single, written by Peet again, with both Peet and Annie singing lead vocal and harmony all the way through. It went to number fifty-two in the charts, and we appeared on TV for the first time on shows like the chart roundup show *Top of the Pops* and *The Old Grey Whistle Test*, a music show where artists performed in really bare-bones setups originally hosted by TV legend "Whispering" Bob Harris.

All during this period, Annie and I were a couple and living in the squat, which was now quite decent. We were still sharing with Paul, and he was a major force behind the band, always promoting us in the shop and getting people down to the gigs. We were still broke, of course, and it was crazy because we had a record deal and a publishing deal, but we had to sign on the dole every week as unemployed! We would see people in the queue, and they would recognize us from the TV and look confused. But we were literally living hand to mouth.

"The Loneliest Man in the World" was the second single on the album and the first song I ever produced. I asked the label to let me produce the song myself. They agreed, but the album was already finished by then, so I had to complete it in four hours, including mixing. A studio was booked, a studio that I had never been in and didn't know. But I did it. I produced my first record. It went to number thirty-two in the UK charts. Now I was a producer. Things started to heat up.

Now when we played gigs, we were pulling five hundred people to a thousand, and we played up and down the country as much as we could and even a few festivals abroad. We began to get lots of reviews and traction as a live band.

We went into the studio to record another album called *Reality Effect*, which had two hit singles in a row, "So Good to Be Back Home" and "I Only Wanna Be with You." The latter we did just for fun, but it ended up being our biggest hit. But even with the hits, to us, we felt it wasn't the right sound.

Annie had dabbled, but she was never a druggy person or a big drinker. Still she had to deal with a lot of it when we were on tour.

We traveled everywhere, always in small cramped vans or minibuses, up and down England, supporting Roxy Music. Then we went all over America and to Australia, France and Germany.

To Annie, though, the Tourists had become a double-edged sword. She'd been drawn toward the world of Joni Mitchell and soul music, Aretha Franklin, Stevie Wonder and Elton John songs. Motown inspired her when she'd first heard it on the radio while she was growing up in Aberdeen. Our band wasn't making that kind of soul music. Our music, which was written by Peet, was psychedelic and guitar-driven. But, regardless, Annie really went for it onstage. She gave it her all. But then we'd have to drive for seven hours, with Annie and me crushed together in a sweaty van with a bunch of guys. Occasionally we would have an overnight hotel, but very seldom. When we had time off, we would still spend every minute of the day together. And on occasion we went on holiday!

One time I booked a holiday in a hurry, because by then we were well-known in the UK. We had been on TV and radio several times and were recognized everywhere we went. This was quite stressful, as we were a couple and we liked keeping to ourselves and having fun in our own private universe. But I couldn't have picked a worse place to go for a couple who wanted to be invisible.

I walked down to the local travel agent to find the cheapest holiday abroad that we could leave for the next day. I don't know whether it was the pressure I put on the agent to find us this holiday in twenty minutes, or a joke he decided to play on us, but he booked us for two weeks on a tiny island off the coast of what was then Yugoslavia.

We took the flight, which arrived as the sun was going down, and we were in high spirits as the coach dropped various people off at their hotels or boardinghouses.

This ride seemed to take forever, and by the time it was our turn to be dropped off, it was pitch-black outside, and we were the only ones left on the bus. This did not bode well. Annie was getting anxious, and when the bus pulled onto a long jetty, there seemed to be nothing there.

Then we heard a voice from below, and there was someone in a small boat beckoning us to climb down the rungs of the jetty wall. I threw our suitcase over the side, and we set off toward a dimly lit island in the distance. It started to feel very romantic and a real holiday at last. When we eventually got shown to our room, we loved it and fell asleep exhausted.

The next morning we got up and read the instructions and the little map that led us to the main reception area and café where breakfast was served. As we walked along this very beautiful twisted path with the sun coming up over the island, I noticed out of the corner of my eye what seemed to be a naked man jumping. I thought nothing of it until we heard cries and shouts, so we both peered through the bushes and there was a volleyball match going in full swing, so to speak, with only one thing missing: clothes!

We laughed, thought that was a bit odd and hurried on to breakfast. I opened the door for Annie, who was met with the sight of about fifty naked and seminaked people queuing with trays for breakfast. I popped my head in and someone shouted out, "Hey, it's the Tourists!"

Yes, we were at a nudist colony, a nature resort, clothing not necessary, and it was an island! Annie was shocked, to say the least, and at first she thought I'd booked this on purpose. We had no idea what to do; the last thing we wanted was to be nude among a bunch of real tourists who recognized us! I had to think fast and said, "Hey, why don't we get a little boat ride to another island for the day, and then we'll figure it out?"

We went to the boatman, wearing as little as possible to try to fit in, and people were asking for photos all the way. He took us to what I understood to be a beach on Red Island. Once we were dropped off, we crossed a bridge, found the beach and guess what. It was another nudist beach, but at least you could lie down on a towel. So we decided to stay for a while and hid behind a rock in case we were recognized again.

Actually, everyone was really cool here, apart from one guy, a huge naked man with a big belly, lots of chest hair and a chain with a gold medallion, who was smoking a big fat cigar. He wouldn't sit or lie down; he just kept walking up and down, checking out all the naked women, and I could see he was pissing everyone off.

We were lying there quietly, beginning to relax at last, when we heard a bloodcurdling scream, and everyone looked up, shocked to see medallion guy running out of the ocean with a giant Portuguese man-of-war jellyfish clinging between his legs. Everyone burst out laughing and cheering as he ran up the beach, screaming and clutching wildly at his scrotum. There was fun to be had here after all! In fact it never fails to cause Annie to cry with laughter when we recount our visit fully clothed with some of the tourists to a local farm. We signed up for as many things like this as possible to avoid our island and our pals in the nudist colony, as it wasn't simply a matter of beaches and playgrounds for the unclothed but rather a self-contained community with their own supermarket, bank, restaurant and laundry (for which there was less than the usual need).

The farm trip took a turn for the worse when we were all greeted with a customary drink of wine mixed with garlic and fresh cow's blood, which tasted awful but was ridiculously potent. Needless to say, I drank quite a lot of it.

I don't remember much else about the evening but evidently I did the Elton John room trick again, somehow finding bedsheets and wrapping them around my head and torso, spinning wildly back into the barn where the feast was taking place.

Annie was in stitches while the other guests cheered me on, laughing and banging on the tables with their empty goblets, as I pranced and pirouetted, doing my best Isadora Duncan impersonation in the center of the room.

Evidently the bus ride home was one of Annie's most embarrassing moments. She kept her head down all the way as I chatted wildly, delighted to have made new friends, forging strong bonds and making flagrant promises to meet them all tomorrow at breakfast. Worst hangover I ever had.

I remember when the Tourists played Los Angeles, we had four whole days off. I decided I wanted to visit Ann Zadik, the lady who was kind enough to let me sleep on her floor back when I first signed to Island Music and whom Pam had come to visit. She was still living in Laguna Beach. It sounded exotic, and I wanted to see what it was like outside of Santa Monica Boulevard or the Sunset Strip. I wanted to see somewhere in California that wasn't about hipsters and hangers-on, dopers and dropouts and grungy LA rock and roll.

We decided to take a public bus, so we got up early and crept out of the hotel only to bump into John Belushi in the car park. As we didn't live in the States, we had no idea who he was or that he was a big star from *Saturday Night Live*. But he approached us—I'm sure because we looked different. Annie had bright spiky blond hair and a leather jacket, and we both had this kind of punky thing going.

He said, "Hey, do you want some of this?" He opened up a large crumpled packet of cocaine on top of a car. It was about eight in the morning, in broad daylight, with people walking by to work. Annie was like "Whoa!"

I answered, "No, it's all right, mate." Belushi was persisting, "Come on." He'd obviously been up all night and we both wandered off, feeling sorry for him. I knew how he must have felt, having been there many times myself.

So we took a bus from Hollywood to Laguna Beach. We were amazed when we arrived. It seemed like some kind of paradise. It was the first time I'd ever been anywhere like this, and we wandered around just stunned at how beautiful it was. Ann and her husband, Tom, took us to a flea market on a giant parking lot. It was enormous, it went on for ages and it was filled with all this stuff we didn't even understand. American stuff. We had a great day. It was such a relief away from the band, being in the same discussions and situations with the guys in a van or in a hotel. It was just the two of us, and we felt like we could relax and breathe.

When we got back to Hollywood, we checked to see if Peet was okay. He wasn't. There were two girls in his room, and some kind of drug deal had gone down. I think it was heroin, as they were all nodding off and couldn't really speak. We felt like "Oh, God, back to reality." From then on it all started to collapse around Peet, and it was very sad to watch.

We flew from the States to Montserrat in the Caribbean to make our last album, *Luminous Basement*, at George Martin's studio. We were the second band ever to record there after Earth, Wind and Fire, and that album was much more weird and trippy.

It was my first experience of the Caribbean, which I fell in love with immediately. We arrived on this tiny little plane, and everything was really bizarre, because Peet and Annie were not really getting on. They were very different personalities from the beginning, and I think he didn't want Annie to be in the band in the first place, and Annie always found it hard to relate to him. Peet was an amazingly sweet character when he wasn't drinking, but as soon as alcohol took hold, he became a different person. Anyway, making the album in Montserrat was not a good experience at all—the studio and accommodation were stunning, beautiful, but there was trouble brewing in paradise, and we were worn-out.

We were overworked, and things got overheated. Stopping recording sessions to do photo shoots in the jungle for the UK press was not our idea of fun, and the whole band was on edge most of the time. Annie and I kind of retreated into our world and became detached from the whole recording process. Again Peet had written some great material. "Walls and Foundations" and "All Life's Tragedies" are to this day really strong songs, but the experience recording them was painful.

The first song that Annie and I ever wrote wasn't really a song; it was an instrumental we composed during our time in Montserrat. It was a sound collage, really, called "From the Middle Room," a very experimental track, electronic and weird, and nothing like the rest of the Tourists' music. We did it while recording the Tourists album *Luminous Basement*, but nobody was in the studio: no Peet, no producer,

just me and Annie and the engineer. I said, "Let's just experiment," and
we got the guy to record our sonic doodling.

Then I suggested, "How about making it sound all phased and
jungly?" and we recorded the crickets outside and brought in this weird
psychedelic harpsichord sound. It was pure experimentation. We put it
on the B-side of the single, which was a luminous kind of fluorescent
yellow see-through vinyl. The reason we called it "From the Middle
Room" was that Annie and I were still living in the squat, and our room
was called the middle room. If somebody said, "Where's my guitar?"
we'd say, "It's in the middle room." "Where's Dave and Annie?"
"They're in the middle room." So we called it that. It was our own
private joke. And that record was, I can see now, the beginning of Annie
and me thinking about Eurythmics. That was the start. That was the
moment.

We left for Australia to promote the album by way of exotic Thailand, except it became more nightmarish than exotic because of Peet's
habit. First, we were stuck in Thailand longer than we had planned,
so Peet's planning of "how much gear he had to last him until he got
to Australia" didn't pan out. In Bangkok, he must have tried to do a
deal, and the people came in his room and threw his suitcase out the
window and ripped him off. So he ended up buying just two bottles of
ginseng whiskey and drinking them instead. He was in a terrible state.

Things didn't improve Down Under, and the Tourists virtually
imploded. We had just arrived, and that very same night Peet over-
dosed in Sydney. He was deathly ill. The next morning we were about
to do TV and radio, when our tour manager told us that Peet couldn't
make it because he'd been found on the floor of a junkie hangout in
Sydney's funky King's Cross area, having convulsions and frothing at
the mouth. Luckily, he had his passport and room key with him—
miraculously neither was stolen—and someone called the hotel.

The next day he flew home and we prayed he'd find some way of
recovering. We realized it was impossible to keep this band together

with our lead singer in such bad shape. Peet wrote all the songs as well as singing them. Without him there was no band. We fulfilled a few obligations that we were committed to do on this Australian promotion tour, not sure whether Peet was coming back or if our band had any future.

One day in the middle of all this confusion, while we were still in Australia, I was walking around outside, and I stepped on a bracelet lying in the street. It was an inexpensive chunky kind of bracelet, costume jewelry at best, and I walked around the corner and there was the sign of a pawnbroker, the Three Balls. So I went in and said, "Look, I've got this bracelet."

He said, "Where'd you get it?"

I said, "Well, I was walking down the road, down there, and it was on the ground. It was nobody's."

And he was going, "You sure about that?"

I said, "Yeah!"

He looked at it and told me with typical Aussie candor that it was worth sod all. But he had a little plastic 8mm cine camera there, and I asked him if he would trade me for it. He said, "Yep." I didn't even know if it worked. I needed a battery that could go in the handle. I said, "Do you have any film for it?" He said, "Well, I don't know if it's for that camera, but we've got boxes of film." He gave me three or four film cartridges. I put one in the camera, it worked and I walked out of the shop, filming. A film I have to this day.

I went back to the hotel room and told Annie about my new camera and how I'd exchanged it for a bracelet I'd found in the street. She said, "I can't believe you bought a camera when there's so many things we really need." I said, "Yeah, but I think we could probably shoot and make little films with it."

This trip had so many insane things happen in one week. We flew to Perth, taking off from Melbourne, and one of our plane's wings caught fire. People were screaming, and the pilot said we had to circle for at least thirty minutes, jettisoning fuel. It was terrifying, and when we landed back down in Melbourne airport, we were met by dozens of fire trucks. If that wasn't bad enough, once we reboarded our flight to Perth, it was another terrible flight with awful turbulence. When we finally arrived, our nerves were frayed to shreds.

Then, when the airport doors opened, we were hit with a bombshell. A voice over the PA announced John Lennon had been shot and killed, and everyone just broke down in tears. It was December 8, 1980. A day a lot of us will never forget.

On the plane back to England, we were convinced that the Tourists were over and that we'd lost Peet for good. Annie and I sat next to each other and discussed the situation. We were exhausted and had been in each other's company constantly, so we decided we should give each other a break. Considering how tight the two of us had been, how close and closeted and loving and codependent, it was an intense moment and an alarming decision to even consider. We both agreed, pulled down our eyeshades and went to sleep.

When we got back home, we were still sort of together, but I began to get really ill. This strange thing happened with my lung, and it was terribly painful. It became difficult to breathe at times, and it had been happening more and more frequently since the car accident back in Germany with Jude. As much as the idea freaked me, I knew I had to go to hospital.

Once there it was decided I needed this big operation, which would result in a huge scar. They punctured my lung, but I had to be awake. It was a nightmare and real, not some acid-flashback nightmare. The doctor had to lean over me with a needle and force it into my chest. This took a lot of force and precision to penetrate the chest wall yet stop before puncturing the lung. Then they said they had to do a major operation, because I'd had both lungs collapse at different times. If both sides collapse at the same time, it's curtains. I had no idea how painful this was going to be or how long the recuperation would last;

this at a time when Annie and I had decided not to be together. I had never felt so alone. But when Annie saw my pathetic and depleted state, she decided she'd better look after me. This whole story is in our song "17 Again," which was written years later for the album *Peace*:

Yea though we ventured through the valley of the stars
You and all your jewelry
And my bleeding heart
Who couldn't be together and who could not be apart
We should've jumped out of that airplane after all
Flying skyways overhead
It wasn't hard to fall
And I had so many crashes that I couldn't feel at all

It explains everything. I was completely knackered. Annie was really scared and worried about me but trying her best to look after me. I kept saying, "I don't feel right." I would literally pass out in my own bed. When doctors do this kind of operation, they move your rib cage, so imagine that pain.

We were no longer supposed to be together as a couple, but as I slowly recovered, Annie would try to help me walk to the corner shop and back, even though it was like walking around with an octogenarian, as I was so weak from the operation.

Then she went off to Scotland to see her parents, and the separation was official and final. I made a couple of friends, and I slowly got back into feeling semi-okay.

Then I went up to Sunderland to see my dad. I met a great girl called Toni Halliday, who was a sixteen-year-old singer-songwriter who had very spiky white blond hair and a beautiful smile, and I could see she had a real edge, a lot of attitude. We got on really well and became friends. I slowly started to get my own little group of other friends around, but I still felt that I didn't want to admit the breakup with Annie was a reality. I would tell everyone, "Well, we seem to have broken up," but it seemed pretty weird to me.

Our friends would say, "We don't get it. We always thought of you two as a couple. It was always Dave and Annie, and wherever you went, whether you were in a restaurant, or at the record shop, or on the road, or at a jumble sale or a car boot sale, it was Dave and Annie. So why are you separating?"

I remember we were desperately confused about it. Annie was crying all the time, and she knew we couldn't be together, yet it was so painful to be apart. It was a very confusing time.

I'd met this man in the hospital, Mr. Fogle, who was in the bed next to me. This sounds crazy, but he was a magician and his wife was his assistant. They would perform magic shows to entertain the troops in war zones, in Germany or in Africa, and he used to do a trick of catching a bullet in his teeth. But some dopey soldier guy got up on the stage and shot a real bullet at him, into his head. The audience was thinking it was part of the joke. But his head was gushing blood. His wife, the magician's assistant, was saying, "No, this is not a joke." But the crowd was laughing more, because they thought she was part of it too till they realized it was real, and everybody freaked out and he was put in a helicopter. He had an emergency operation. Half of his skull was missing. And he was in the bed next to me.

He would blow his nose as I shuffled past him to go to the bathroom. He had a white hankie with black spots. But when he shook it, it was a black hankie with white spots. But he never told me he was a magician. I was on these heavy post-op sedation drugs, and I thought I was going mad. But then he told me his story and why he was there. He'd invented something called the Fogle Scope. He thought he was going to die and wanted to know if I could help him get it on the market to help his kids. It was like the last desperate act of a dying man.

After we were both out of the hospital, Annie and I went to see him on his birthday. I'd always written nice letters to him. When we arrived, his wife took Annie and me aside and said, "He's not got long.

He's dying." Then the two of them showed us their scrapbook of their lives, starting with when they had first gotten together back when they were young. She had been his assistant ever since. It was so sad.

Annie and I were looking at the scrapbook, and we were also a couple who worked together, and who were now breaking up, looking at this sweet older couple, and everything they'd been through. I remember I was driving back to the house, which was absurd, as I couldn't really see the road, because the drugs I was still on from the hospital were so strong. Annie was really affected from being at that couple's house. We barely made it home. We realized, *Okay, we are going through some intense shit together*, because we were obviously so sensitive and emotional. We knew we shouldn't put ourselves in that kind of situation again, or anything like that, at least until I could get over this operation. And, ever so slowly, I did get over it.

CHAPTER:5

IN THE GARDEN

When we met, Annie was only twenty-one, studying flute and harpsichord at the Royal Academy, living on her own and working as a waitress. Then boom, straight into a relationship with me where we lived together and formed a band, made records and toured all over the world. Now she was twenty-five, and it was the most intense time of her life, and of mine, because we became slightly successful, but it wasn't the kind of success we wanted. It was not the band we wanted to be in, and not the music we wanted to play. So the band had broken up, and our relationship was falling apart.

It seemed like everything was turning to dust, and Annie went up to Scotland to stay with her parents and I stayed alone in our flat. But at those times when everything seems empty and hopeless, for some reason I feel calm. The same goes for when everything is totally chaotic and out of control—I feel the same sense of calm.

I'm either nuts or somewhere along the line I learned that behind every *no* there is a big *yes* waiting to come out. So I started to experiment on my own with a little tiny synthesizer and a drum machine, recording to a little four-track, and for some reason, I felt overwhelmed with joy. Like a child, I was lost in wonder and could see infinite possibilities. Just doing this every day made me feel so inspired, and I started to come up with a vision of a band built around just Annie and me, the two of us, electronic. I started playing ideas to her on the phone, and she would be listening up in Aberdeen in her parents' house. She loved them. We never stopped talking about music and creativity—she would whisper, "Oh, that sounds really good."

I could hear in her voice that something was sparking, igniting a flame.

When she came back to London, we experimented constantly together. It wasn't easy when Annie and I broke up romantically, but we never broke up as musical partners. So we broke up but we didn't break up. We were apart but still together. It was confusing because we were so used to constantly being in each other's company, sometimes twenty-four hours straight; we lived together, and we were in a band together; we were inseparable. And we were best friends. We didn't argue ever. In the whole of our relationship, we didn't argue once! But it got to the point where we felt like we were smothered by each other by being together constantly. It became what the French call a "folie à deux," which means when two people are in each other's company too much, and it becomes insular and slightly crazy. It gets to where you don't really want to go out to see other people. You stay in all the time.

Annie and I were so close that when the reality finally kicked in that we had really split up, it was devastating. It felt like having my right arm cut off or one side of my brain removed.

It's not easy, this transition from lovers to something else. How do you break up with someone when you are still together? We both agreed we could do this, but we didn't realize the real magnitude of stress this would create. It was hard for people to accept why we had split. Everyone was confused, because they knew us as Dave and Annie. We were a pair. So even when we were separated, people didn't accept it; our friends, and the public, all thought we were inseparable but gradually we adjusted.

Annie moved into a flat upstairs, which was a bit crazy, as we could hear each other walking about or playing music and to have any other guest would be extremely awkward. Anyway, we still saw each other every ten minutes for a cup of tea or a chat. During this period I was still not fully recovered from my operation and a little weak. Annie was really sweet and would come downstairs and start making some home cooking again—spaghetti Bolognese, shepherd's pie or a healthy soup—while I carried on twiddling knobs and making strange beats and noises down the corridor.

Looking back we didn't split up like a normal couple or at least the way it seems to play out for most people. We carried on being practically the same with each other and never asked each other where we'd been or who we had been with. All those usual jealous emotions seemed to have escaped us—well, at least during this first year apart.

She eventually moved to a flat at the bottom of the street, and I stayed in the one we had shared. She was a whole street away now, which seemed like another city. We started to build a new life with this arrangement. I started to get back on my feet again, able to go out and meet a friend for a glass of lager, and to understand the situation. "Okay, we are not living together anymore, but we are making music. As a duo."

It was never easy for us to see each other with different girlfriends or boyfriends, but I learned to adjust to Annie being with other people and I always was friendly and tried to make them feel welcome in the room. If they played tennis, we'd play tennis together. If they played music, we'd jam on instruments and get to know one another.

But no matter who our partners were, Annie and I would always be seen to be a couple when we were together. So doors would open for us instead of for our separate partners, and heads would turn to see us and whomever we were with would feel a bit left out. It was an odd situation to deal with, and not unlike what my mum or my dad had to face. Long after they were divorced and remarried, they were always labeled, even by me, as Jack and Sadie.

The music we were creating was nothing at all like pop; it was a whole other world. We would put on our "pop" police hats and immediately wipe and discard anything that sounded too commercial. In my bedroom, I was recording on a simple four-track cassette Portastudio, making really good little demos. Annie and I were enjoying the fact that we could experiment and do anything.

Annie and I struggled on and slowly started to evolve a plan. We would be a duo and would call ourselves Eurythmics, much to the bafflement of the people at RCA records, who couldn't even pronounce the word. I remember at one meeting an executive said, "Isn't that a sexually transmitted disease?"

The name actually stemmed from the fact Annie had studied Dalcroze Eurhythmics, a well-known method of teaching music developed in the early twentieth century by Swiss musician and educator Émile Jaques-Dalcroze. Dalcroze Eurhythmics teaches concepts of rhythm, structure and musical expression through physical movement. Dalcroze discovered that moving your body in time with the music through specific exercises leads to improved understanding of musical concepts, improvisation, and overall musicianship. Actually we liked the name because it had "Eur" for "Europe" and "rhythm" in the middle; we took the "h" out before the "y" to change Eurhythmics into Eurythmics.

We recorded our first album with the famous German producer Conny Plank in his studio in the tiny village of Wolperath near Cologne. The album was dark and moody. We didn't think at all about whether it would be successful; we just hid away in the middle of the German countryside and smoldered. It was like we knew something was being born but were not sure what yet. We had interesting avant-garde musicians play with us: Holger Czukay and Jaki Liebezeit (both of the band Can), Marcus Stockhausen and Robert Görl from D.A.F. We also had drummer Clem Burke (of Blondie) and Roger Pomphrey, a friend from Crouch End. A couple of the songs were cowritten by Roger: "English Summer" (featuring lots of rain sounds recorded especially) and "Caveman Head."

We called the album *In the Garden*. We always thought about music visually and often explained later in interviews we wanted to create the feeling of beauty and sadness together, like in a garden when the roses have just peaked and are turning bloodred—a kind of sweet decay. We even went so far as to try to capture that on the album cover: beautiful photographs taken by Peter Ashworth with Annie and me looking like emotional refugees in an overgrown garden; on photos inside the cover, Annie and I wore animal masks, and you could see we were going through a transformation.

The album kind of creeped out, as the label was not sure what to think of it, but some people took notice that something very different was emerging from the two of us.

In 1981 we performed our debut single, "Never Gonna Cry Again," on *The Old Grey Whistle Test*. We were introduced by Annie Nightingale, and this was our first public performance. It was a strange performance, with me on bass, Clem Burke on drums, Roger on guitar. Toward the end of "Never Gonna Cry Again," Holger Czukay wandered across the stage, playing a French horn, much to the bewilderment of the TV audience.

My favorite song on *In the Garden* is "Take Me to Your Heart," so simple but it got under your skin and showed the early signs of what Annie and I could write together. What came next was to be an avalanche of music, but first, we were learning how to do everything ourselves, with no money, just a whole lot of inspiration, determination and, of course, love.

We realized that if we had only a small amount of money—enough to buy the right equipment—we could make a record on our own without a producer or anything.

Adam Williams helped us make this transition. He was really a lovely guy, and he understood that Annie and I were this quirky couple who had ideas and wanted to get them down on tape. He was the bassist in a band called the Selecter, which was part of the Britsh two-tone ska- and reggae-inspired movement with bands like the Specials and Madness. Adam was obsessed with reggae bass playing. But he'd also learned how to record on an eight-track, and he knew the minimum amount of equipment we would need to put it together, and it would cost about five thousand pounds, which, to us, was a small fortune, as Annie and I didn't have that much money between us.

I suggested we visit our local bank manager. Annie wasn't too sure this was going to work. A—we didn't look like the kind of people banks lend money to, and B—how would we explain what we wanted to use it for? So I went prepared with pictures cut out of newspapers and magazines of the exact equipment we wanted to buy and information about how much each piece cost. When we were invited into the bank manager's tiny office, we were both nervous, so I just went into overdrive, talking excitedly about how we could make masterpieces on this equipment, and we would save so many studio bills that if we had success, we would make a lot more money because we wouldn't have so much unrecouped debt to the label.

Annie sat quietly, looking very serious, and to our amazement, the bank manager stood up and said, "That sounds like a very good plan," and agreed to the loan. We were stunned. I remember Annie and me standing outside the bank with him shaking our hands when out of the corner of my eye I saw my friend Ashley pull up, wildly waving to us, driving a car with nine cats in it! Ashley had his own form of "situationist art" at the time. He stopped, jumped out of the car, carrying three of his feline friends, and made us all hold them while he began snapping Polaroids. Here we were, standing with the bank manager, who now had a cat on his head, with Annie and me looking dead serious, holding cats on either side.

I was hissing, "Not now, Ashley!" through clenched teeth. But, come to think of it, it was perfect synergy, like a piece of voodoo art: a spell had been cast. I wish I had copies of those Polaroids today, but Ashley disappeared with them and the cats and drove off.

The manager slowly backed into his bank, looking nervously from side to side, wondering what was going to happen next, and seriously worrying about the decision he'd just made to finance these two strange young people whose friend had just photographed him with a cat on his head. It was turning into *Dog Day Afternoon*, except the manager wanted to get back in the bank rather than get out.

We bought all the gear on the list, and Adam and I set about putting together the studio in a small loft space we had rented above Falconer's Picture Framing Factory in Chalk Farm.

Conny Plank had shown me how to operate lots of stuff in his studio, but his was a much bigger deal—twenty-four track—and Conny had built a mixing recording desk, and it was very complicated. What we bought with our bank loan was a simple-to-operate TEAC eight-track recorder and a secondhand Revox two-track recorder to mix down onto. We had minimal other equipment: a Klark Teknik spring reverb, a Bel noise reduction system, a Roland space echo and our pride and joy, a Soundcraft secondhand desk with sixteen inputs, meaning we could record and mix our own records for the first time.

Hallelujah!

The Loft was a very tiny, cramped space, and you had to duck most of the time because it had eaves and huge beams. There was one tiny circular window that looked out over Camden Town. When they would make the picture frames, the guillotine sound slicing the wood made a loud clunk in the studio, so if we were recording with a microphone, we'd have to wait between executions.

Adam knew all about the specific equipment we bought and quickly showed me the ropes. I was very excited, as I thought for now it could do everything we wanted. It was possible to do our own music now. It was very self-contained, and we could record with Adam being the engineer. Since he wasn't always around, I also learned to do it all myself. By experimenting with Adam and alone, I learned every trick you could do with delay and echo and using a compressor. We actually just used the noise reduction switched in and out as a compressor at the time.

I learned that anything is possible if you ignore the rules. If I wanted to distort the drum machine, no one could stop me; if I wanted to mix the sound of the street with the guitar, that was fine too.

Once I had this freedom, I would go into the studio on my own for hours. I'd work twenty hours in a row, easy. Annie would be back in her little flat. She'd come in, and I would play this stuff that was just insane, bonkers stuff, very weird and totally experimental. There would be monks chanting against drum loops, and I would be playing weird instruments I'd bought in Camden Market, like Thai stringed instruments or Moroccan percussion. But she was always great about it, always interested, because she loved being experimental too. I'd get other kids of all nationalities in from the street to shout or make noises to record. It was very important for me to experiment to the point of extreme madness and then reel it all back into the *Sweet Dreams* album.

I was so obsessed with recording, I would go to the studio all the time and switch on all the gear like lighting up a TARDIS, and I'd invite people up. I don't think Annie even knew how many people I asked up there to record. Just to experiment, and learn how to record music. I'd meet some guys who were a duo in Camden Market and invite them too. And I'd be the engineer and record them and help program a beat and play instruments. For me it was a massive learning experience. And, of course, other people wanted to have a day off or an evening off or a weekend off, but I knew I'd be in there until three in the morning, going cross-eyed trying to learn all of this stuff.

Annie and I came up with a manifesto, which we nailed to the wall of our tiny loft there in the factory. We separated likes and don't likes or dos and don'ts, listing everything from music to visuals—how to present to the world our thing.

We had:

LIKES

Motown
Electronic
Soul
Andy Warhol
Dub Music
Gilbert and George

And so on.

You can see that from this list came the birth of the *Sweet Dreams* album. It gave us a path, which we followed. It had our influences—soul and electronic music, two disparate musical traditions that, when combined, gave us our signature: electronic textures with a soulful voice on top.

We stated our lifelong allegiance to the British artists Gilbert and George, who are among the most influential artists to hail from Britain. Theirs is what Annie and I based our look on, the image of the two of them in matching suits. So Annie and I wore identical suits. Like us, they did everything together. They went to college together, lived together and worked together. They posed as living sculptures. They were the most significant British conceptual artists of their time. They had a lasting influence on us in every way, the understanding that art is work and work is art.

Right at the start, we bought matching suits. We extended that philosophy through all our years together, and in everything we did. Almost twenty years later, when there was an exhibition of our photos, Annie and I wore matching outfits, went, sat down and never moved. We sat still as statues and silent. All influenced by Gilbert and George.

That original inspiration lived on in our work and our art forever.

Eventually, we began to organically discover our own signature style in the mixture of electronic and acoustic sounds. We'd use a drum machine groove but augmented by a real shaker. Or we would mix a real electric guitar with street recordings we'd make. Every song became a sonic collage. Even "Sweet Dreams" has that signature. Everybody thinks it's totally electronic, but there are several organic sounds mixed in there. There's a track on there of Annie and me playing glass milk bottles with sticks.

This was a weird time in our lives. Annie and I had broken up, but we spent hours and hours together every day in the studio. We learned early on that when we worked together, we could create something special, unlike what we would do on our own. She once said, "I think to combine the sum of both of our parts was actually greater than our two individual selves." I think one of the reasons Annie and I became such an explosive recording-and-songwriting duo is that she had studied classical music at the same time I'd been learning everything from Robert Johnson and Delta Blues music all the way through Stax, Motown, and via the West Coast Crosby, Stills and Nash–type music. She had studied all the classical composers but was also deeply influenced by a whole spectrum of British and American sixties pop music, rock, folk as well as Motown that she'd grown up with as a young teenage girl in Aberdeen. I had studied blues, soul and pop, and I'd also learned how to play most styles of music. I knew all the chords to songs by the Beatles, the Clash, the Staple Singers, the Rolling Stones, Marvin Gaye, Sam Cooke and the legendary Robert Johnson.

When the two of us came together, it was like this mad hybrid of knowing the whole gamut of music, so we felt we could do anything, and then we'd do it. Sometimes we'd work until one in the morning and then drive home together and go to our separate places. Then we'd get up in the morning and go back to the tiny studio for hours upon hours. This went on for months. It seemed like years. But in reality it was about eight months of experimentation.

Occasionally this would result in something great, and we honed it on those passages that became "Love Is a Stranger," "Sweet Dreams," "This Is the House" and "The Walk." None of those is a conventional pop song, but they are undeniably infectious. Even before we released them, we realized this, because people who came to watch and listen to us working would then walk around all day singing them. This would lead us to celebrating and ordering jugs of margaritas from the restaurant in the street below, getting blind drunk and dancing around in our cramped studio, delirious with the music we had just made.

CHAPTER:6

HOLD YOUR HEAD UP, MOVING ON

Annie was now living on her own in a tiny bedsit again and feeling very lonely and emotionally down. She was curled up one day on the floor of the studio in a kind of fetal position, saying, "Oh, nothing works. Nothing will ever come of what we're doing. It's just no good. I don't know why we're here. . . ."

Though I felt sorry for the way she was feeling, I was also excited because I started to get a rhythm going on this drum machine we'd found in Bridgwater. It was a weird prototype that we'd heard about, so Adam and I had driven two hundred miles outside of London and slept on somebody's floor just to acquire it. I was completely fascinated and obsessed with recording and experimenting on it. This was not like drum machines nowadays; this was quite complicated to operate. It had analog and synthesized drum sounds and a tiny visual monitor. We were recording only on an eight-track tape recorder and one of the tracks had to be used to record time code to sync up to the drum machine. On the first beat, I'd tuned one of the tom-tom drums down so low, it sounded like an African drum, and it landed on top of a four-on-the-floor bass drum pattern I'd programmed in. But I couldn't get the fucking thing to stop, and it was deafening and blasting on the first beat of every bar: "Boom dum dum dum. Boom dum dum dum." It was like driving an out-of-control steam engine.

The sound of these drums woke Annie up out of her depression. She picked her head up, asked, "What's that?" and went straight to the keyboard. She started playing this great riff with a string sound on the Kurzweil, and it locked in with my weird drum pattern. I grabbed our Roland SH-101 synthesizer and started playing "Um-dit-um-dit-um-dit-um" with her "Doom dum dum dum dum dum dum dum." These three sounds together—the keyboard, the drum and the synthesizer—were the only tracks happening, yet they created this monstrous feeling. We were very, very excited!

Annie immediately started to get some ideas for lyrics and went down to this little empty room below the studio to write. Shortly after, she came out with: "Sweet dreams are made of this!" Incredible! And could there be a more appropriate title?

Very quickly the song was getting constructed, and then we realized it was just doing the same thing all the time, so I suggested there had to be another section, and that section should be positive. In the middle we added these chord changes rising upward with "Hold your head up, moving on. Keep your head up, moving on."

When Annie was really excited about something, a lightbulb would go off in her head, and the race to the end was always incredible. She was singing, "Some of them want to use you. Some of them want to get used by you. Some of them want to abuse you." All of these great lines she was coming up with off the top of her head. In the space of literally twenty minutes, Annie changed from being down on the floor to leaping about the room. A major hit was born!

To us it was a massive breakthrough, but I remember later some famous publishers coming to hear it, and they didn't get it at all. They just kept saying, "I don't understand this song. It doesn't have a chorus." But the thing is, it just goes from beginning to end, and the whole song is a chorus. There is not one note that is not a hook.

I was so excited about the song, I drew a storyboard of the video and marched down to the record label to show them the concept. I'd based a lot of it on Luis Buñuel– and Salvador Dalí–type surrealist movie imagery. A few people were saying, "Dave, why the cow? Annie is so good-looking."

Those people should go buy a copy of the book *Purple Cow* by Seth Godin, about how to make your business remarkable. It was written twenty years after I had the purple cow in our video—which certainly did the trick and made my whole life remarkable. You can see me operating the actual drum computer we used in the recording in the video of "Sweet Dreams." I carried it into the field full of cows, and in the boardroom, when the cow turns her head to mine and our eyes meet, it's a very surreal moment.

When we played live, unlike the record that faded out on the riff, we always ended the song with the "Keep your head up" section. In fact we always ended our concerts with "Sweet Dreams" but the last line we always sang was "Keep your head up."

Today, more than thirty years later, "Sweet Dreams" is everywhere. It has been recorded and performed live by hundreds of deejays, singers and rappers, including Beyoncé, Marilyn Manson, Pink, Nas, David Guetta, Avicii—the list goes on. It's been played on just about every radio station in the world, and to this day it's being played on the radio, in a concert, in a club, somewhere every second of every minute of every day. EDM (Electronic Dance Music) festivals around the world often feature various deejays' versions blasting during the high point of their sets. Somewhere right now, as you are reading this, there are drunken karaoke versions being sung in Japanese, Russian, and Italian. It follows me around every day, everywhere I go. Trying on clothes in a boutique, buying organic veggies at the market, riding an elevator or driving past someone else's car and hearing it on their radio. Sometimes it's like that, you know? Something that took a very short piece of time to create and not even a few hours to produce becomes the lightning rod that affects the rest of your life.

Having the studio to create in every day, Annie and I started to become amazingly creative songwriting partners, true collaborators, and we began to write all our songs together like Rodgers and Hammerstein, Jagger and Richards, Lennon and McCartney, and Marr and Morrissey. I'm not sure exactly how these other songwriters worked together, but all I know is they must have recognized that when they did, sparks would fly. Annie and I played different roles and didn't step on each other's toes. I was always experimenting at the desk or on an instrument, and Annie would sit behind me with a notepad, thinking or writing furiously. It's a kind of alchemy that occurs, a magical process of making something out of nothing. One minute a song doesn't exist, and twenty minutes later it does. We always knew within ten or twenty minutes if it was worth pursuing an idea, and we very rarely disagreed. Once or twice I would fight for something but usually we were on the same page.

Our recording process was that much easier because by default I had become the record producer, and that meant we could do anything. We could play all the instruments between us, record ourselves, make mistakes and not care, just laugh about it.

Freedom at last!

Sometimes I would program the drums, play the bass on synth or real bass, play the guitars and other keyboard parts, engineer myself recording the sounds and Annie's vocals and keyboard parts and then mix it all in a few hours, a magic feeling, as for once we were in full control!

Usually there was no one in the room while we were writing, as whoever was working with us would tactfully make an exit when they felt something was brewing. Then, when we recorded, there would be one engineer—someone we trusted not to break the spell; people we knew and felt comfortable with. We didn't go looking for an engineer through the record label or a studio, and we didn't use expensive studios or expensive equipment. We were always about keeping it close or DIY.

I also had the role as manager all the way through the first two albums, *In the Garden* and *Sweet Dreams*. This meant having to deal with the record label, figure out schedules for performing and organize how we would actually stage this strange music we were making.

We loved putting our shows together, from choosing great players to thinking about the stage set or the intro music. We were involved in every aspect, literally. A true collaborative partnership.

Most of our first concerts were very experimental. I would come up with ideas of how to play with just three people onstage, operating even the lights ourselves while performing. Adam Williams and I were convinced that we could have the mixing desk onstage behind Annie and me so we could get the same mix as the audience, and Adam could use the desk like an instrument, doing a kind of dub mix to what we were actually doing live. It sounded amazing sometimes and terrible other times. The audience was often confused about what was going on.

Annie could sing and then add a harmony to the delay coming back. It was all being performed in real time, but I remember that on a college tour, some of the students would ask afterward if we were actually playing or miming! This was partly because the sound was so perfect that it didn't seem real.

Today artists like Björk or Lorde use prerecorded sound to augment their live sound. Even bands like the Foo Fighters or U2 use loops or prerecorded tracks along with their live sound. But back then it was highly unusual. Sometimes it worked, and sometimes it would be on the edge of catastrophe.

Only Annie's performance skills salvaged us from a perpetual train wreck. In order to play as just three people, I invented a crazy setup using a lighting boom stand and balancing my double-neck guitar and bass with counterweights on the other side. I'd use a see-through fishing line to create the illusion of the guitar being suspended in midair.

Our sound was very strange at those early shows and the songs were strange too, with titles like "4/4 in Leather." It was all about being as free and as crazy as we wanted after being stuck in a band. We didn't want to be put in any box and categorized in any way, so we just went slightly mental. It was a very useful creative process, and we were proving a lot to ourselves; we were not afraid of anything. After what seemed to be a long period of experimentation in our tiny rented space above the picture framers in Chalk Farm, we got this out of our system. We started to write songs, one after another, and recorded them. We wouldn't make demos of the songs. The demos were the masters.

We never did preproduction or anything like that. We would be recording while we were writing. The songwriting, the recording, the performance—all of it was one single process.

Our work ethic became almost like a mission that only the two of us could understand, and to explain it to a third party seemed a bit pointless. I believe we were so distraught that we had separated as a couple that in a way we had to prove, to ourselves and to each other, that it all meant something. There can't be that much love between two people that it could just vanish into thin air. That's why you can hear it in our music. Performing live was a very emotional experience for both of us and for the audience.

Annie has a very distinctive kind of voice, very soulful and powerful, and unique. There's something about the tone of certain voices, whether it's Bob Dylan's or Joss Stone's, Bryan Ferry's, Sinéad O'Connor's or Mick Jagger's. It just sounds like them immediately. As soon as Mick Jagger starts singing, you know it couldn't be anybody else. Annie has that quality that is unmistakably Annie Lennox. You know instantly it's them because they are not actually singing with their voices; they are singing with their souls. When you're writing and working with people who have that quality in their voices, it'd be very easy to be lazy and just use any old song because it's going to sound good anyway. But

Annie and I were obsessed with not using any old song. We wanted it to be a great song. Unless you pair a great voice with a great song, you will never reach the world, and that's what we always aimed for—not in a "rule the world" way; we just wanted to touch people, no matter who they were or where they were from.

The sound of music coming out of the radio or ghetto blaster or fancy sound system had to be consistent, so when I was mixing any record, I would have a little portable ghetto blaster and a crappy radio as well as some good speakers and some monster speakers, constantly switching between them. I'd even go so far as to add some compression and broadcast to a car and drive around listening as if the music was on the radio.

With Eurythmics, and with all my productions, I'm one of those old-fashioned record producers who likes to make music around the voice. Back in the fifties, if you heard a Patsy Cline record, everything was built around the singer. The musicians are great, the arrangements superb, but they're all following the singer. Back then, or even before that, it was the conductor of the orchestra or the bandleader who was really producing the record. The music was going down on one track or two tracks in one take, so the balance between the singer and the music had to be perfect so you could hear every word, but still hear and feel those great parts those musicians were playing.

That's the way I look at it today. People want to hear and feel the emotion in the human voice, and for me that's the most important thing to get right. There came a point in music when you could have forty-eight tracks, then seventy-two tracks or so, and just create a giant wall of music. And not a good wall of sound, like Phil Spector's—which was crafted always around the singer—but just a big wall with no dynamics that would overcome the voice. I believed in following the voice on its journey, and that's still my thing. The success of Adele is no surprise, as everything is built around her voice.

Eurythmics always had a stylistic freedom most bands don't have. We weren't restricted to the sound of the band, whereas the Heartbreakers are going to sound like the Heartbreakers, and the Stones are going to sound like the Stones. We could sound like anything and be anything we wanted. So we'd record a song with an orchestra and an accordion, and the next thing is totally electronic, and the next one is Stax soul with a horn section. We were entirely in control.

The record label never questioned us or said, "You can't do that," because they'd hear it and go, "Holy shit, that sounds great!" So we had more freedom, in terms of sound and production, than a normal band. And that freedom is reflected in every album, and every song, that desire to do something different each time.

In a lot of songwriting collaborations, one person writes solely the words and the other solely the music, like Elton John and Bernie Taupin. Annie and I recorded at the same time, like making a sound collage. Sometimes I would kick off a song by starting to make a whole section of music, but Annie would sometimes come in with an idea straightaway that she'd worked out on a keyboard, and we would go from there. But usually we didn't try to work on anything until we sat in the room together.

I must say Annie is a genius songwriter in her own right. I was a kind of catalyst in a way, a trigger to explore and explode a wealth of songs and styles. But Annie, like many songwriters, can become prone to writer's block, and if you dwell on writer's block, it can be torturous. When we wrote together, I thought I could break that spell and used what I would call "breaking the plane," which could be anything from taking a walk to standing on your head. It doesn't matter what it is as long as it changes the train of thought. Brian Eno created a pack of cards called Oblique Strategies, which is useful for breaking through creative blocks.

Annie has within her the talent and instincts and ability to write some of the greatest songs ever, and she already has. But she might not necessarily feel like doing it all the time, which I understand, as there are many other things in life that overwhelm us all, particularly if you have become a mother and a known figure.

Annie is a brilliant lyricist, vocalist and tunesmith. I recognized

Annie as a writer within seconds when she first played her old harmonium and sang for me alone in her tiny room in Camden Town. Those songs she played on that harmonium were astounding. I knew I was in the presence of greatness, and I was not confused about it. The clever trick of great singers, such as Frank Sinatra, was choosing the right songs to sing—even better for Annie and me was that we could write the right songs for her to sing. We would spend time making sure it was the right key for her to sing in, where the song is resonating through her whole body. We'd keep altering the key slightly, taking it down a half step, to where she didn't have to sing powerfully, but the sound was melancholy and cutting at the same time.

An aspect of our lives that most people don't understand is that the conversation between Annie and me, and between all songwriters, artists and musicians, never stops. It's a constant thing. People think that we make an album or do a tour and then stop, take a break and put the music away. But it never happens. Whether it's us or Mick Jagger or David Byrne, or whoever it is, it's a never-ending conversation. Being an artist means you don't have a five-day week and then stop for the sixth day. Being an artist involves every day of the week, nonstop, from the minute you wake up until you go to bed.

People also think that famous musicians—whether it's Bono, Leonard Cohen, Alicia Keyes, Rihanna or Annie—know or believe they are great and never question it. Not true! I have never heard someone come offstage and go, "I was amazing." No. They are all extremely self-critical, very aware of what wasn't right, what went wrong. I think it's the same with great athletes. They don't finish and say, "I've just run the best race of my life." They analyze what they did wrong to get it better the next time.

This close collaboration with Annie made it easy for me to write songs with many other artists. One of the secrets to my ability to collaborate with so many other talents is that I take all the pressure away. As Mick Jagger said, there's no angst. It's done out of joy. Stevie Nicks was very happy when she realized this, and said, "Oh, hang on. We can just have fun and not worry?"

And I said, "Yeah, you know why? Because if we don't like it, nobody will ever hear it."

People have gotten used to the pattern of having to make a new album at the same time they're touring, and the record company is waiting for it, so there is a lot of pressure. Suddenly they have a handful of weeks to write and record twelve new songs. The pressure is remarkable and not conducive at all to writing good songs.

So when I come along and say, "Well, you know, it doesn't really matter if you don't like it. Nobody will ever hear it. We'll just throw it away, burn it. It doesn't make a difference," suddenly it's a whole new world. There is no pressure, and you're allowed to make mistakes, and you know everything is fine. You don't have to think everything is precious. When you're relaxed, great things happen, and you can capture something truly amazing. And this creates momentum, because you use that energy and it leads to more ideas and inspiration. People get excited, and it becomes fun. And when you're having fun making music, it's infectious, for yourself and everyone around you. And it's also much nicer for your family when you, eventually, get home. When I say nothing matters and we can burn it, it's a kind of reverse psychology. Often your collaborator will say, "Oh, but I really like that! Let's keep it," or "Let's put it on the track."

With me and Annie, on any Eurythmics tracks, we always hit the nail on the head with this dynamic of despair and hope at the same time. It would be really dark, and then boom, it would transform musically and lyrically and in every way. And those two things together made a magic vibe.

Necessity is the mother of invention, and in the early Eurythmics days, that's what it was all about. We had hardly any instruments or equipment and very little knowledge of how to operate what we had! We had the drum computer that I used for "Sweet Dreams," and I was constantly messing around with it. We had a couple of monophonic synthesizers and a Vox Continental organ, and we sometimes borrowed Reynard Falconer's Oberheim polyphonic synthesizer. When we were tourists—not the Tourists—in Japan, I bought this crazy new electronic instrument called an Omnichord made by Suzuki. It had just come out and was kind of a cross between a toy and an instrument. You could play chords by pressing down buttons with one hand and, with the other, touch or tap on another section, which looked like a flat hair comb, and hear an electronic harp sound. This toy/instrument gave Annie and me hours of fun and drove nearly everyone else mad! The only other person I met who was in love with this weird machine was Brian Eno, who carried one everywhere.

So, needless to say, the backing track to "Love Is a Stranger" is an odd mix of sounds. The track I was building had a kind of frenzied disco drumbeat with the high hat speeding along doing sixteen hits to the bar like an out-of-control train set. The Roland SH-01 synthesizer was playing straightforward pulsing notes, eight notes to the bar. The weird tinkly harp sound from the Omnichord was answering this aggressive beat with a seductive feminine type of sound, and with only three tracks being used, it sounded eerily complete. At the time it sounded urgent and exciting because we had been through walls of guitar sounds for many years, and now this was new and radical!

Annie's sultry voice against this strange marriage of heavy drum and toy harp gave the song a different dimension, almost like an invitation to a dangerous place. Annie sounded both vulnerable and dominant and the lyrics "Love is a stranger in an open car to tempt you in and drive you far away" sounded scary and seductive at the same time.

When Annie lays down a vocal, it's a special moment, because something happens between her mouth and the microphone, a lot like when the camera falls in love with an actress. The microphone likes her, and with the right one and a good balance in her headphones, she can play with her sound and be herself one minute and within a second flip into a character and out again, even if it's just for one word like "obsession." This vocal, like many other songs we recorded, was only one take and was, as always, remarkable.

We were very experimental at the time, and the *Sweet Dreams* album was a collection of the more normal-sounding songs. Many of our other songs were very odd and more for ourselves. I don't think the record label ever even heard them until we gave them as extra tracks on our ultimate collection. "Love Is a Stranger" on the *Sweet Dreams* album was a deviation and has some very odd things about it. It never changes chords when you expect it to, and its structure is strange, with two sections that are neither verses nor choruses. As in "Sweet Dreams" there is no distinction between verse and chorus; there are just different sections that seem to fit together. I played a little guitar melody with a wibbly-wobbly sound that had nothing to do with anything else going on. All the way through, I made these grunting, breathing-type sounds— God knows why. It just seemed like a good idea at the time. We had our own little studio setup and were in our own little world, so we could do whatever we wanted.

The accompanying video to "Love Is a Stranger" was our foray into surrealist-type filmmaking, and Annie plays three separate extreme characters. The first character is a glamorous call girl (guess who is her chauffeur) paying a visit to a client at what looks like an expensive house. We actually used my mother's apartment! Annie then rips off her wig and takes on an androgynous sneering persona, almost Mick Jagger as a gangster in the movie *Performance*, while spitting out the lyrics "It's gilt-edged, glamorous and sleek by design." She then turns into a dangerous-looking PVC-clad female in a black wig, brandishing a pair of scissors.

You have to remember that at the time videos were quite a new thing, and we were very excited about making them. We would obsess over every detail. For instance, in the "scissors" scene, there are cut-up photographs of specific dead singers on the floor and floating in the bath. Everything we did, even though it may have started out from instinct, had a discipline, thought process and reason behind it, right down to the last film frame and musical note.

The year 1983 is a blur, because we did so many things in that time. I remember Annie and I were in San Francisco the morning after playing the Kabuki Theatre, in my room in a Japanese hotel called the Mikado, and we got a phone call saying that Eurythmics had gone to number one on the *Billboard* chart with "Sweet Dreams."

We really didn't know what to do. We were ecstatic, jumping up and down and looking out the window down on San Francisco! We were so far from home.

America is a complicated place for an English person. For a start, we have a national health service in England for anybody on the street. No matter who you are, if you fall down, you can have a major operation, no charge. If your child is sick, you go to the hospital. When we arrived in America, we got insurance, and then we realized, *Hang on, you have to pay on top of that and on top of that and on top of that and on top of that*. It could be frightening.

Then on the TV they are selling fear constantly. They say, "Oh, have you saved up enough for your pension? You thought you were living to sixty, but you might live till ninety. That's thirty years with no money!" And then the next ad comes on. "Are you finding it irritable to go to sleep? Why not try this drug?" We'd never seen commercials like it. In Britain the BBC was not allowed to have commercials. And on commercial TV, they were very benign: "Try drinking Ovaltine. It has a gentle chocolate flavor, and it might help you get an easy sleep." That was probably the hardest sell you'd get.

So, for the first few years, we resisted even putting the TV on! The first time Annie and I arrived in America, we were in a really cheap hotel, and the guy came and said, "You've got to lock your door in your room not just with the door lock but with the bolt."

We asked, "Okay, but why?"

And he said, "'Cause people burst in."

And we went, "Oh, great."

In the early days, after "Sweet Dreams" hit it big, we'd be so busy on the road—doing interviews for radio stations, playing live concerts, doing TV appearances—that we hardly had any time to think. Not a lot of people know this, but nearly every album we made took only three or four weeks, including writing most of the songs from scratch, so recording was squeezed in between all the other stuff. I would have a portable studio on the road, and we would often put down sketches of ideas in my hotel room. (We even made entire records in hotel rooms!)

Songs, like other things in the universe, will find you if you're open. If you're not open, they don't find you. So we both stayed open—open to experiment, to whatever might come. I might be over in a corner strumming on a guitar or messing around with a synthesizer. I'm usually pushing things forward or monitoring the progress, I suppose. With Annie I often play the role of an enabler. I enable a song to be born.

We released two albums in 1983, *Sweet Dreams* and *Touch*. We started the writing of "Here Comes the Rain Again" when we were at the notorious Mayflower Hotel in New York, in a corner room overlooking Central Park. We used to like to stay in this hotel, I think, because of the windows looking onto the park and the fact that other bands stayed there, so you didn't feel like an alien surrounded by a bunch of suits.

I'd been out on Forty-sixth Street and bought a tiny little keyboard—a really tiny little thing. I think it was one of the early Casio keyboards, about twenty inches long with very small keys. It was an overcast day. Annie was hanging out in my room, and I was playing some little riff on the keyboard, sitting on the window ledge, and Annie was saying, "Oh, let me have a go at that keyboard." But I had just bought it, and a bit like a kid I said, "I'm playing with it now." Anyway, we had this fight over the keyboard, like two seven-year-olds. I managed to win the fight and keep the keyboard. I was playing these little melancholy A minor–ish chords with a B note in it. I kept on playing this riff while Annie looked out the window at the slate gray sky above the New York skyline, and sang spontaneously, "Here comes the rain again." And that was all we needed.

Like with a lot of our songs, we needed only to start with that one line, that one atmosphere, that one note or that intro melody. And the rest of it became a puzzle with missing pieces we filled in. That goes for many—in fact, most—of the songs Annie and I wrote. The feeling or the atmosphere was everything for us. If what we were creating didn't have that something, we would abandon it very quickly.

The making of our *Touch* album was interesting, because it started with our purchase of a studio—except it wasn't a studio; it was an old church. I always marched into crazy schemes like this, and the strangest things would unfold. I was again walking up the street in Crouch End, just like the auspicious day I met Paul Jacobs. I was passing by a church when an older guy, with white hair and beard, leaned out of the church door and whistled at me, beckoning me to cross the road. I was curious, so I went over to see what he wanted.

He said, "Hey, son, are you looking for somewhere?" The more I looked at him, the more he looked like a wizard. So I said, "Well, yeah!"

We had just been told we had to move out of the picture-framing factory because we were behind on the rent, and we were in the middle of recording the *Sweet Dreams* album. He said, "Come inside and look at this."

It was getting a bit spooky, but in for a penny, in for a pound. I went in, and he said he and his mate owned the whole church, and we could use the front office to work in, if I wanted it, for free.

I was confused, but elated. He had just solved our problem in one word: free. Then I thought, *Hang on, there must be a catch*; but there wasn't! By some weird chance, these guys were so thrilled that we would make music in their church that they were happy to do anything for us. They converted sections of it, with their bare hands, in the middle of the night lit by floodlights, to create a little studio for us.

The men turned out to be Bob Bura and John Hardwick, famous British animators of beloved children's TV shows such as *Camberwick Green* and the very odd *Captain Pugwash*. So here we were set up in an old church vestry, making weird electronic noises while Bura and Hardwick were building us a recording studio at no charge. We couldn't fathom our good fortune. We just thought somehow we'd been blessed, and I guess we were, in so many ways.

I remember one day when they were busy building the studio, I decided to go visit my ex, Pam, in her flat. It was quite early in the day, and she answered the door in a robe and said, "Ah, come in. Oh, look, you might like this guy I'm in bed with. He does music, as well. He's called Michael." So we went in the bedroom, and she said, "This is my ex-husband, Dave." Michael said, "Good to meet ya."

I sat down on the side of the bed and said, "What kind of music do you do?" He replied, "Well, I'm in all sorts of experimental bands, but I also do string arrangements and orchestrations." I said, "Oh, shit, yeah, great! Look, Annie and I have written a song called 'Here Comes the Rain Again,' and I imagine a big old string arrangement on it."

He said, "Well, how does it go?'" So I am sitting in bed with a cup of tea next to my ex-wife, and I'm going, "Hang on. Pam, do you have a guitar lying around?" And then I'm playing the chords of our new song. He said, "Oh, okay, I could probably write something up. What kind of thing do you hear in it?" I didn't know anything about orchestration, so I said, "Well, the way I hear it is just loads of strings in the old Motown style, loads of violins." I didn't really know, so I said, "How about twelve cellos and sixteen violins?"

Michael said, "Well, it doesn't really work like that. You probably have violas in the middle." He was being really nice to me, probably thinking, *This guy is nuts*, but because I was this crazy sort of rock/pop–type person he seemed to be into the idea. He said, "I get what ya mean. I'll write something and book the players." I said, "Okay, great. We've got this church to record in."

The trouble was, when the orchestra arrived, there was no room for them. The section Bura and Hardwick had built for us had a little, tiny corridor-shaped control room up a spiral staircase, and a tiny booth for Annie to sing in. The booth was built inside the giant church hall with no way to get into it. But Michael was so sweet, he said, "Well, fucking hell, we will make this work." We had a corridor leading to the church door where the cello players sat all in a row. There was a bathroom with viola players and the violinists were in the kitchen.

Jon Bavin engineered, and I don't know how he didn't have a nervous breakdown while we were trying to do it. There were microphone leads everywhere, trailing down the spiral staircase, hanging down into the hall. Ambient mics in the kitchen and bathroom all leading back to our small Soundcraft desk—but somehow the string sound was incredible—the mixture of the different rooms and our limited capabilities made it sound like an old sixties Motown string sound, exactly what I'd imagined when I had no clue how to do it.

So how we made that record is a miracle. I was playing a big Gretsch Country Club guitar with a Bigsby tremolo arm, along with programmed drums and sequencers. We had a live orchestra all over the church, each with separate sections that poor Michael had to run around conducting. Yet it all came together, and the sound of it was fantastic.

A lot of people thought my guitar playing was a programmed synthesizer sequencer, but I played like that to sound like a sequencer. I'd put my right hand on the bridge and play those patterns, that kind of spot-on playing. I always had to learn spot-on guitar playing because I was playing with things that were rigidly locked in. Then I'd have to do the same thing on the bass and track it. And I basically just made it up as I went along.

While I was in New York, I'd heard of a company that made this insane device called a Voyetra, which was one of the first sampling heads that you could plug into a keyboard. I got one. Annie wasn't into technology. But what was so great about working with her was that she would let me go and experiment, and was always interested in the sounds.

She'd come in and say, "What's going on?" I'd been spending four hours or so trying to get the Voyetra to work. I plugged it in, and the very first sound I got on it was like a steel drum calypso. Annie said, "Oh, that's fantastic." She immediately began playing it, and with that sound, we wrote "Right by Your Side" in about ten minutes.

That song became another big hit. The lyrics again mixed joy with sadness. It had those beautiful lines:

Give me two strong arms to protect myself
Give me so much love that I forget myself
I need to swing from limb to limb
To relieve this mess I'm in
'Cause when depression starts to win
I need to be right by your side.

I wanted to play the guitar with it, because I'd been listening like crazy to King Sunny Adé, the West African legend. So I slowed the tape down to half speed, played a normal-speed solo slow so that when you sped it up, it sounded like King Sunny Adé.

The music was so uplifting that Annie and I started dancing around the studio. It was a really upbeat calypso thing, and then we thought, "Well, we need horns on this." So, in London, we were starting to get musicians from all over the place.

Annie and I had had experienced producers forever restricting our creativity, stopping experiments and saying, "No, that— You can't do that. Oh, that's crazy." So like me she liked to go as far out as we could. I would be just thinking of the craziest idea—the most extreme experiment—and Annie would never say, "Oh, stop that experiment." She'd always sit there, smiling, listening to it, taking it in, and then, at one point she'd go, "Oh, that bit's great."

Now I would do a similar thing with her words, her journal of poetry. Sometimes when working on a song, she would get fed up and say she couldn't think of anything. And I'd take a peek into her journal, and though she'd say, "It's no use. There's nothing good in there," I would persist. And I would look and always find something brilliant and say, "Well, for a start, the first lines you have written here are fantastic."

"What? Why?"

I'd tell her why and play it with some chords, and she'd perk up. Suddenly she'd open her mouth and start singing, and it would sound incredible. And she'd say, "Oh, it is pretty good. I'll carry on," and she'd sit in a corner and furiously write all of it. So it was totally true collaboration from the beginning to the end.

When it came time to mix any of these tracks we made, back then we had no automation like they have now. These days, you can do a digital mix and save it just like you save a Word document, and then go in and change it if you need to. Not in those days. Then you did a physical mix to tape—moving the faders in real time—and if you didn't like it, you had to do it again.

Also, these mixes were complex, so it took many of us at the recording desk at the same time to move all the faders at the right moment. It would often be four of us: Annie, me, Jon Bavin and another assistant.

Often I might have three things on one track: maybe a guitar line, a rhythm part and then bass. So, with the chart in front of us, I'd say, "Annie, you've got these three faders, right? And at one minute, ten seconds, you've gotta mute that one and bring that one in."

So we had to do this over and over because somebody would make a mistake, and we'd have to start over from the beginning again, but we never got angry at whoever made the error. We'd just laugh. The person who did it would go, "Uh-oh," and that would mean we'd have to start all over again.

We were deep into the Thatcher years. Maggie was voted prime minister again, with a landslide win for the Conservative Party. It was 1983 and the music charts were full of eclectic but classic songs: Michael Jackson's "Billie Jean," David Bowie's "Let's Dance" and

"China Girl," Culture Club with "Karma Chameleon," the Police's "Every Breath You Take," Prince's "Little Red Corvette" and "1999" and the Clash's "Rock the Casbah."

Yes, 1983 was one long, crazy year, and the competition was fierce.

Without us knowing much about MTV and the power it was soon to have, we had already filmed many videos to go with our singles; we had videos up our sleeves for "Love Is a Stranger," "Sweet Dreams," "Who's That Girl?" "Right by Your Side" and "Here Comes the Rain Again." We unleashed an avalanche, all of which became monster MTV hits as well as global radio and chart hits. The difference before MTV was you could be hugely famous but not really recognized on the street much, but when you were on the TV once every three hours, your face became as familiar as a newscaster's.

We had released two albums back to back, toured the world extensively and become a household name globally. In fact, we had already sold millions of albums, and royalties had just started to arrive in large amounts.

CHAPTER:7

CAUTIOUS CELEBRATION

At first I was unsure how much money we would (or could) make as artists. I remember calling our lawyer and asking if he thought it was okay for me to buy a new car. I'll always remember his reply, which was a classic British answer. "Dave," he said, "I think you have reason for cautious celebration." I hung up, wondering how the hell I would celebrate cautiously. I soon found out.

A week before Christmas I was told that because of tax laws in England, unless I was out of the country the following year and paid strict attention to rules and regulations, I would be in huge debt. We'd been working flat-out, touring on *Sweet Dreams* and recording our new album, *Touch*. But the old managers of the Tourists wanted a cut, and we had to settle with them out of court for a huge sum; that, plus the amount of tax I would have to pay, meant that instead of having any money, I would be in massive debt.

But since I was going to be touring nearly all of the next year, 1984, I was told that if I came into the UK only at certain times and for no longer than a few weeks, it would all work out. We planned an immense world tour to support *Touch*. And then we were going to record another album, which we would do in France, and when not there, I would be in America.

They also told me I could not have a residence in England. They said I just had to get out of the country and stay out.

Back then I had been to the Caribbean only once, to the tiny island of Montserrat. But I had a sense about the place. Even before then I used to think, *Someday I am going to go to Barbados.* I even told *The Sunderland Echo* newspaper in an interview I gave when I was seventeen years old that one day I was going to live in Barbados. This was entirely based on the fact that a family friend had been there and described it as exotic. Exotic sounded good to me—so on the verge of being rich and famous, I booked myself in at the Treasure Beach Hotel, certainly a better choice of tax haven than the Isle of Man, which was once described as fifty thousand alcoholics clinging to a rock. On the day I was leaving, a whole bunch of people came around to my flat in London to say good-bye, wish me well and get free stuff. I started giving most of my things away: boxes of my favorite vinyl albums, clothes and books. I gave my car to my brother, who sweetly turned up to help organize my departure.

Kathy Valentine from the Go-Go's was visiting me at the time. Poly Styrene from X-Ray Spex, who was now a Krishna, also dropped by with some other Krishnas. A lady from across the street, a journalist for *The Times*, was there, drinking vodka even though it was only ten a.m. When I eventually left in a black cab, I looked up at the surreal gathering waving me off as I headed for the airport and the great blue yonder.

I got to Barbados late at night, and was driven to the hotel. I went to my bedroom and crashed out. When I woke up the next morning, I was completely confused. So I got up and I went and sat on the beach, look-ing at the sea. It was Christmas and I was thinking, "This is weird. It's now Christmas Day. And I'm on the beach, looking at this turquoise sea. And I actually have some money."

It was a weird feeling—no Annie, no family or friends, just me,

(L to R) 1. In a folk club looking about ten years old. 2. Stewart & Harrison. 3. Playing for my mum in the kitchen. 4. The first photo shoot for Longdancer.

IF
IT WAS
SO SIMPLE

Longdancer

Dave Stewart   Kai Olsson   Steve Sproxton   Brian Harrison

(L to R) 1. From our UK tour with Elton John. 2. Pam and me tripping in a field. 3. Me and Jude Henderson in Holland. 4. Sadista Sisters poster. 5. Longdancer's first album.

(L to R) 1. Paul Jacobs, who introduced me to Annie. 2. Paul's record shop and, above, the squat where Annie and I lived. 3. Annie in the back street. 4. Annie having tea with my mum, Sadie. 5. Annie on the rocks. 6. Christmas day in Aberdeen with Annie's family.

(L to R) 1. Annie on our strange camping trip. 2. Peet Coombes, Annie and me celebrating. 3. The Tourists playing a rock festival. 4. The Tourists playing the Hope and Anchor in London, 1978. 5. A candid snap of Annie touring the USA with the Tourists.

(L to R) 1. Luxurious accommodations in Los Angeles. 2. She promised it wouldn't hurt.
3. Annie en route to Oz. 4. Annie at CBGB's NYC.

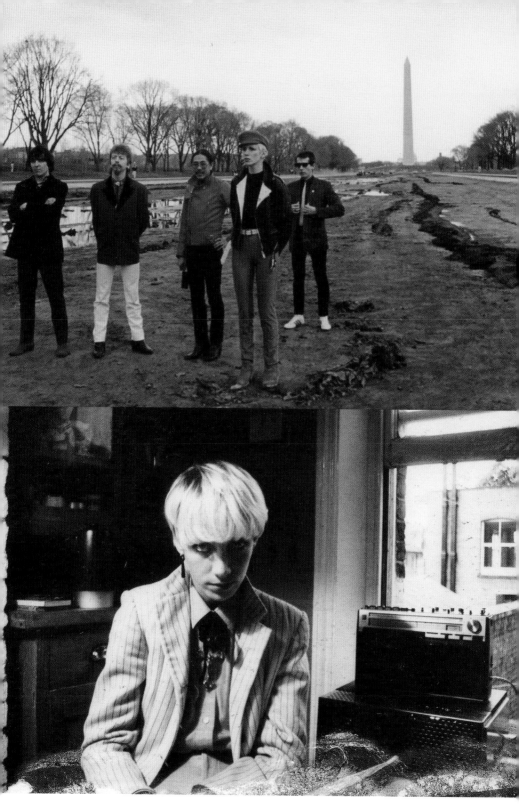

The Tourists in Washington, DC.
Back home at the squat.

(L to R) 1. A mini collage of Annie and me on a cheap holiday and Annie holding the Tourists album. 2. Annie in Oz. 3. Annie, Paul and me (the Three Musketeers). 4. Too much blood, wine and garlic. 5. Annie waking up and realizing we had checked into a nudist retreat.

(L to R) 1 to 3. Hard at work with Conny Plank in his studio. 4. Self-portrait of the artist as a young man. 5. Mixing *Sweet Dreams* in Picture Framing Factory. 6. Our poster on a wall in Soho London, 1983. 7. Mirror image. 8. A still from the "Love Is a Stranger" video.

(L to R) 1. Annie and me onstage during the Revenge World Tour. 2. With the legendary Aretha Franklin after recording "Sisters Are Doing It for Themselves." 3. Stevie Wonder playing me ideas on harmonica.

to R) 1. Just after coming offstage at the Grammy Awards, 1984. 2. One of the hundreds of
ur personalities. 3. Annie being made up as a man in secret before our iconic Grammys
erformance. 4. Me as the Sun King. 5. Bright Annie, moody Dave.

(L to R) 1. Always holding on to each other. 2. All smiles after winning the MTV Video Music Award for Best New Artist in 1984. 3. Princess Diana backstage with Eurythmics tour jackets for her boys.

Onstage with Annie during our acoustic set.
Being inducted into UK Music Hall of Fame in 2005.

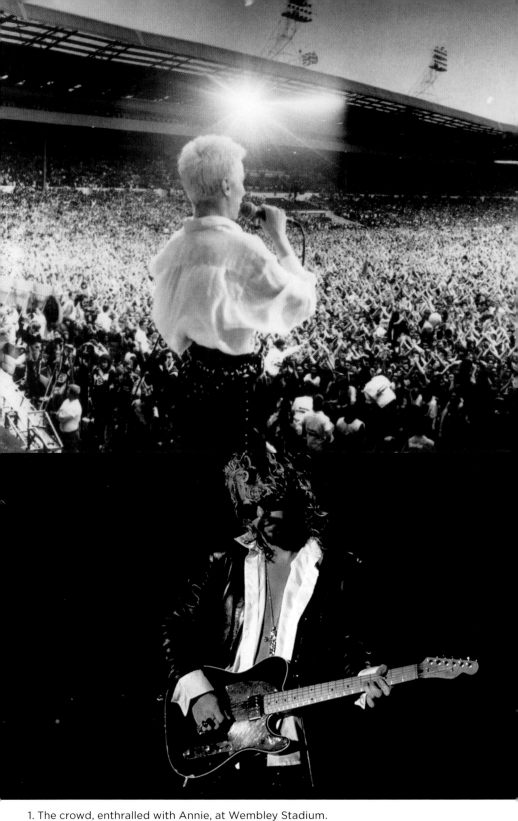

1. The crowd, enthralled with Annie, at Wembley Stadium.
2. Playing live on the Revenge Tour; we played to more than 230,000 people in Australia alon

y boots and Annie taking a break.

myself and I alone, on the beach. Annie and I were not together, though we'd just had this massive success with *Sweet Dreams*, and were now huge, known all over the world. There was nothing but an empty beach and an empty me, looking out at the big empty sea.

Except suddenly this tiny little dot appeared, and it got bigger and bigger. I saw that it was a rowboat with two people in it. They came right up to the beach, to where I was sitting. I took a good look and said, "Eileen?"

"Dave!" she replied. It was Eileen Gregory, an old friend I'd known for years, and she happened to arrive right on that spot, on the beach. She had just sailed across the Atlantic Ocean with her boyfriend. From that day on, we worked together. From the end of 1983 all the way through until 1997, she ran my film company, Radioactive Films. Later she ran my recording studio with her husband, Phil Gregory, and she also ran my American company, Eligible Music, U.S.A.

I decided to make a film paying homage to those great blues artists who inspired me when I was fourteen years old, sent me on vinyl by my cousin Ian in Memphis. I had to try to find out who and what was left of that blues tradition. I asked Eileen to help, and my brother, John, who had been running Oil Factory, a production company in London, for a few years. They came on as producers, and Eileen went off on a field trip to try to contact these various musicians.

We got in touch with Robert Palmer, the *New York Times* music critic and an expert on the blues who wrote the book *Deep Blues*. I said, "Well, why don't we make *Deep Blues*, the film?"

With Robert Palmer's help, we found amazing blues artists such as R. L. Burnside, Roosevelt "Booba" Barnes, Jessie Mae Hemphill, Big Jack Johnson, Junior Kimbrough, Booker T. and more. The great documentary director Robert Mugge agreed to come on board to direct. I financed the whole movie and was executive producer. I flew to Memphis for the start of filming and hooked up again with my cousin Ian, who hadn't changed a bit. His accent was still as thick as ever, and he helped us navigate Memphis and the Delta area.

But when I arrived the producers said, "Just one thing. We want you to be in it." I was dead set against it. I thought this would ruin the movie. I was a quirky English guy, and all these artists were the real Delta blues players who had been playing for decades and were all in their seventies. I was in awe of them.

But the producers convinced me that having me in the film would enable it to get attention and distribution; they were afraid it would never get distributed otherwise, so I agreed.

Jack White has since told me it's his favorite film. Lots of people I meet say, "Oh, my God, *Deep Blues* completely blew my mind." It influenced a lot of acts like the Black Keys and Gary Clark Jr. It's the only film that captured all of these Delta blues artists while they were still playing out live in juke joints and everything. I think many of them are still alive now.

There are so many great performances in the film. R. L. Burnside taught me how to play the song "Jumper on the Line" on his front porch. I was sitting thinking this was unreal after being a kid in Sunderland listening to Mississippi blues through my dad's homemade record player. Now I was in Mississippi listening to the real deal only two feet away from me, and you know what? I was as electrified and stunned as the first time I ever heard it. Financing this film, I think, was one of the most important things I've ever done.

This all lay in the future. By the time 1983 ended, Annie and I couldn't go anywhere together without being bombarded with autograph requests and harassed in every country we visited. Not only had we released two albums in the same year, but we started the grueling Touch Tour, which went from October 1983 till September 1984. The attention was a strange thing to cope with, and for the first time, we realized that we needed some kind of protection.

Sometime just before the Sweet Dreams Tour, Annie was on the full front cover of *Rolling Stone* with the heading EURYTHMICS: SWEET DREAMS OF SUCCESS. This was massive for us at the time. So many covers were just of Annie, including our album covers, which we both decided on. I didn't mind this at all. I was just so thankful that I had a partner who was so attractive, inventive and highly photogenic. I'm not a conventionally handsome-looking guy at all, and at the time, I usually looked as if I'd just seen a ghost, with out-of-control hair and a messy beard. I knew my role and I liked it. I created situations. I took risks at every corner. I was the dice man and I just kept rolling.

John Lydon, aka Johnny Rotten, once said, "I like crazy people, especially those who don't see the risk." And Kevin Spacey said, "Sometimes it's the crazy people who turn out to be not so crazy." So I played the crazy person, the weirdo, the eccentric—which wasn't hard, as I am those things—but always in the back of my mind, I had a calm and stable place where I could make reasonably sane decisions, having to make hundreds of decisions a day as Eurythmics producer, co-songwriter, performer. Up until the end of our first Sweet Dreams Tour, I was even acting as the manager.

Doing all that and touring almost killed me. If it hadn't been for a guy called Jack Stevens, a young A&R guy at RCA records, we would never have had a tour or even had the *Sweet Dreams* album come out.

Jack was our great ally, and he fought tooth and nail to keep us at the label after *In the Garden* failed to find a big audience. I worked together with him, battling against the label to allow us to be the way we wanted. Because he was young and edgy, they took notice and thought perhaps he knew something they didn't, and he did. Jack knew that we could be huge but that we had been doing everything ourselves. He was the first real help we had, and I was, more often than not, in his office conspiring and brainstorming our next steps. Jack introduced us to Laurence Stevens, who was fresh out of college, and he remained our artwork collaborator throughout our career. So at the end of the Sweet Dreams Tour, I was introduced to Kenny Smith by good friend and fellow guitarist John Turnbull. Kenny was married to John's ex-wife, Sandra, and I suggested Kenny be our tour manager and Annie had Sandra as her personal assistant. We were getting a team together now and things got a bit easier.

By the time the Touch Tour rolled out and I had left the country, we had amassed a small fortune and had bought the entire church from Bura and Hardwick. We also bought the house and shop next door to house our management company and had created D&A Ltd. And by now Kenny was acting as our manager in the UK, but we signed on with a legendary American manager, Gary Kurfirst, who managed Talking Heads, the B-52's and the Ramones, all bands I adored.

We then made a very different arrangement for our management and created a UK management company that would take 10 percent of UK and ROW (rest of world) earnings and 5 percent of USA earnings and a USA manager who took 10 percent of USA earnings and 5 percent of ROW earnings. Gary wasn't happy with this, as it was less than his usual percentage, but it meant everyone had to see what the other earned. It was our bid to try not to be left in the dark, as our past experience with management had not been something we wanted to repeat.

We were determined to avoid what happened to most bands, which was to end up broke. My father gave me an amazing piece of advice after reading our record contracts and management contracts, each the size of a telephone directory. He told me that even though he was a certified accountant, quite honestly, he didn't have a clue what those contracts meant.

The only advice he offered was: "Make sure you and Annie get the money first. Then pay everyone else." In other words, stay in control. This pearl of wisdom was invaluable. Because we kept our recording costs very low and we didn't employ outside producers, as I was mostly producing, those royalty checks started pouring into the same bank account in Crouch End, where only eighteen months earlier we had just five thousand borrowed pounds to record the *Sweet Dreams* album. We were now set to conquer the world.

CHAPTER: 8

U.S. OF A.

We started 1984 with a bang. Annie was on the front cover of *Newsweek* with Boy George and the headline BRITAIN ROCKS AMERICA AGAIN, and we started the second leg of the Touch Tour on January 27, 1984, in Australia, on the same bill as Talking Heads, Simple Minds and the Pretenders.

On the way to Australia, we stopped in Bali for a few days, and a crazy thing happened. I went to sleep in a tree house–type hotel room dazed from the journey and woke up rather early with jet lag. I couldn't find anyone or even the reception of the hotel compound. I wandered out of the grounds and decided to stroll along the road to what looked like a village in the distance. Soon a couple of kids started walking beside me, and they were pointing and shouting. Then there were ten, then twenty, and when I finally got to some small huts/shops, I was surrounded by people chanting something I couldn't really understand.

Eventually they pushed and pulled and dragged me into a kind of bootleg cassette shop. The walls were covered with posters, but one big one in the middle was just of me, and it said "PUNK 83." I was so confused and they kept chanting, "Punk 83!!" wild with delight. Then they showed me the number one selling tape, which again was my face, and it was called "Punk 83." I checked the song titles but not one was Eurythmics, nor was it punk music. It was random pop songs from American bands. But that was my face on the cover, oddly.

This, fused with jet lag in a foreign land and being about a mile from the hotel at six a.m., was getting to be a bit much. I marched back and arrived to see Chrissie Hynde looking as confused as I was, as I wandered in with hordes of kids chanting, "Punk 83, Punk 83!" Chrissie called me Punk 83 all the way through that Australian trip.

This was my first taste of being around loads of different bands and musicians. I was in heaven, and I went on to be best friends with many of them, and made records with lots of them over the years.

We arrived back in the States to perform "Sweet Dreams" on the twenty-sixth annual Grammy Awards as Best New Artist nominees. Our band was made up of a mixture of the members of Talking Heads, the B-52's and the Brothers Johnson. We did the rehearsals low-key, not letting on that Annie was going to perform as a handsome man, almost an Elvis look-alike in a suit and wig, chewing on a matchstick. When John Denver announced us, his jaw dropped as we walked out. We could see the audience's mouths gaping open as Annie swaggered through the song with a woman's voice coming out of a man's body. When we finished there was stunned silence. Thank the Lord for canned applause.

We were howling laughing backstage, even more so when Boy George picked up his award and said, "Thank you, America; you've got taste, style and you know a good drag queen when you see one."

Later at the post–Grammy Party, Colonel Tom Parker—yes, Elvis's manager—came up to us just as our new manager, Gary Kurfirst, was talking to us. The Colonel said, "You guys were great. Do you have a manager?" and before we could say, "Yes, he's here," he said, "Get rid of him. I can get you three months in Vegas." We all stood looking at the ground, not knowing what to say, but as he left, Gary said, "Fuck! That was the Colonel and he just sacked me!" We had no idea who he was. We thought he was just a scary, grumpy old man.

Annie and I were asked by Richard Branson to record the sound track to the movie *1984*. Annie and I decided to record in Chris Blackwell's studio, Compass Point, in Nassau in the Bahamas. In theory this was a good idea, away from the public eye where we'd be able to concentrate on making great experimental music. There was, however, the distraction of being in a stunning location.

Before the sessions started, I had hired a Jeep and was driving with the top down along the coast road. For the first time in my life I felt like I'd arrived somewhere and that all this madness had actually turned into something amazing. It was okay to relax for a moment and enjoy some success. I remember breathing deeply, looking at the sea shimmering on my left, the swaying palm trees, the warm sun on my skin.

But suddenly things shifted. Out of the corner of my eye, I saw a black dot getting bigger and bigger. Then bang, and something was colliding with my face: skidding wheels, sunglasses flying, the car in hyperdrive and then juddering to a halt, the Jeep now hanging terrifyingly over a precipice.

Yes, a fucking overripe plum decided to embark from its tree and smash into my face right on my Ray-Bans, covering me in plum juice.

I sat in the car, my heart beating like the clappers. I started giggling uncontrollably and eventually broke into full hysterical laughter. I could see the headlines: EURYTHMIC DAVE STEWART KILLED BY FLYING PLUM! It was like a Zen monk hitting me on the head with a wooden spoon and saying, "Now, clean your bowl."

After our second album, I soon realized that a trend was starting of remixing tracks for clubs. As soon as we had a hit with *Touch*, the record company got Jellybean Benitez and François Kevorkian to do remixes of all of the songs. They put out an album called *Touch Dance*, completely without our consent. It seemed as if they didn't know how long we were going to last, so they wanted to exploit a good thing while they could. Tons of our fans bought the album, thinking it was *Touch*. It really upset Annie, this album with all these remixes with a weird cover and our name on it. The real album *Touch* had "Here Comes the Rain Again" and other epic songs.

I had met this guy called E. T. Thorngren, who was the in-house mixer for Sugar Hill Records. He had mixed legendary songs like "White Lines." So I brought him to Nassau to work on our sound track album, as he was a master of soundscapes. That was when I learned all about using delays and dub mixing.

He was in the midst of mixing the landmark Bob Marley album full of hits, *Legends*. I would go in the room where he was working, and it was thrilling. He would say, "Listen to this," and let us hear bits captured on tape. Once there was a track of the musicians recorded on a mic where there was meant to be singing, and they were all talking and you could hear people go, "Ah, pass the spliff!" It was like being there with Bob Marley and his crew.

We worked long hours creating a unique movie score, only to find out the director Michael Radford had not actually been informed that we were doing it. At the time we kept asking to talk to him, as we needed to see the locked-off cut of the film with timecode. We became bewildered by the communication process, but we were in Nassau and there was obviously no Internet or e-mail back then. We plowed on regardless and delivered what we felt to be a very strong piece of work.

Unbeknownst to us, Michael had commissioned his own orchestral score. So two versions of the film were released, one featuring our music and the "director's cut," which replaced most of our music with the orchestral score. This turned into a bit of a controversy when

Radford complained that our score had been *foisted on him* by Richard Branson in an acceptance speech. It was another flying plum, as we were innocent in the whole affair. We issued a statement saying we were as much in the dark as he was. Years later he apologized to Annie for what happened, and Annie explained that we had no knowledge of the other score until he made his speech! Nevertheless I love the album, and "Julia" is one of my favorite recordings. "Sex Crime," the single from the album, was banned on the radio in the USA, but it went Top Ten in fifteen countries around the rest of the world.

We continued touring in America for the remainder of 1984. When Annie and I played the Wiltern Theatre in Los Angeles, the place was absolutely packed with half of the LA music industry and a host of famous musicians. There was hardly room for the general public.

It was a wild show. Sam, from Sam and Dave, leapt onstage and sang with us, and the crowd went nuts. There were a lot of musicians and singers backstage, and one of them was Stevie Nicks.

Backstage was pretty small, and a lot of musicians who came to the show were milling about and talking. Stevie was in my dressing room doorway, wearing a faux-fur coat just like the one Annie had on the first time I met her. Underneath she wore a black lace dress and she had long, flowing hair. I didn't know who she was, but there was something about her that I was instantly attracted to. Stevie remembers that I looked her straight in the eye and said, "I want to be your boyfriend." Little did I know that the day before, Joe Walsh and Stevie had had a big fight and had broken up.

She invited me back to her house for a party, and ten minutes later, still in full sweaty leather stage gear, I was in the back of a limo with Stevie and her three backing singers, who were her best friends—always by her side on- and offstage. I had no idea where I was going, and at that time there were no cell phones, so I had kind of parted from my touring group. I'd even forgotten which hotel we were staying in and had no way of getting in touch with the tour manager or management company in New York until the next morning.

We drove to Stevie's home in Beverly Hills. When we got there it wasn't really a party: just Stevie and her singers being very speedy, laughing and talking. The house seemed enormous to me, so I wandered around, and when I came back to the living room, they had all disappeared into a bathroom for what seemed like hours. Actually it was hours. At around three in the morning, I ended up saying to myself, "Okay, I'm really tired now and I have no idea where I am or which hotel Annie and the band are staying in."

I just went to bed in one of the four bedrooms upstairs. I didn't know this but the backing singers had a bedroom each and the last one was Stevie's. I woke up at about five a.m. to the sound of doors rustling open and in the half-light saw Stevie opening and closing closets, as if it was the middle of the afternoon. Obviously they were all still wide-awake, aided, I imagine, by what we in England call "marching powder."

Stevie went back in the bathroom and about an hour later came out in a long Victorian nightdress and quietly slipped into the other side of the bed. Stevie is an incredibly talented, soulful and beautiful woman. There was a fair amount of what I'd call skirmishing that went on. I remember at one point actually falling backward out of bed onto the floor, which made us both laugh hysterically.

Stevie recently told me that all she could see when she came out of the bathroom that night was a mound of black leather and chains on the floor and a wild head of hair poking out of the bedcovers. I remember making love once, but she later told me we made love twice. And then she said, "I remember clearly because I was wide-awake, wired on cocaine." It was all very good-humored and sweet, but it was also very romantic in a rock-and-roll kind of way.

I was woken up at about nine thirty a.m. by Stevie saying I had to leave because someone might have been coming around to collect their clothes, and things could get tricky. I didn't like the sound of "tricky," so I phoned my management, found out where the band was staying and jumped in a cab still half asleep. The band had already left the hotel when I arrived. Later that day I managed to get a flight to San Francisco, just in time for the sound check, right before the gig.

After the show, using my little Portastudio, I started to create a track with a drum machine, a tiny synthesizer and this Coral Sitar guitar that I'd bought somewhere on the road, which has sympathetic strings that make it sound like a real sitar. I came up with this whole track but without any words, and then the line came to me. I was singing it with the music and it fit well: "Don't come around here no more. Don't come around here no more . . ." I had that with the music, but no other lyrics.

I was reflecting on what had just happened in the last twenty-four hours. I really liked Stevie, and she seemed vulnerable and fragile when I was leaving that morning. I was thinking about that and the situation she was in and I started singing, "Don't come around here no more."

After San Francisco we had some time off, and I decided to go back to LA to see Stevie again. Jimmy Iovine, the great producer who went on to start Interscope Records in the early nineties, had invited me to stay with him at his house, and this was where it got interesting. I had no idea of the complexity of the relationships among Jimmy, Stevie Nicks and Tom Petty at the time. But I was soon to find out more than I ever imagined.

Jimmy had been living with Stevie in 1981 when he was producing her album *Bella Donna*, which was a huge success. Now he was working on her next album, except this time around they were not together. Stevie said later that it was because she was so addicted to drugs at that time.

I played Jimmy the demo of "Don't Come Around Here No More," and he said, "Wow! This is gonna be great. Let's make it for Stevie's album."

I jumped at the chance to work with Stevie, and we went right into the studio a few days later. When we started recording, Stevie was acting strangely and not really coming out of the bathroom much. There seemed to have been quite a bit of friction between them. I had no idea that it was because they had been living together and were now broken up. Finally, Stevie appeared with her lyric book and started to sing into the microphone.

The sound of her voice gave me goose bumps. I was mesmerized until Jimmy said, "She's reciting fucking Shakespeare!" He did have a point; it was kind of Shakespearean and very odd. So Jimmy, Stevie and I were standing around the piano, and he was trying to get Stevie to change the lyrics. Jimmy knew the chorus was a hit, and he didn't want it to get lost. Stevie was upset and the discussion became very tense.

He was saying, "Can you stop arguing with me in front of my friend David? You don't really know him." And she said, "Your friend? What are you talking about? We slept together the other night."

I turned white and stared at the floor, wondering what was coming next. Fortunately Stevie turned, walked out the door and left the studio. I thought Jimmy was going to ask, "What does that mean?" But he just said, "I know what we should do. We should get Tom Petty down here to finish writing the song with you. He's great." He immediately dialed Tom's number to ask him down to the studio.

Previously, Jimmy had been saying to Tom, "Who do you think is an interesting songwriter at the moment?" I think Tom said, "Well, the only person I've heard is that Dave Stewart guy with Annie Lennox. He seems to have an angle on collaborating and how to make records sound different."

I'd seen Tom perform in England, and I knew he had written loads of songs. I thought he was cool and creative, and I was excited to see where he'd take the song. Tom arrived and said, "Let's hear it." After listening to it, he went in the studio and he was trying some stuff. He was singing, "Don't come around here no more"—he got the chorus I had written. He goes, "Okay, that fits this."

We didn't have to change the key. Then he sang, "Stop walkin' down my street," and then "I'm givin' up . . . on waiting any longer." Jimmy was going, "Fucking hell, it's a smash! We've gotta record it now."

Tom Petty was truly the coolest cat I'd ever met. We hit it off immediately, and within twenty minutes we got the song somewhat finished. Then another silence emerged. With just a few eyebrow raises from Tom, I started to understand the new situation I was in. Tom is very sensitive and finely tuned. He said to Jimmy, "I think I should sing this song," and then they started having a kind of argument among themselves—well, not a real argument, but a strange conversation. Tom and Stevie had done a duet of Tom's song called "Stop Draggin' My Heart Around." Jimmy had put it on Stevie's album. It was a huge success for her, but not for Tom, as it kind of stopped his album in its tracks. I think Tom saw history repeating itself and decided he wanted to put this one on his album. So he said, "Well, let's go to my garage and do it." It was all very confusing because we were in a famous studio. Prince was in the room next door working. But before I knew it, I was in a car with Tom, driving to the garage underneath his house. We got the tape and started playing it. Jimmy came to the garage, as well. So it was Jimmy and I now producing this track together with Tom. But the thing I was soon realizing was, *Well, hang on, there's no band on this*—but it's Tom Petty and the Heartbreakers.

The next day, after Tom and I had worked in his garage studio, he got the Heartbreakers together and they recorded the song. At first, when they heard "Don't Come Around Here No More," they didn't like it. They said, "God, what kind of music is this? Hang on! We're not playing on it. What's going on?" The Heartbreakers must have thought I was some alien from outer space. Here they were, busy making an album called *Southern Accents* about coming from Florida, and along came this quirky Englishman playing music with sitars. They were totally confused, but Benmont Tench, the keyboardist, knew there was something to the song and he was very friendly. One by one the band warmed to me. After we had made the record and then shot the video, we all became friends and started to hang out.

The actual recording is half of my original four-track demo and a string quartet through most of the song. So I had an idea to bring the Heartbreakers into the song. I said, "How about the band, at the end, they sort of take over, and it's like you've been on a trip?" And that's what we did. Two-thirds of the way through, the band comes in double time, starting with a female singer trying to hit an almost-impossible-to-reach high note, almost a scream. In Tom's book, *Conversations with Tom Petty*, he recalled me shocking the vocalist into the note by leaping naked into the studio, which worked! After that note, the whole band comes crashing in. Everybody played great and the whole experience was a trip.

I remember I was sitting at home at the kitchen table with Jimmy when the phone rang. I could hear him kind of having a mini argument, and he came back and said, "Fucking hell, that was your manager, and he was shouting at me on the phone, saying, 'What the hell are you doing with my artist?'" My manager found out that Jimmy had me writing a song for this person and that person. He probably thought what was going on was out of his control. I think Annie, quite rightly, was going, "Well, hang on a minute. We're Eurythmics and we're a duo. Dave shouldn't be doing this."

Remember, Annie and I had been collaborating for years, but this was the first time the whole world was responding to our music in a big way, and I didn't want to dilute that. So on many occasions, I told Jimmy, "Just put my credit down as Boo Boo Watkins or Jean Guiot or whatever you want to call me."

In fact it didn't impact badly on Eurythmics. Instead, it opened me up to understand different kinds of music and particularly American music, because I was now in a studio with fine American musicians.

It helped Eurythmics in a way, because when we did certain songs, I would use some of the Heartbreakers as players.

Stevie remembers coming back to the studio later on and hearing Tom singing "Don't Come Around Here No More," which he'd recorded instead of her. She said, "Even though I was deeply hurt, I knew it was a great song and that Tom deserved to sing it. He sounded great singing it and I told him so. I said nothing about feeling wounded. I kept those feelings to myself."

I mentioned to Tom that it'd be great to make a really unusual video, like a Mad Hatter's Tea Party from *Alice in Wonderland*. It just reminded me of how my whole trip to Los Angeles had been "Dave in Wonderland." Everyone loved the concept, and the video was created and directed by the brilliant director Jeff Stein. He put together an Escheresque set with forced perspective, using black-and-white tiles juxtaposed with wild-colored costumes for the band.

In the beginning of the video, it's me as the caterpillar, sitting on a giant mushroom, playing the sitar and smoking a hookah pipe. I've got these crazy long fake fingernails that I use to summon Alice up the mushroom steps. I offer her a poisonous cupcake. With some smoke, I blow her tumbling down the steps and she lands at Mad Tom's Tea Party. The video's ending actually caused quite a stir because Alice gets cut up like she's a birthday cake. MTV had thousands of complaints because it looked like the guys were cutting up the real Alice with real knives, the high scream adding to the horror.

We had to do two edits—one with Alice being eaten and one without. Still, it was a huge hit on MTV, the radio and all the charts. It put a massive spotlight on Tom in this new video arena. From then on people wondered what he was going to do in the next video and the next.

I've written a number of songs with Tom. He has an amazing sense of melody. It just comes out of his mouth without really sounding like he's trying. He kind of throws it away, but then it's right under your skin and you can't get it out of your head. He's also a great wordsmith, a true artist and a brilliant songwriter. Tom Petty and the Heartbreakers have been around for more than thirty years and they're still going strong. They sell out everywhere they play to audiences of all ages who love their authenticity. They're one of the last great American rock bands.

After I collaborated on "Don't Come Around Here No More," the Touch Tour picked up again, and by then I had my base in Los Angeles, living in Jimmy's guesthouse. We went to Japan for a couple of weeks, where we played to overly enthusiastic fans who gave us gifts everywhere we went. Then we were back on the road in the U.S., playing bigger venues, ending with three nights at the Greek Theatre in LA.

This was a glorious moment; in one year we had conquered America. I was exhausted but ecstatic. I decided to enjoy myself being free, single and on top of the world! Jimmy threw a massive birthday party for me. I was thirty-two years old and up for anything.

The next month or two was an amazing time, and through our success, I met everyone. I arranged to meet Madonna at the Mayflower Hotel and we went up to my room to drink some champagne and noodle about on the keyboard. It was interesting to me that Madonna said she didn't really like minor chords and she liked everything to be upbeat in a major key. The next day she came to see me play with Annie at Forest Hill Stadium, along with Talking Heads and the B-52's. It was August 3, 1984. She stood on the side of the stage and watched our whole set. And afterward, back in our caravan, she said she didn't think Annie gave out enough to the audience. But Annie always gives out in a different way, though I must admit we did end our set in the most depressing way with a song called "Jennifer," about a girl who's floating dead under the water.

A few weeks later Madonna came out to visit me at my guest house at Jimmy's house. I was in the Jacuzzi when she arrived. I was playing new mixes of "Don't Come Around Here No More" I'd just written with Tom Petty. She listened to it all the way through and afterward said, "Hmm. It's not really my kind of music, but it does sound like a hit." Later that same day, Bruce Springsteen nabbed me to listen to the new album he was recording. He had a small barbecue at his house in LA but took me up to his bedroom and played me rough mixes of the *Born in the U.S.A.* album. I remember both of us sitting on the bedroom floor in front of his stereo, with the Boss anxiously biting his nails and listening intently. "What do you think?" he said. I thought somehow I'd managed to slip into another universe where anything and everything was possible.

California dreamin' it was: Bruce Springsteen, Tom Petty, Stevie Nicks, the Eagles, all these characters every day. All Jimmy and I could do was laugh hysterically at our good fortune, knowing where we both had come from. This was the time of our lives, and we knew it.

After touring and traveling from one city to the next for the last year and before that living in a squat and eating baked beans and chips, I was now on top of Mulholland in a beautiful house with a Beverly Hills view, and we were number one with "Sweet Dreams."

I remember thinking, "Well, if we're *numero uno* in the U.S. of A., we must have some money somewhere." I managed to get some money transferred to the USA, even though I didn't have an American bank account. But though it was relaxing, being with Jimmy was also very exciting. I couldn't help but get involved in what he was doing, rebuilding A&M Studios, the former Chaplin movie studio in Hollywood.

Jimmy was also working with many very gifted LA artists, and he would always take me along, the two of us together in his car. We were so in tune with each other's sense of humor that on more than one occasion we crashed the car, or ran off the road, because we were laughing so hysterically.

We would never stop laughing. We laughed about everything: a crazy situation fueled by the fact that we often didn't understand each other—because I was from northeast England and he was a bona fide New Yorker. We would eat at this little Italian place nearly every night, and then return to his house of lunacy.

In England, we're used to calling on friends. Not call them on the phone—I mean physically dropping by, ringing the doorbell, seeing if someone's in. If the door's open, you walk in the kitchen, and you get a slice of bread and jam or put the kettle on. Well, on top of Mulholland, obviously, it was not really like that for most people.

But when Jimmy said Don Henley lived down the road, I figured I'd just walk there and drop by. "Past Jack Nicholson's house, then farther on a bit. Right?"

It was a long walk and a hot California day. I came to this big gate. I couldn't see a bell or anything because I probably didn't realize it was back there where you stopped the car. So I just climbed over the gate, then walked through down the grounds and up toward the house. I couldn't find anyone, so I went around the back to the kitchen and there were Don Henley and his girlfriend making a cup of tea. I opened the door and said, "Hey, how ya doing?" He was shocked, as if encountering a home invasion by hooded gunmen.

He gasped, "What? How did you even get here?"

I told him I'd climbed over the gate. He couldn't get his head around that concept. "You did what?" I was always doing things that were inappropriate in the Los Angeles world. I'd go over to Tom Petty's house and join his daughter Adria for a bowl of Cocoa Puffs before school. He'd say, "How did you even get in here?" And I said, "Well, I just climbed over the gate at the end of this drive." It was a laugh. I obviously was seen as a completely eccentric Englishman who couldn't understand the rules of LA living. Even so, I felt embraced by that whole crowd.

1984 was the year music was selling in bucket loads, with huge single and album sales, in juxtaposition to the unemployment figures that were at a record high of around three million in the UK. Frankie

Goes to Hollywood released their debut single "Relax," which was banned by the BBC for sexually suggestive content but still became a massive anthem. Wham! had their first number one single, after four earlier Top Ten hits, with the upbeat song "Wake Me Up Before You Go-Go." Elton John married his studio engineer, a woman named Renate Blauel, which confused not only me, but half the population. The Smiths had released their first album, and the song "Heaven Knows I'm Miserable Now" is still a favorite of mine. Last but not least, Stevie Wonder, after eighteen years of releasing singles, had his first number one hit with "I Just Called to Say I Love You"—1984 was massive.

It seemed, to most Americans, that Eurythmics had come out of nowhere and now we were everywhere. "Sweet Dreams (Are Made of This)" had already been number one.

"Who's That Girl?" and "Right by Your Side" were also hits and all over the radio. "Here Comes the Rain Again" solidified our success worldwide. For us it was like we'd been tied to a rocket called "Sweet Dreams" and it was shooting us to the moon; we reentered the Earth's atmosphere not only alive and well, but stronger and more determined. There was no way to turn back anyway and there was nothing in our path, so we just clung on to each other and hoped for the best!

CHAPTER:9

WOULD I LIE TO YOU?

I n January 1985, instead of going bigger for our next album, *Be Yourself Tonight*, I suggested we go smaller, back to a tiny room like the old days. I said to Annie, "Let's get right back to the eight-track recording setup that we started with, and let's go to Paris."

So we all went to Paris, and again we had a small room in which we had an electronic drum kit, a few synths, guitars and the original "Sweet Dreams" eight-track tape recorder. It was a tiny room to set up all our equipment in, about fifteen feet by fifteen feet, and this room was located at a youth club in a Paris suburb, the kind where kids met to take ballet lessons and play table tennis.

While we were recording, the French kids didn't actually believe we were making a record. We were just the "crazee Engleesh" people with strange haircuts who locked themselves in a room for twelve hours a day. To make the room more cozy, Annie went out and bought some things at the local market.

Adam Williams set about wiring up our makeshift studio/den, and very soon we were under way. Now, to most artists, when you're on your third album, selling millions and with huge hits all around the world, you'd be going, "Oh, now we're going to record in a big fancy studio somewhere." Instead, here we were in this tiny youth club in Paris, with sequencers, synthesizers, drum machines, Annie's eccentric furnishings and fairy lights.

At first we played around with a lot of typical Eurythmics' experimental sounds that resulted in songs like "Conditioned Soul," but we soon started to play more soul- and bluesy-type experiments. This small intimate space was so conducive for us, because the more we were together, the more the sparks flew.

The UK music show *The Old Grey Whistle Test* came to Paris to film us recording for this latest album. We performed a song we had just written ten minutes before, "I Love You like a Ball and Chain." There's only a drum machine, me on guitar and Annie singing. We performed the song as if we'd known it for years and pumped up the volume. It's an electrifying performance that ends up with me lying on Annie's lap on the sofa, playing the riff and soloing, while Annie is still singing and riffing away full throttle. They filmed the whole thing in one take, all done in five minutes, and it sounded amazing.

During the recording, I asked my mother, who was visiting from London, and our drummer Olle Romo to march on top of pebbles (on the roof) to mix in with the sound of the drum machine. I forgot they were up there marching, and when I eventually remembered, I ran up to see how they were doing, and my mom was breathing heavily, very red in the face but soldiering on.

If we knew we had a TV crew arriving to film us, or we were doing live radio, we would go full force and take no prisoners. It was like a boxing or wrestling match. We had the Muhammad Ali attitude of "We will win in round three, with a knockout. There is no way we can lose." It was like that for us in every way.

In true Dave and Annie style, we had rented apartments on top of each other in Paris. One morning I was having breakfast in my kitchen below Annie's, eating a bowl of cereal, my acoustic guitar on my knee as always. I wanted to make another killer R&B riff, and that was where I came up with the guitar riff for "Would I Lie to You?"—belting it out in my boxer shorts till I had the whole guitar part for the song mapped out in my head. I couldn't wait to play it for Annie. At first she wasn't too sure about, as it sounded too removed from what we were doing, which was true. But the great thing about Annie is, even if she's not sure at first, she will let the experiment develop, whereas some people are too afraid and shut down before even trying.

When we started putting it down, the song had a lot of energy and inspired Annie to come up with the great lyric—"Would I lie to you?"—and a melody with very odd answering harmonies, "Now, would I say something that wasn't true?" These harmonies are very unusual, and Annie is a genius at working them out very quickly in her head.

The song quickly became a fusion between Stax-type R&B and Eurythmics. Olle played a classic R&B drumbeat. Our bass player Dean Garcia played a great solid line, and we soon realized this could be a monster track. Annie's lead vocal was fantastic and a killer to record. Doing it live was especially intense, with the high-octave leaps on the verses.

When we released it as a single, it became a smash hit around the world, hitting number five on the US charts and number one in Australia and always a huge crowd-pleaser live onstage.

When we finished work, we nearly always went to a brasserie to celebrate. One particular night we went to an old Russian restaurant, and I drank so many different kinds of vodka that I was told the next day my Russian dancing was amazing. I wondered why my knees hurt so much.

People started to hear about our little recording camp on the out-skirts of Paris, and visitors made the trek out to see us. Elvis Costello was one such fellow musician, a singer-songwriter extraordinaire. He arrived as we were writing "Adrian," and he ended up singing har-monies all the way through for fun. We liked the sound of it so much, we kept it on the master recording and mixed it. Blended with Annie's voice, it almost sounded a bit like the old Tourist days with Peet and Annie singing together.

Our most complicated production was "There Must Be an Angel." This track has the kitchen sink in it, even though we were still on an eight-track recorder. Olle played the synth drums. Dean on bass. Annie and I played keyboards; then we decided we would have an opera singer and a gospel choir and an orchestra, and we wanted a real harp player. Annie said, "This could be great for Stevie Wonder." I heard it and said, "It would be great for us too, but why don't we ask Stevie to play harmonica on it?" With the songs recorded, we moved camp to Los Angeles to mix the album.

We had sent the song "There Must Be an Angel" to Stevie's people, and when we didn't hear anything, we figured, *Okay, he isn't interested.* It was just a crazy pipe dream, after all. But then while we were in LA, we heard that he received the song and loved it and was happy to come and play a solo. We were, of course, ecstatic.

We were booked into the studio and waiting for him to arrive. We knew about the mythical "Stevie Wonder time," that he doesn't subscribe to normal timekeeping and might be late. So it was ten p.m., then later, eleven p.m., and then it was midnight. We kept working, mixing the track, hoping he would arrive.

But by two a.m. we were completely knackered and jet-lagged and figuring this day was done, we went back to the Sunset Marquis, where we were staying. At four a.m. the phone rang in my room. It was a frantic guy, sounding like he was having a panic attack. "Hurry! Get back here! Stevie is here!"

"Stevie Wonder?"

"Yes, STEVIE WONDER!!"

I roused Annie, who was asleep, and we got a car and went back to the studio. And there was Stevie, in all his glory. He was the nicest soul you could meet, all pure spirit. He had his hair all in braids bound with beautiful gold beads and looked resplendent. When he'd play, he'd shake his head and all the beads would sound like a percussion instrument, so he had someone who would tie his braids with a piece of cloth while he played.

He said to play the track, and he'd play along on harmonica. And so we did, and when he got to the solo section, he played a beautifully melodic, gorgeous Stevie Wonder harmonica solo. The kind of solo only this one man could make. As soon as he began, you knew it could be no one else making that sound.

But just to be safe, when he was done, I said, "Great. How 'bout doing another?" I wanted to protect us, in case there was anything wrong with the first one. I didn't really think he could improve on what he had done but we always do several takes of things like this.

Stevie had a facial expression that said, "But I just nailed it, you know." Then he did the next take, but instead of playing a solo, he played an Irish jig. He knew we had it in the can. And we did. And to this day I play that track—with Stevie Wonder doing a harmonica solo on our song—and it is breathtaking. It sounds as great as it did that night, that very late night.

When we wrote "Sisters Are Doin' It for Themselves," I was playing a kind of gospel-blues-soul riff on the guitar. Annie immediately connected with the melody and came up with perfect lyrics in a heartbeat. She would sometimes have a whole poem written out, like: "There was a time when they used to say that behind every great man there had to be a great woman."

We thought, *Oh, my God. This is like a Tina Turner classic.* We soon realized we shouldn't give the song away and someone suggested inviting Aretha Franklin to sing it with Annie. Of course we both loved the idea, and next thing we were on a plane to Detroit along with Don Smith, Tom Petty's engineer, to help.

When we arrived at United Sound recording studios, Don realized he'd left our multitracks on the plane! Luckily they were found, and he went to the airport to retrieve them. Meanwhile Annie and I hung around on the street corner, waiting for Aretha, who was running late. When the Queen of Soul eventually arrived, it was with an entourage of guys and a huge box of chicken wings. Aretha apologized for being late and explained she'd been cooking the wings all night, especially for us. I didn't want to tell her that Annie was in fact a vegan, so I ate as much as I could.

As the session was getting started, Aretha beckoned me into a tiny room the size of a shoe box, with just enough room for me, her and a piano. I thought she wanted to go over the song but instead she started playing and singing "The Way We Were." She had tears streaming down her face, and I was spellbound. When she stopped she didn't say anything and neither did I. There was nothing to say really apart from "Okay, I've heard everything. I can happily die now."

Somehow I had to get Aretha and Annie to connect and humor was the only way. So, making light of the situation, I started to joke around and get Aretha laughing and loosened up. I could see Annie was extremely nervous. (Who wouldn't have been? This was to be a duet around one microphone with the greatest soul singer in the world.) I went into the control room, which was full of Aretha's posse, friends and family.

Just before we started recording, Aretha asked to see me again. She had the lyrics written out and she was looking at Annie with her cropped short hair and said, "Hey, Dave, I wanna ask you something. When it says here 'ringing on their own bells,' you don't mean what I think you mean." Then she started winking and kind of looking at Annie. I realized she was worried that she was going to be singing lyrics about being gay or doing a duet with a gay female icon. At the time "androgyny" was the buzzword, and we were definitely all over the US press as the odd couple, although Aretha had no idea who we were really, just these strange aliens who had landed in Detroit.

I assured her that Annie was not gay, and in fact that we once were a couple and this was more a song about equal rights. Aretha's brother Cecil couldn't get it into his head that we were a duo and assumed that I was Annie's manager and wanted to talk business with me. The session was a bit confusing, but once the track started, the whole room became electric. As soon as Annie opened her mouth, Aretha stood up straight. I could see her thinking, "Okay, this girl can sing."

The whole song went down in a few takes, almost like a sparring match. At the end Aretha and Annie were laughing together, and thankfully we walked out with amazing vocal takes and an anthem for all women. The song was on our album *Be Yourself Tonight*, and we agreed Aretha could have it on her album *Who's Zoomin' Who?*, which gave Aretha her first multiplatinum seller and a whole new audience.

I asked Mike Campbell of the Heartbreakers to play the guitar solo on "Sisters," and he played a memorable one. Even though I was there when he recorded it, I had no idea what notes Mike was playing, so in the music video I just leapt around in the Church Studios like an idiot while Annie and Aretha were filmed onstage in Detroit.

I started to learn all about horn sections. I recorded Tower of Power, and then was a big fan of the band Fishbone. I loved them. I went to see them live, and I remember thinking, "This band is crazy good onstage, leaping about all over the place, playing horns, and the lead singer is fantastic." And so on the video for "Would I Lie to You?" I got half of Fishbone to be the horn players.

I decided to stay in Los Angeles for a while and rented a house on Cherokee Lane in Beverly Hills from Linda Gray (she played Sue Ellen Ewing on the TV series *Dallas*). I'd agreed to produce Feargal Sharkey's solo album, his first departure from the pop-punk band the Undertones. I had all the great players around me in LA, so I invited him over from Ireland to stay in the house and work with me in the studio.

On the second or third day of recording, I was at the mixing desk when the studio receptionist rang through and said, "I have Bob Dylan on the phone for you." My first reaction was that this was Feargal messing around. I answered saying, "Ha, Feargal. Good joke!"

But when I heard the voice on the other end of the line, it was unmistakable. After years of hearing this voice come out of my dad's gramophone and every stereo I ever owned, learning his songs over and over and spending nights just discussing every nuance of a Dylan song, I was now connected to him by this twisted wire. Every word was like an electric shock to my brain.

In fact, all I can remember is Dylan saying something like "Do you wanna meet up and talk about films and stuff?" I knew a family-owned Thai restaurant called the Talesai on Sunset, so I arranged to meet him there that evening. At first it was kind of awkward, and in a way he grilled me about various filmmakers and styles of film. We drank some sake and beer, and then we got to talking about music and videos. He said he hated making videos for songs. I said Annie and I liked doing them and considered them short vignettes or little movies.

Dylan then suggested I follow him to a great club to hang out for a while. Never would I have imagined Dylan going to clubs. The drive went on and on, and I was following his beaten-up old car for what seemed like an hour. We were off any map I'd ever used, and we ended up miles into East LA. He pulled into what looked like a disused parking lot, more like a junkyard. He got out and motioned me to go toward what looked like a boarded-up building. He gave a few taps, and a door swung open with a loud "Bobby!"

Dylan bent down and picked up this sweet lady, who was about three feet tall and wearing a full wedding dress. She wrapped her arms around him, and we stumbled into a dark room with loud mariachi music blasting out of tinny speakers with people dancing and laughing and in good spirits. It was an explosion of joy, and they all knew Bob.

It made perfect sense, as he can't go anywhere really to have fun because he gets bombarded with fans and autograph hunters. So we sat there and women were coming over to talk. Bob leaned over to me and said, "Just drink out of the bottle," meaning not out of a glass. After an hour had passed, we'd both drunk a few beers and were surrounded by cheerful, beautiful women. He turned around and said to me, "So, why don't we shoot some film to a couple of my songs?"

I said, "Sure. When?"

He said tomorrow and pointed at one female Latina and said, "She'll be in it." Then he pointed at another raven-haired girl, and said he wanted her to look like a young Elizabeth Taylor in a different song. I looked at my watch and hopefully suggested tomorrow, meaning thirty-six hours away, as it was already three in the morning. He smiled and nodded yes.

The next day I managed to get it together with Dom and Nic, two great young aspiring filmmakers. We rented the Hollywood United Methodist Church on the corner of Highland and Franklin and we shot two music videos in a row for "When the Night Comes Falling from the Sky" and "Emotionally Yours" from Dylan's album *Empire Burlesque.*

After that, I went back into the studio and completed Feargal Sharkey's album. Feargal and I cowrote some of the songs with my old friend the poet Tim Daly. One of the songs we recorded I had heard first when Maria McKee, the young lead singer from the country-rock band Lone Justice, played it on a piano in my bedroom. Jimmy was producing the Lone Justice album, but somehow this song had been rejected. When I first heard it, I asked Maria to play it again all the way through, and I recorded it on my cassette recorder. I knew it was a hit for sure. I played it for Feargal and suggested, "Let's record this as an out-and-out pop song," as it was kind of a country ballad on the demo. He loved it, and off we went recording "A Good Heart."

The song was a hit! It went to number one for two weeks in the UK and was a hit all around the world.

loved the opportunity to collaborate with all sorts of artists and often push them outside of their comfort zones to record different and experimental music. Daryl Hall from the megapopular duo Hall & Oates was branching out to record a solo album, *Three Hearts in the Happy Ending Machine*, in 1985. He wanted to experiment and do something very different from the Hall & Oates sound, so he chose me to write and produce with him. Things sparked off the very first day of our recording, and we became great friends.

Daryl arrived in London to start work at the Church Studios in Crouch End. For some reason, Daryl and I decided to celebrate the starting of the album by taking some psilocybin mushrooms, also known as magic mushrooms or 'shrooms. They can cause a kind of euphoria, an altered thinking process in which you lose time and hallucinate, depending on the amount. We decided the safest thing was to make tea with the mushrooms so we could sip the tea, until we felt it was the right time to start experimenting. The one drawback of this oblique strategy was that once we started sipping, we lost track of time or how much we'd sipped, and we fell on the floor in uncontrollable fits of laughter.

This was a bonding moment for Daryl and me, but not for T-Bone Wolk, the late great bass player who had come to help in the production and make sure everything went smoothly for Daryl. T-Bone was an amazing musician and a beautiful guy, but very unsure about this experiment, in which he didn't partake. In fact, he was saying, "Guys, please don't. That's a bad idea. This is the first day of recording."

We promised him we would be fine. Of course, within an hour of taking the mushrooms, we couldn't do anything except laugh, so we decided to go back to my house. All the way there, T-Bone was going, "Oh, guys, I knew you shouldn't have taken that stuff," and he was looking really fed up with us, sitting on the jump seat in the London black cab. He wanted to get to work, and now he was dealing with us.

Meanwhile, Daryl and I couldn't stop laughing in the back of the car. We were giggling hysterically. We got to my house, and Nida, my wonderful Thai housekeeper, had made this amazing-smelling fish soup. We were both suddenly entranced by the exotic aroma and were going, "Oh, my God, what an amazing smell!"

Then, all of a sudden, I went, "Oh, no, I've got a fish bone in my throat." I couldn't breathe, and started to panic. Daryl came to my rescue and said, "Let's have a look." I lay down on the table, clutching my throat. Daryl was saying, "Hang on. Do you have a torch?"

He got on his hands and knees on the table, leaning over me with a giant flashlight, the industrial kind you use in a garage, and he was trying to stick it down my throat. He was trying to see the fish bone that got stuck. He started yelling, "We'd better go to the hospital." I was just choking and screaming, "Get it out, Daryl!" And we'd only just met. This was the first day of recording.

Meanwhile, T-Bone was getting more and more exasperated, pulling his hat off, going, "Guys, guys, you've not even eaten the soup. There's no fish in your mouth." Nida was confused, as she hadn't even poured a bowl out yet. We hadn't even eaten anything. It was all a hallucination.

And that was how the album started.

We carried on the next day in the church without the help of the 'shrooms and things started coming together. In fact, it sounded fantastic. I then suggested we go to Paris and record with my great friend Manu Guiot at the Studio Grande Armée, where Annie and I later worked on both our *Revenge* and *Savage* albums.

We carried on having so much fun there. I don't think Daryl had ever laughed so much. We ended up making a great album. For one of the songs I got the guy who lived across the road and had a guitar shop to play Daryl this instrumental he would play whenever I went to look at guitars. Daryl loved it, and we made it into a song called "Dreamtime."

As usual, I was surrounded by chaos, as I was working on a few things at the same time. Dylan was visiting me at home a lot during the Daryl sessions, and Bob wrote a completely different set of words to "Dreamtime" for fun, while he was in my basement.

"Dreamtime" became Daryl's first Top Ten solo single in America, reaching number five on the *Billboard* Hot 100. The next single, "Foolish Pride," also went Top Forty in the US. On a side note, SSL, the famous manufacturer of high-end mixing consoles, used the album for many years to demonstrate the quality of sound produced. It must have been the shrooms.

I was a guest on Daryl's show, *Live from Daryl's House*, a few years ago. We played "Dreamtime" and a couple of songs from that album. Then I played some songs from my albums *The Blackbird Diaries* and *Greetings from the Gutter*. Over dinner we reflected about that time and you can see it on the *Live from Daryl's House* episode with me. We were just crying, laughing again, talking about the fish incident and all of the mad things that happened to us in London, Paris and New York City during the making of the album.

Our next Eurythmics album, *Be Yourself Tonight*, came out in February 1985, which unfortunately was the same year that our record label, RCA, got a new head. His name was José Menéndez. The aforementioned Gary Kurfirst was managing us in America at the time, a man with good taste. He had met with Menéndez, and came back in a panic. He said, "Oh, no, I can't even talk to this guy!"

José Menéndez was the same guy who was later killed by his own kids, Lyle and Erik Menéndez. But that didn't happen until 1989, four years later. Annie and I were delivering *Be Yourself Tonight*, which we knew was huge. Gary was saying Menéndez didn't have any clue about us or how best to promote our records and that he didn't know anything about music at all. Annie asked, "Oh, what are we going to do?" I said, "I'll have a meeting with him."

I went to New York to meet him. He was a huge Cuban guy, and he had listened to the new album and wanted to talk about it. Wonderful!

"Hey, Dave," he says. "It's a lovely album. Good work! It reminds me of *Ghostbusters!*"

I was like, "*Ghostbusters?* What the hell was he talking about?"

Then I discovered Menéndez had come from Hertz Rent-a-Car, where he had been CEO. And now he was the CEO of RCA Records. I mean, how did you hire somebody who had been running a car rental company to run a record label?

It was at that moment that he said, "I have an idea for you and Annie. We've been talking to Burger King, and we're going to put your album out with them and they'll have a CD free with a meal. They'll make little plastic Dave and Annie toys!" That was when I saw the future of the whole music business, and it was burger-shaped. In the record business, the money never did seem to add up. We could never work out why we were selling out all these huge theaters and arenas four nights in a row and weren't making it in record sales.

I was talking to Tom Petty and explaining to him that we would have four hits off our album and sold-out tours, all over the world, and we would sell a comparable number of albums. In Australia we would sell six hundred thousand and in Norway and Sweden about five hundred thousand albums. And then, in America, we'd sell a million. But we should have been selling about five million. Tom Petty was going, "And that doesn't make sense because you're on the radio all the time, and you're selling out all these huge venues, so you should be selling three to five million."

Well, there has never been a full investigation about this, but we found out that José Menéndez was printing up vinyl records in South America, shipping them in and selling them, not on the RCA label but through a record store chain. All the money, I think, was going into the soft porn industry in Los Angeles, and he was getting it out through a high-end talcum-powder-and-soap company. Talk about laundering money! So we never knew the actual sales or numbers; all of it was twisted.

José was very much about success and power. I remember meeting his elder son, Lyle, who wanted to be a champion tennis player. I think he was all right at tennis, but his dad was very mean and strict with him. I think he had both sons terrified. I can totally believe that because he was scary to me.

CHAPTER:10

REVENGE

1986 was the year of *Revenge*, which Annie and I recorded in the middle of the countryside in north Germany at our dear friend Conny Plank's studio. Conny had recorded *In the Garden*, and had such a positive and ongoing impact on our music that it seemed right to return. His studio in Germany was a good place to get away from everything and focus.

I went to that studio with a mission: to make a record that had an epic, arena-type sound to it so we could really get our teeth into it when we played live. I started to play more guitar on this album, and it was made with a band feel, as opposed to the sound of a duo.

It was Conny who inspired me to become a producer. Back when we recorded Eurythmics' first album, *In the Garden*, he demystified the craft of recording and made it a fun and experimental creative process. He let me play on the board, which is something most engineers or producers never do. They say, "The band sits back there," and it's like they're in charge of flying the airplane, and you're not allowed in the cockpit. But Conny let me in the cockpit every day, and it was thrilling. He was forever showing me all sorts of mad things, and he encouraged experiments. Like "Let's put this microphone down the farmyard well, and record the echo from the water, and let's take the bass drum, detune the skin and hit it with a mallet but put the microphone fifteen feet away in the big room."

He taught me anything is possible. He would say, "You want to distort it? We'll distort it." Whereas the old way of thinking was "No, no, you can't distort the thing!"

Conny was always teaching us that there are no rules. His studio was in the middle of nowhere and it was just a little farmhouse with a tiny barn that he'd converted. Conny and his wife, Christa, had just had a little boy, Stefan, who is a lovely man now and who has released rare oddities of his dad's recordings in Germany.

I think the main lesson I learned from my time with Conny in his studio is that all that matters is the sound, not how you achieve it. You have to try stuff out to see if you like it. So go get a can and put some split peas in it and shake it with a bag of pencils, and then put that through a delay. And see what you have. It doesn't matter what it is that you're banging or recording or whether the guitar cost five dollars at a thrift shop—you can make it sound amazing.

Before digital sampling and sequencers, Conny worked with Holger Czukay, who created "Persian Love Song" by cutting up bits of tape to make loops. Holger used tape editing as an instrument. It was fascinating to watch and I used this approach over the years.

I asked Clem Burke to play with us again. He is a fantastic rock-and-roll, pop, classic drummer who is very dramatic. If you're building from a verse into a chorus, he really gives it stick. He doesn't hold back or try to be jazzy or too subtle. He's all about the fact that we are making pop and rock music, and you need to feel it.

Take a song like "Thorn in My Side" for example. Even with just me on a twelve-string acoustic, Annie's voice and Clem's drumming, he made the whole thing sound electrifying. Annie was channeling her anger and was so focused when she opened her mouth and delivered her cutting lyrics, "Thorn in my side, you know that's all you ever were," that it was icy cold yet burning with passion. She carried on and did the whole song in one single take.

Then we moved to Paris to do more lead vocals, saxophone and other overdubs, as it was our favorite city and we always did great work there. Once we set up camp at Studio de la Grande Armée, my old Sunderland pal Eric Scott came and painted our portraits for the cover of the album. It was quite surreal as he painted every day in my small apartment, while I was at the studio working, and when I came home at night, there would be a little bit more of me, or Annie, on the canvas. Our album cover was coming together in front of our very own eyes.

"The Miracle of Love" on *Revenge* started, as do most of my songs, on an acoustic guitar. I love playing acoustic guitar. Sometimes just a very simple line along with the right chord inversion is all I need, and the rest of the song structure just flows. I also love playing music with friends in the kitchen.

I started working on it back in London. I had a house with a stone kitchen floor, and it had a great natural reverb. I played the "Miracle of Love" opening riff on acoustic guitar in my kitchen every morning for a few days. I wanted Annie to come back from holiday so I could play it to her. I had the guitar riff, chords, chorus, melody and the line "The miracle of love will take away your pain, when the miracle of love comes your way again." But I had no idea what to say after that, and it was driving me crazy.

Annie eventually came home, and within minutes of me playing the idea with her at the piano, she worked out the melody of the verse. She then nailed the lyrics like the genius she is, coming up with lines like "They say the greatest coward can hurt the most ferociously."

You see, there is something very moving about certain inversions of chord changes and the way they play against the timbre of someone's voice. Not only does Annie have a distinctive sound to her voice; she has another element that is soaked in emotion and moves people to tears. It's a mixture of the sound she makes with her voice and the fact that she comes from Aberdeen, Scotland, where the musical heritage is littered with haunting airs. It is hard to explain how such sadness and beauty can come from the melodies and chord changes in Scottish or Irish airs; you just have to listen to them and feel it. It's something instinctive to Annie, and coming from the northeast of England myself, I easily relate. We both grew up where the sky was filled with varying shades of gray and where a freezing northern wind blew. I think these elements added to the dynamic between us when we wrote ballads. We both knew when something had the chill factor.

Our old friend Michael Kamen composed the string arrangement. The instrumental in the middle reminds me of those big open skies on a windy day, with the soaring strings, backward guitars and forward guitars. Annie added some great subtle ad-libs toward the end of the song, and the strings do an ascending movement that gives me goose bumps.

By the time we recorded *Revenge*, Annie and I had already been through so much together as a couple, but we still also shared whatever was going on with each of our personal lives. It was almost impossible for us not to share everything we were thinking and feeling; we discussed everything as part of the creative process. It was sometimes very painful and difficult for us and the people around us, yet in a way it was because of our unique relationship that the songs were so full of emotion: sometimes angry, sometimes full of tenderness, but always intense.

When *Revenge* was finally finished, we went straight into making three music videos in a row. Just like the recording, I wanted the first videos to be performance-based with the band, so "Thorn in My Side" and "When Tomorrow Comes" were made with our newfound band members, as a precursor to our live shows.

Along with the video producer Billy Poveda, I directed and shot the music video for "The Miracle of Love" using an 8mm cine camera in the back garden of the construction site that was to be my home on Balboa Avenue in Encino, California. It was intercut with some disturbing war and riot footage, and I inserted a nuclear explosion every time Annie sang "The Miracle of Love" as the ultimate juxtaposition.

My favorite image ever of Annie is on the footage at the end of this video. I was using a long lens, and she didn't know I was shooting her. When she realized it, she smiled and started to laugh. That is always the image I think of when I miss Annie. In a few split seconds I captured on film everything I love about her. For a long time, we always finished Eurythmics' shows with this song, and it was always emotional. People of all ages would be looking up with tears streaming down their faces.

"Missionary Man," also on *Revenge*, has become one of our most famous and beloved songs in the USA. Around the time when Annie and I wrote it, life had become a little complex for me. I was working with a revolving door of amazing prolific artists, and it was probably driving Annie crazy. It was unintentional, but I was just open to anything, and of course when you are open to anything, anything can happen.

On one particular morning something very peculiar did happen. I went down to the kitchen in my home in London, in Maida Vale, and standing outside in the street I could see my mom talking to this little lady who was showing her a piece of paper. My mom was pointing to my house.

Mom came to the door and said, "Look, this lady's lost and she's very upset. She was going for an interview." She had just come to England and didn't speak much English, and she was lost with a piece of paper she didn't comprehend. My mom kept saying, "Well, my son will give you a job." And I said, "Okay."

So she came in and she seemed so sweet and was so upset that she was lost. I said, "Don't worry. Let's have a cup of tea." Her name was Nida and she was from Thailand. At the time I didn't need a nanny or a cook, or anybody really. I was a single guy and was always out or on tour. But she turned out to be the greatest cook and the best nanny in the world! Nida became one of the most important people in my life, and she worked for me from that day onward for twenty-seven years, until she retired.

It wasn't easy going at first. I had to get used to her, and she had to get used to me. I had my mum teach her how to make scrambled eggs for breakfast instead of her favorite Thai breakfast, oil of black snake. Slowly Nida was introduced to the awfully boring ways of the Western diet. We had a few misunderstandings too, like the time she threw ten thousand pounds in cash in the dustbin on the day the garbage truck came. I had it in a carrier bag to buy a rare guitar from a guy who wanted cash. Nida had to get used to the bedlam that was my single life.

It was a steep learning curve for her when this was a typical forty-eight hours in my life: I woke up to the doorbell ringing in my London house. I stepped over Jeff Lynne, who was asleep on the floor, and went downstairs. I looked out the middle floor window, and there was the brilliant Kevin Godley and Lol Creme (the art rock band 10cc) with a film crew in tow. I opened the door and they said, "You've forgotten, haven't you?" And I had. I think it was something to do with a Jukebox TV idea, very ahead of its time. Anyway, they came in and we all sat around having a cup of tea. Jeff Lynne left and George Harrison wandered into the kitchen, much to the amazement of Kevin and Lol. The film crew left and Mick Jagger arrived. Mick sat down at the piano in the middle room and started to play and sing a new version of "Memory Motel" as a song for a TV series I created called Beyond the Groove. It sounded amazing. Satisfied we were in agreement on the song, Mick left. Ten minutes later Robert Plant rang the doorbell. He had arrived to talk about an idea he had for Toni Halliday to sing on his solo album. Poor Nida had no idea who anyone was, but she started to get used to the idea that this was a crazy musician's life, and she learned to love it.

But it doesn't end there. Around noon the next day, I headed for the Church Studios, where Annie and I were experimenting with "Missionary Man," when Bob Dylan arrived. Annie pulled out some lyrics she'd been writing and read it like a poem to Bob, and we both thought it would sound great with his voice singing it. Annie and I also sent Robert Plant a different version of "Here Comes the Rain Again," as we thought it was a good idea for him to sing! Talk about being presumptuous!

Bob didn't say much about the song, though, as he was extremely shy, and Annie was very shy too. So to break the plane I just began jamming around until Bob and I decided to go back to my place and listen to some music we had recorded. I had this Japanese-style hibachi cooking table, where you could sit around and cook things in the middle, so Bob, his girlfriend and I were sitting around the table while Nida was cooking, throwing prawns and vegetables on the hot plate, and we were drinking shots of tequila. Bob was wearing my big Mexican sombrero, and we were playing back the tracks we had recorded on my cassette player while Bob made up lyrics on the spot as he was singing along.

Just then the doorbell rang and it was Annie. She came in and immediately started singing harmonies along with Bob. We had a boom box on the kitchen table blasting out the tracks, the prawns and steak sizzling, Bob and Annie singing.

A friend who was down visiting from Sunderland was kind of speechless, because it was his first visit and he couldn't get his head around the fact that Bob Dylan was singing along to a cassette, in a sombrero, in my kitchen. I have since found the cassette tape of us doing that, and I labeled it the Mexican kitchen tapes.

The next day Bob spent a few hours in my basement playing R. L. Burnside–type blues guitar into my Portastudio, with Nida bringing us Thai snacks and cups of tea, which she'd now mastered. What a whirlwind existence to bring sweet Nida into, but she caught on quickly.

Bob and I became close friends after enough long days and nights of playing and hanging out. On another occasion we had been jamming at the Church Studios when Bob wanted to leave. I suggested that "Big Kenny" drive him. Big Kenny worked as a bodyguard at a London nightclub, and I'd met him one night when a famous video producer suggested that I was a bit tipsy and needed a ride home. Kenny drove me home in his bright turquoise Rolls-Royce.

Kenny was big—in fact, huge—yet the gentlest soul you could ever meet. He worked for me for many years after that as security at the Church Studios. So on this particular day when Bob wanted to leave early, I told Big Ken to pull the car round the front and take Bob back to his hotel in Mayfair in central London.

I thought nothing of it till about two hours later when someone shouted, "Bob Dylan on the phone for Dave from a pay phone!" I thought that was odd. I got on the phone and Bob was describing his whereabouts and it sounded like he was in Luton, which is far outside of London.

I asked to speak to Kenny, and when he came on the phone, he was panicked and told me, "Bob don't say nothing, Dave. I couldn't read the signs, a few wrong turnings and I'm lost."

I had forgotten that I always told Kenny the directions until he memorized any route, as he was dyslexic and had great difficulty reading. In fact my mum was homeschooling him to help him with it.

I said, "Don't worry. Put Bob back on." I told Bob the problem. What happened next was the sweetest thing. According to Big Kenny, Bob got in the front seat next to him and pulled out the A-to-Z map of London and proceeded to direct them all the way to Mayfair. Along the way Bob told Kenny his life story from his childhood through to megastardom. What any journalist would have given to be in that backseat!

These were the times. I had all-night jam sessions with the craziest combinations of artists and people we had met along the way; I had produced records for some of them. One time it was me on bass, Joni Mitchell on drums, Daryl Hall on guitar and Clem Burke on piano. It sounded terrible. Annie must have thought I'd gone mad half the time, but I wouldn't have changed it for the world. All of it was invaluable experience for years to come.

At this point in our career, I'd seen how the biggest acts approached a stage show and knew we had to step up into the arena, so to speak. This had a lot to do with the music you made and the way you presented it in a larger-than-life kind of way. The Stones had been doing this for years, but in the eighties' quirky music scene, this kind of act had almost disappeared. The bands that were storming their way through America were aware of creating a real show and making live films like U2's *Under a Blood Red Sky*, from their 1983 Red Rocks concert, or Talking Heads' *Stop Making Sense* concert movie from 1984.

So in 1985/1986 I was looking to produce an album that would be great to build a live show around and for a group of musicians who could pull it off. This came together for us on the *Revenge* album. We searched for the perfect band lineup to play our live shows. We had Clem Burke on drums and Patrick Seymour on keyboards, and then were lucky enough to get Chucho Merchán on bass, Jimmy "Z" Zavala on harmonica and saxophone and Joniece Jamison on backing vocals. These musicians were not only amazing performers, but, just as important, great people to be around. We had wonderful times together as we traveled the world.

The Revenge Tour was the biggest and longest tour we had ever attempted, lasting over a year, but each time I played the opening bars of "Thorn in My Side," I felt the same excitement as when we first put it down in the studio. It was a rush to the head.

"Missionary Man," the opening track, became a linchpin song on the Revenge Tour. I wanted to create a spiritual feeling at the opening of the song. I felt like an alchemist cooking up a weird brew of blues, rock and voodoo, with a strange mixture of guitars, synthesizers, backward noises and harmonica that spiraled toward the opening line, "Well, I was born an original sinner."

Annie delivered such a focused and intense vocal on "Missionary Man" that, even though the song had explosive drums and a wall of guitars, she cut right through it like a knife.

The video for "Missionary Man," directed by my longtime friend Willy Smax, was set in an alchemist's laboratory. The opening sequence shows a serpent weaving its way around these glass tubes, and I throw an apple into the glass cauldron, where a new Annie forms inside. We were always visually playing with what was happening in our world and mixing it with fantasy or surrealism. In this case, we were reinventing ourselves as a rock band and playing with the imagery; we had unusual black leather outfits made and wore matching black leather boots.

Annie is such a brilliant performer that sometimes I was so busy watching her, I would forget what I was doing. When you're onstage with someone like that, time stands still. Looking back at concert footage from Berlin, Rome, Sydney, Tokyo and San Francisco, no matter which concert, or which song, you can see that by this time we had it down. The minute the curtain opened, we came out like caged animals. Annie and I loved figuring out the opening of the show, always with something unusual.

Revenge had an amazing opening. Instead of a curtain we wanted the stage to be covered with stretched PVC, which looked like a pair of jeans with a zipper. We asked Ana Maria, our bass player Chucho Merchán's girlfriend at the time, to sit in the audience near the front. As the lights went down, Ana would run and jump over the security barriers (with the security guys in on the plot of course), and she would climb up on the stage and start to scale up the large zipper—as our taped intro started saying "Sex, ss-sex." Panning across in stereo "Sex! Ss-ss-sex."

The crowd would be going wild as the security guards were trying to pull Ana down, but of course she climbed to the top rung and hung on the ring pull. The zip started to come down, opening up the PVC jeans, while shafts of white light came through. By this time the crowd was going crazy and let out a deafening roar as Annie and I leapt through the opening in the jeans just as they tore apart, and launched into "Sex Crime."

Revenge was our biggest album. Now, with "Missionary Man" this quirky electro duo from the UK won a Grammy for Best Rock Vocal Performance by a Group and were number one on the Billboard charts. I was the "man with a mission," as the song says, and we mutated from pop stars into rock stars overnight. The album and the tour broke us in a big way, in every country. Now we were not only playing indoor arenas; we were also doing outdoor stadiums. The Revenge Tour went on and on and on for over a year from 1986 to '87.

We had leather stage outfits with long frock coats covered in pearl buttons like the Pearly King and Queen except we added studs and leather trousers with long leather riding boots. One thing we didn't take into consideration was how hot the stage would be under the lights, and how hot and heavy our clothes were. So by the second number we would be dripping with sweat. We plowed on through the whole year, though, wearing this gear, and I must have lost ten pounds.

The Revenge Tour concert movie had a very unusual opening: there are many pieces of broken mirror, and I put them back together to form seven whole mirrors. It's all one long shot on a crane that starts with me and slowly reveals the whole band in different rooms, acting out their personalities before the show. Eventually the camera rises so high that you see we are all caged in a little room, waiting to be let out of jail, and then we burst on the stage. We had become one step removed from ourselves. I'm sure people, when they saw it, thought, *WTF!?*

I remember we had a premier of the concert film in Los Angeles and my guest was Jodie Foster. I was going mental because the cinema sound was atrocious and she kept telling me, "Calm down, it's all right. I'm trying to watch it." And I'm saying, "Yeah, but I want to hear it as well."

We went far enough down the path into that world of rock and roll, which, I suppose, throws you into sort of semi-extreme behavior. We never imagined we would become this huge, but slowly we started to realize everything was becoming bigger and bigger, and we were flying about the world with a massive crew of people, followed on the road by a big convoy of trucks.

Every night there would be lots of people we knew at the show, as we had played those cities so many times before. In Sydney, for instance, we played eight sold-out nights in a row at Sydney Entertainment Center, with thirteen thousand screaming fans every show. So every night, after the concert, there was a party. Well, it seemed like a party but mostly it was in my head. Sometimes I wouldn't want to bother leaving my dressing room, as that's where the party started, and I never got out.

Michael Hutchence from INXS attended our Sydney shows, and at the time he was going out with Kylie Minogue. That party ended up with the three of us in my hotel suite at the Sebel Townhouse. Michael was passed out on my bed, and I was trying to help Kylie, who was throwing up in the bathroom. Eventually she seemed okay, so I went back to trying to work out the chords to "Walk like an Egyptian." This was the new normal.

I first met Jack Nicholson when he came to a concert at the Greek Theatre. All three nights he stood on the side of the stage screaming instructions to us—that we couldn't hear of course—till we came offstage before the encores. Then he put his arms around us both, and with the same worrying grin he had when he breaks through the bathroom door in *The Shining*, he proceeded to tell us to "Walk back onstage. Hold hands. Stare at the audience for at least two minutes. Totally still, don't move. Don't say a word." So we did and the audience slowly went bananas till they were standing on their seats, screaming and chanting. The longer we stood still, the wilder the audience became. From then on he told everyone he was our manager. I didn't mind. He was and is a genius.

After one of the shows Jack asked me to come back to his place, so I did with my girlfriend at the time. There was just Jack, his friend, and me and my girlfriend. It was chill and quiet after the deafening noise of being onstage. I just started to feel relaxed when suddenly I could smell burning. For some reason my girlfriend had set fire to an expensive sculpture, made of hundred-dollar bills, on Jack's coffee table. I thought this was going to end badly, but instead Jack just watched it burn with a slight smile and a glint in his eye.

The night ended well, though, with my girlfriend and me in his outdoor Jacuzzi at four in the morning, with Jack in a bathrobe conducting

Beethoven for us, which was blasting out of the stereo. The whole time I was nervous because he was standing on the thin ledge of the Jacuzzi wall, with his back to a thousand-foot drop off his cliffside backyard. He was getting more and more animated with his conducting. One inch the wrong way, and he would have fallen to his death.

By this time I had become good friends with Jack. We were both completely open-minded, creative people who wanted to push boundaries and experiment in whatever we were doing, including partying. At another show in Boston, he arrived in my dressing room backstage with Michelle Pfeiffer. They were in the middle of shooting *The Witches of Eastwick*. The combination of alcohol mixed with strong reefer had gotten to Jack, and unbeknownst to us he had locked himself in one of the bathrooms. It wasn't till we were all leaving and Michelle was confused as to where he had gone that we began a search. Eventually we found one locked door. Chucho, our bass player, was at the keyhole, saying, "Jack, are you in there?"

He heard a groan and said, "Oh, my God, are you okay? Jack, you're my hero." Then he heard Jack whispering back through the keyhole, "Sorry about that, man." We had to get security to screw the door off and help him out, looking a pale shade of green, but still with that impish grin.

Annie and I had been on the road for years by now, and we had been broken up for about six years. I'd been out with various people, but it was really hard trying to be in a relationship on the road and in a huge band. Annie had massive problems with this too. You either had to say good-bye or bring them along, and being on the road as a guest gets old after more than a few days. The other person doesn't get the thrill of playing every night and that exhilarating rush of adrenaline that comes with it that keeps you awake half the night. Eventually the two worlds collide, or they give in to your world and become confused about who they are, or you contemplate packing it all in to try to have a normal relationship, which must have crossed Annie's mind many times during the years of touring.

During this time I was conflicted. I loved my life and everything about it, but now I was nearly thirty-five years old and had been doing this for twenty years, albeit in all shapes and sizes. Now we couldn't really get any bigger, so in the back of mind I had a question continually popping up: "What's next?"

Before the tour started, I was in LA at the Sunset Marquis, picking up Bob Geldof and Paula Yates to fly off to Vegas for their wedding when I saw that Siobhan Fahey from Bananarama was arriving. Everybody kind of knew one another from being in the same world.

Bananarama had been in the charts solidly for ages. I liked their music but I'd only met Siobhan once when they appeared in the Eurythmics video for "Who's That Girl?" so I called her room to introduce myself. We realized that we'd both be in New York at the same time and we arranged to meet for dinner.

In New York, I wasn't sure what kind of outing to plan or what she might like, so I just asked the concierge at the hotel, "What kind of meal should we eat? Chinese?" And he told us where to go. I figured he must have known what he was doing.

We decided to get one of these horse-drawn carriages to take us to the restaurant and then we felt really bad because it's not the best thing for a horse to be riding around on a New York street. We went to the Chinese restaurant and there was nobody in it. New York, Chinatown and Chinese restaurants are usually packed, so I'm going, "God, this concierge, he's throwing us a bum steer, right?" This was not good.

Everything seemed slightly off-kilter all night. Then I was talking to Siobhan across the table and behind her was this commotion. I didn't know what it was at first, but it was a deaf couple having an argument. Siobhan couldn't really hear them apart from a few noises, and they were the only other people in the restaurant. It all was very strange. The evening was morphing from a date into a very bizarre outing. Then we had the discomfort of bumping into each other in the MTV green room when both our bands were there at the same time, and I think the others had guessed about our secret date.

That was how our relationship began and we started talking to each other a lot. Trouble was, I was just starting this bloody huge tour and she was in her band and they were having a huge global hit with "Venus," so they were all over the place themselves.

Bananarama already had big hits in America, like "Cruel Summer" and "Robert De Niro's Waiting," and now Siobhan was a devil in a red PVC catsuit in the "Venus" video, which I saw everywhere I went.

We kept in touch and arranged to meet again in London, and we got on really well. We had fun. I loved her sense of humor and we laughed a lot. It was a relief for me to be in a whole different world with her and it was probably the same for Siobhan. Being with the same people day in and day out can be tiring, even if you love them dearly. But then I had to leave for LA to shoot videos and rehearse for the Revenge Tour.

I was writing with Bob Geldof at the same time. Bob had just created and organized the Live Aid charity concerts, which raised more than two hundred million dollars. He'd been handling logistics and business for this event and was creatively unfulfilled. He had lost any confidence to make music again, which he knew he needed to do to feed his soul. I met him at an awards dinner and asked what he was doing musically. He was so pleased that someone wanted to talk to him about his music and not his efforts in Africa that he decided to come to see me in Paris, where I was living at the time. He stayed with me in Montparnasse for a short while just to chill out and get away from England and the tabloids.

I had to go back to America for rehearsals with Eurythmics and to shoot videos for our finished album *Be Yourself Tonight*. Bob decided to come too, and he lived with me in a house I rented in the Valley. We had such a great and crazy time. The second day Bob was there I realized we needed someone to help around the house, as we were not the best chefs in the world. I decided to fly in Nida from London. You are probably wondering what all this has to do with Bob and me writing a song, but I don't actually write songs. I just kind of create chaos, and all of a sudden, a song starts to emerge. There is usually someone around who is very good fun to share the chaos with, and this time it was Bob. There was a perfect storm brewing!

Nida arrived in the afternoon while we were out, and I had forgotten to tell her the security code to the house. Unbeknownst to us, she was trying to explain the situation to the security patrol car guys, in broken English, while the alarm was deafening the entire neighborhood. When we arrived, I had about ten people in tow and Nida was crying on the step with the alarm still going off. I opened the door with my key but the alarm refused to stop. Bob went and got an ax from the backyard and proceeded to chop through all the wires around the security system, immediately severing the lights, cable and most of the household appliances. But there was silence at last.

Nida cheered up quickly. My friends had brought wine and we found candles. Bob drove Nida to the supermarket, and somehow she prepared a Thai feast for twelve on a gas stove in twenty minutes. I was extremely impressed, and Nida has been my favorite chef ever since. So we ate and drank in candlelight into the early hours of the morning until I passed out, leaving a few stragglers behind.

The next morning I was a bit hungover. I sat down and started tinkering on this very out-of-tune upright piano that came with the house. Bob stumbled into the room in his boxer shorts, looking like he'd just had a fight with a hairbrush and said, "What's that song?" I mumbled, "I dunno," and wandered into the kitchen to see if Nida had magically whipped up breakfast without electricity. (She still has a problem with breakfasts!) Anyway, I heard Bob playing the chords and that was the beginning of the song "This Is the World Calling" coming together, right there in the blinding-headache morning light, in the debris from the night before, with Bob in his boxers and me sitting cross-legged, eating Cheerios with apple juice instead of milk. There was no milk left, because Bob had drunk it.

We fiddled around with the song during the day, and Bob came up with some great words. Then we decided the Husky dog that came with the house looked too hot in all that fur. The temperature in the San

Fernando Valley is over 100 degrees Fahrenheit in the summertime, and this dog could barely walk and hated the heat. So we took him for a haircut. The dog was very old, so we gently lifted him into the back of my Jeep and drove along Ventura Boulevard, looking for a pet shop to help the dog out. Against the pet shop owner's advice, Bob persuaded the man to shear the dog. We really felt we'd done a good deed and were driving home with the dog looking a lot cooler in the back when at a stoplight some kids shouted, "Hey, Bob Geldof and Dave Stewart are in that Jeep." People started coming up to us and the dog panicked; he must have thought they were looking at his new haircut. He tried to jump out of the Jeep, but fell badly on his nose, which started bleeding.

Now the kids were chanting, "Geldof and Stewart, they've killed the dog." This wasn't going to look good in the tabloids: GELDOF SAVES AFRICA, THEN KILLS DOG. So we scooped him up and scampered back home. In the end the dog was okay, although the pet shop guy knew the owners of the house and called them to report their dog's new hairdo. They went nuts about us ruining their dog's Husky look. Bob had a good old row with them about how it was stupid to have a Husky in the heat, and then they saw the ax next to the loose wires and stopped arguing, went home and called the Realtor to say I had to move out or they would call the police.

I got someone to fix the electrics, and we had the song nearly finished on the wonky piano, so we decided to record it the next day. The only problem was, I was shooting a video with Annie for "Missionary Man" at A&M Studios. I booked the recording studio next door to where we were filming for "This Is the World Calling" so we could record at the same time. So during the "Missionary Man" breaks, I would run across the lot into the studio and carry on producing the track. We had called too many people to come down and play: we had myself and U2's the Edge on guitar, Larry from U2 on drums, and Clem Burke on drums too. We had a few female backing vocalists and three bass players. The word got out, and it was turned into a circus because everyone loved Bob and wanted to help on his first track since Live Aid.

In the middle of it all the weirdest thing happened. An extremely official-looking chap arrived, completely out of place, looking a little bit like somebody from the FBI. I saw him at the front desk saying, "I'd like to have a word with Mr. Geldof." I thought, "Oh, shit, it's because of the dog. He's from PETA or maybe it's about Bob's handiwork with the ax." I rushed passed him and burst in the studio saying, "The police have come for Bob!"

Bob was like "Oh, geez, I've done something. I'm gonna get arrested or something." Anyway, the man came in and said he needed to talk to Bob alone and they went into a small lounge room. We could see through the glass and Bob looked dead serious. We were thinking, "Oh, shit. He's gonna get roped in for something." Bob came out, all smiles, and shook the guy's hand, and the guy left. We said, "Well?" In his thickest mock country Irish accent, he said, "Bejaeezus! Oi'm gonna get feckin knighted by the Queen of England." Ha! And we all played a jig and fell about laughing. This guy had actually been sent by the Queen with a little red briefcase, very official, to say, "You're going to become a Sir." And now he is Sir Bob Geldof.

This was during the peak of craziness, and just when we thought it couldn't get any worse or better, it did. . . . Bob and I had agreed to perform at this event for Amnesty International in the LA Forum that happened to be that very same day. We said we would perform as the Brothers of Doom because for some mad reason, and with our sort of warped sense of humor, we invented this duo to turn up as special guests. We were in the studio recording and had completely forgotten that we'd agreed to perform that night. All of a sudden I heard, "They've called from the Forum and they're wondering where you are for the sound check." This was now about seven p.m. We were like, "Shit!"

I grabbed my acoustic guitar and got a yellow cab, and we went dashing down toward the Forum, jumping out of the cab when we arrived because we were so late. Then the car drove off with my bleeding guitar in it!

I asked Jackson Browne if I could borrow one of his guitars. There was a rack of them, so I hurriedly picked one up, as we literally had to go straight onstage. In the car we had decided we were going to sing "Redemption Song" by Bob Marley and one of Geldof's songs to keep it simple. As we get onstage I was putting the guitar on as they were announcing, "And now special guests, the Brothers of Doom," and I realize I've picked up a left-handed guitar.

Bob walked up to the mic and says, "We are the Brothers of Doom and we'd like to sing for you a Bob Marley song, 'Redemption Song,'" while I'm busy looking at my hands trying to figure out how to play D and G upside down. Bob looks at me, going, "Fuckin' start the song, ya bastard!" With fifteen thousand people waiting, I'm saying, "Keep talking, ya twat." He's looking at me like I'm a loser. Very funny, but we managed to get through it. At the end of the night we got a cab back to the house, and we were completely shattered and starving, as we'd forgotten to eat.

So, we went to this twenty-four-hour diner called Twain's on the corner of Coldwater Canyon and Ventura Boulevard, and it was just the two of us at the counter. The place was completely empty and we were laughing hysterically, asking, "What the fuck happened today?" You know, we'd been making a video, recording a song, getting told Bob was gonna be knighted by the Queen, playing live at the LA Forum, and it was now two in the morning and we were on our own, giggling and eating dried cheesecake with cups of old black joe.

Bob and I were recently going through this story and laughing. He said, "Oh, but you don't remember? There was a great end to the story." And I said, "What's that?" And he said, "At Twain's Diner, I pulled the waitress!"

In the midst of this madness Siobhan came and stayed with me for about a week. We drove all over the place in my open-top Jeep, just feeling free and doing what we pleased.

I had the wooden outside structure of a house I was building that was to become the Encino house and studio. So we went there and sort of walked around the outside, in and out of the wooden structure, and I said, "We could live here." I didn't know if she was really involved with somebody else. She said she had been seeing someone in London for a while, but I got the feeling it wasn't going smoothly, so I didn't ask much about him.

Anyway, we started going out with each other, prior to the Revenge Tour. When I came back to London to rehearse for the tour, we hung around with each other again and she took me to meet her parents. It was the first time I'd been in a family setting for years, and it felt good. I felt like the family gave me a tick of approval! I was going away the next day and I'd just bought a car. I don't really drive cars that much, but for some reason I had bought a sports car. I said to Siobhan, "I'm going away and I don't want to leave the car in the street; do you want to have it while I'm away?" She said, "Not really. I don't want the responsibility of it." I liked that.

I flew off to start the Revenge World Tour, and I was thinking, "God, here we go again. I've met somebody I like but now I'm away for ten months." In fact the tour lasted almost a year. Kenny, our UK manager, knew that I was besotted with Siobhan and took some sweet Polaroids of her for me. She'd written things underneath each one, like "Looking forward to seeing you again." I thought, "Jeez, I really like this girl. This is getting mad."

By the time we got to Brisbane in February 1987, I was feeling low. I was exhausted and a weird depression sank in. I'd never really experienced that feeling before, so I didn't really know what it was. Unbeknownst to me, the promoter had put a personal bodyguard by the name of Tony Quinn in the hotel room next to me, with an adjoining door.

Tony was to become an amazing person in my life, but at this point,

I had no idea he was even there. We had a few days off, and I was just moping around my room, feeling trapped and down about the length of the tour we were about to set off on and missing Siobhan.

Now, this was very unlike me, and it was the first time I'd ever felt anything but excitement and enthusiasm about touring, so I was confused with mixed emotions.

I rang Matthew, our tour manager, and said I had a headache and needed some tablets, and he told me there was a guy next door who would get me anything I wanted. Tony had been told by the promoter that I was a wild one and to expect anything, at any time, day or night. When I knocked on his door, he answered in a nanosecond. I thought Tony too small to be my bodyguard, but was later to find out he was kickboxing champion of Australia, hence the speed of answering my knock on the door.

He dashed out to get some headache pills, only to get stuck halfway down the side of the hotel in one of those capsule-shaped exterior elevators. The damn thing had broken down, and there was nothing he could do about it. I waited for a few hours, thinking the guy was slow. In the meantime a friend from the UK had sent a message saying he was in Brisbane, and he wanted to go out on the town.

When Tony eventually got back, I asked him to book a car, and he gave my friend and me a tour of the underbelly, the other side of Brisbane. We wanted to go to the worst areas and see what it was like: a terrible bar or a really awful club or house party where no one would know me and where we could have a drink and a catch-up. The first place we stopped at, my friend tried to open his door, but it was jammed. He kept saying, "The bloody door won't open," pushing it as hard as he could. I could see Tony waving outside, so I wound down the window and he said, "Leave the door, mate. It's jammed against a body. A guy just got stabbed."

We thought, *Okay, this is the right part of town.* So we got out the door on my side. Tony was nervously suggesting other places, but we said, "No, this is fine." We went to a bar where we were immediately invited to a house party. Never one to turn down an adventure, I directed Tony to drive us where the action was.

When we arrived at the house, the place was full of hookers and guys with cocaine, a guns-on-the-table scene, but I could see that Tony had an aura around him like a force field. Still, it was a little too much action, so we left that place rather sharpish and went to a more regular dodgy/seedy club where I started talking to Tony. I liked him a lot, and he worked for me from that day for the next twenty-five years, starting as my bodyguard and ending up running my office.

In fact, by the time we got to Melbourne on the tour, Tony was invaluable, so I'd already proposed he leave Australia and come live with me in the USA when the tour was over. So, on a night off in Melbourne, I was back in my room around midnight. Frank Infante, the guitarist from Blondie, was in my suite, shaking under a blanket on my sofa as he was in shock from a small plane crash earlier that day. He had been in a two-seater light aircraft, and they'd had to do a forced landing on a beach. Also in my room was Claude Gassian, a great French photographer friend whom we had flown out to document some of the tour.

I'd been having Shinkendo Japanese sword lessons on the tour. Don't ask me why. Claude and I were playing with these dangerous swords, and the door was ajar, and suddenly Tony appeared with his girlfriend, just as I managed to miss Claude and slice the chandelier above my bed.

Tony, unfazed, waited till the last of the glass beads had stopped bouncing around the room and announced, "Hey, I just got engaged to my girlfriend." I was still standing on the bed wielding the sword and she was in a baby doll nightdress, covered in bits of chandelier. I said, "Cool. Is she coming to America too?" Frank just looked up from the sofa at the mess and said, "Congratulations!"

I invited Siobhan to join me in Japan and she came, even though it was a long way to fly from London. I was there at the airport in Tokyo to greet her when she arrived. She had on this really cozy duffel coat that she had been wearing in the Polaroids, and her whole demeanor was fuzzy and warm with a comforting, homey feel, after the crazy rock-and-roll lifestyle I'd fallen into, constantly touring the world.

She was totally jet-lagged, so we nestled in the back of the black sedan and were driven back to my hotel, her sweet face lit by the odd neon of Tokyo's streetlights. I had totally forgotten that a documentary crew, filming Annie and me for the whole of the Japanese tour, was waiting back at the hotel. It wasn't going too well with the film because Annie wasn't feeling good, so they kept filming me more than was necessary.

Now I had brought Siobhan in, so they were trying to film us in the room together, like cinéma vérité. They were shooting everything that was going on in my room. Siobhan was disorientated, to say the least. It was a bit awkward, because they were all there with their crew and they had come all the way from France. The filmmaker was the well-respected documentarian Amos Gitai, and his assistant director was Uri, whom Annie later married.

It was a weird time for Siobhan and for us as a couple, as we were just getting to know each other. Annie and I had to play these shows, and we had to do interviews, and we were being filmed in a documentary. Siobhan just had to be in the hotel or come to the gig and be on the side of the stage or backstage. She'd been to Japan a few times before with Bananarama. They were really well-known there too, and Siobhan knew some places to go in Tokyo, so it wasn't as bad as it could have been.

Siobhan stayed on the tour and we battled through it. While we were in Japan, she discovered she was pregnant and we decided we would get married and stick together. I remember we rang her parents and said, "We're getting married!" We omitted the pregnant part and they were thrilled.

We decided to tie the knot as soon as the tour was over. I'd just come up with the idea of recording Eurythmics' next album in a huge empty château in France. I'd seen hundreds of them to rent in a magazine called *Châteaux Demeures*, which I'd bought in the Nice airport, and they looked insanely cheap to buy. I suggested to Siobhan that we get married in a château, because we would never be able to find anywhere better—and at this point I had the trusty Tony Quinn working for me, so organizing a wedding in a château would be no problem.

With TQ anything was possible! I was crazy about Siobhan and thrilled to be starting a family, so getting married in a château seemed like a promising start to our life together.

CHAPTER:11

SAVAGE

Our next album, and adventure, was *Savage*. We were trying to decide where to make it. I knew that to rent a big recording studio would cost about forty thousand pounds. At the same time, I had sent my ex-wife Pam's husband, Olivier, on a mission to find a country house or an old château in France not far from Paris, and he discovered the Château Dangu, in Normandy. It would cost the same to rent for three months as a big studio, except in the château you could do many things that you couldn't do in a studio.

The château had been moved stone by stone from Paris by Napoleon's political adviser, and it was stunning, with a beautiful long driveway. It was surrounded by woods and the view from every window was magnificent. It had twenty-eight bedrooms, massive drawing rooms, dining rooms and a sweeping staircase that went on and on.

Most of the château was beautiful and well preserved, but upstairs it was kind of ramshackle and falling apart, perfect for the photos and video that we shot in those areas. All the album cover and all the artwork photos were shot there. It was a perfect location. You could do everything in this château, and we did, using every different part of it.

I brought our drummer Olle Romo, who I knew was a genius. I really needed him because I had already purchased a Synclavier from the producer Jack Nitzsche and Olle was one of the only guys who would know how to program the damn thing. It was immense and quite an amazing new kind of synthesizer, which had a polyphonic digital sampling system. It was also a lot of trouble to use it.

I couldn't comprehend a thing about it, so while Olle worked out how to use it, I would ride around the château on a bicycle and have the window open into the *fumoir*, or smoking room. Olle would put speakers on the window so I could hear. For ages, it seemed, there would be nothing, and then I could hear something working. I'd pull up to the window and go, "Anything happening yet?" It was like trying to start an old car. It could take eight hours to just get something going.

Suddenly Olle would go, "Yeah, yeah, I've got something." We'd fed in some sounds that Conny Plank and I had recorded in Japan, tapping on bamboo trees and all that kind of stuff.

We made all the tracks for the album *Savage* right there in the *fumoir*. Once the Synclavier and mixing desk were in there, it was tiny, with hardly enough room to swing a cat. Annie didn't really like coming to the château much. She came a few times, but she was really settled in Paris and working through a relationship that I didn't feel she should have started in the first place. She couldn't really concentrate on making this album right then. So I worked without her for the first time ever in our recording career. I was confident in my own talent and judgment, but it still seemed strange.

Annie didn't like the tracks, however, when I first played the music to her. Normally we were together writing songs and making records in the same room. We'd be critiquing each other as we went along and we'd get rid of things we didn't like immediately. But here I had just been left working on my own with Olle, so Annie would hear whole finished pieces and not be sure how to respond. Amazingly, though, once I returned to Paris, she got into it and all her vocals came together in a few days.

She finished all the lyrics she was writing and was on fire. We didn't erase one track, and when she sang the words to the title track, it was an astounding mixture of vocal soundscape and lyrical genius. When she finished we all applauded her in the control room and played it back ten times or more.

The first single we gave the record company was "I Love to Listen to Beethoven." By this time Eurythmics had already had about fifteen hit singles and sold about fifty million albums. The label never really had a say in anything we did from "Sweet Dreams" onward. We delivered this new song and we said, "Look. This is our first single." There's not even a chorus or a hook, and it starts with Annie talking, saying,

Take a girl like that
And put her in a natural setting
Like a café for example.
Along comes the boy
And he's looking for trouble
With a girl like that
With a girl like that.
Who knows what they'll decide to do?
Who knows what they'll get up to?
I'd love to know.
Wouldn't you?

Then the only melody is on the one line "I love to listen to Beethoven." I'm sure the record company was thinking, "How do we get this on the radio?" Annie and I never thought "Beethoven" would be a hit. That was the whole idea. We were trying to reel it back in, because

Revenge had become so immense, and we were starting to feel too much like a rock-and-roll band.

For *Savage* we decided to make something very odd and very experimental, to get back to electronic strangeness. We wanted to put out something surreal and nonsensical, something that would shatter people's perceptions of who we were and what we had become, and it certainly did the trick. In a way it was like committing commercial suicide.

At the time it sold about two million albums. It was electronic and experimental and spawned great songs. It's Annie's favorite album and the favorite of many fans. There is a lot of powerful songwriting on it because Annie did pour her heart out, since she'd been through some rough times over the past five years.

Experimenting has always been at the heart of our work, and our success. The courage to experiment, to break rules, to make something different—that's what keeps things exciting.

Einstein said, "If at first the idea is not absurd, then there is no hope for it." I'm from that world. It's not an experiment if you know it's going to work. You have to take a chance. You've got to put things in and stir it up and see what it's like.

That's what the *Sweet Dreams* album was too, a huge experiment. The album was a long and complicated experiment, and some of it was torturous for Annie because I was in the midst of trying to understand and learn how to record. Some of the songs were born out of total mistakes, magic mistakes.

I'd get anybody in, friends, people off the street; we'd make sounds like a Balinese instrument with a drum machine. I'd reverse the tape, see what it's like, and then make everything distorted or send it through the telephone and back onto the tape. Much of the time, Annie was unsure whether we were going to be completely lost at sea and fail miserably, or whether we would land somewhere meaningful. Never was there any guarantee. This is the nature of an experiment. Every day we leapt off the diving board into the unknown, and I still do today!

———

During the making of *Savage*, my mom lived in the château with us and so did Nida; they got along because they both loved to cook. Siobhan was there most of the time, though periodically she would have to go to London to visit her sisters or to shoot a video, as Bananarama had a new album called *WOW!* coming out. Amazingly she did all the videos and promotion while she was pregnant, but it doesn't really show, partly due to her sprightly figure. Later on they needed some camera trickery, as she was getting more and more pregnant.

She was about six months pregnant when we got married, but you couldn't really see it much because Siobhan was very slim and a really great dancer, which she proved once again at the post-wedding party. Our wedding was way more over-the-top than even Elton John's Rocket Records launch party, in fact. We were ensconced in a château, and I was probably having delusions of grandeur.

All of our wedding guests were either flown in or came on rented buses from London, and we filled up the surrounding area's hotels and guesthouses. There was a huge marquee tent, with chefs and a full staff brought over from the UK to cope with all the meals, and another huge marquee tent for the party after the ceremony and the wedding dinner. The Fureys turned up to play at the wedding. I hadn't seen them since I ran away with them. This, of course, delighted the Irish contingent, who were all there in full force to celebrate. Siobhan's mum and dad even got up to sing with the band, and Annie did too!

After we got married we spent a few days in Nice with Pam and her husband, which Siobhan was confused about, as she later pointed out that it's highly unusual to invite your ex-wife to join you on your honeymoon. In retrospect I agree it is.

Pam's husband was French and they were helping me find land in the perfect spot to build a house—which we did by flying around in a helicopter and landing on beautiful pieces of land, then asking the homeowners if we could buy the property. How crazy was that?

After the honeymoon we flew off to LA to move into the house in Encino. Not long after this, on November 26, 1987, Sam, our first son, was born, at Cedars-Sinai Medical Center.

The funny thing was that because we did this in LA we had to have all those birthing classes where the mother and father are together, and we learned to breathe and push, et cetera. Siobhan and I couldn't stop laughing at how sort of LA hippie dippy it was. It was also partly nervous laughter on our part, as our instructress would say, "Let's breathe together, and hey, maybe she should have a water birth!" And we said, "No fucking way."

It was a traumatic time for me, though I suppose more so for Siobhan. I was very worried about cutting the cord, which I'd been told was a must-do, to join in the experience. I'd already had premonitions of fainting while I did that, so I asked if it was possible that I didn't cut the cord, but on the day, in slow motion, I saw the doctor handing me the scissors and I started to pass out. The doctor was confused when he came to visit thirty minutes later because Siobhan was fine sitting up in a chair, holding Sam, and I had fainted on the bed.

Suddenly, there was Sam. It was like, bloody hell, the weight and responsibility hits you. Suddenly you're a parent and in charge of this tiny baby, and everything seems dangerous. Before the birth, you're thinking, *Oh, yeah, we're going to have a baby.* But you don't really know what it means, and then you have a baby and you go, "Oh, I see. This is serious."

What was amazing was that less than a month after Sam's birth, Siobhan was skiing on a holiday we took in Vancouver. I was proud, thinking how fit she was. Later she told me it was a crazy idea that nearly killed her. We booked a totally over-the-top Christmas log cabin and took Nida along to help. Luckily it turned out that Nida was crazy about babies and she was a godsend.

It was kind of surreal because Siobhan was in a pop group that had just released their fourth hit album and I was in a pop duo that had released five hit albums in a row. And now we had a baby and we were in Vancouver at a Christmas cabin with a bunch of straight people. We were both thinking, "Where are we? Who are we? What just happened?"

Babies change so quickly, and they start to get a personality really fast, so by the time Sam was three months, he was adored by us and everybody around him. He became a remarkable, sweet little child. Siobhan and I were crazy about him, and Nida was ecstatic about having a baby in her life again. We all called him the golden boy because he had beautiful golden hair and was adorable.

Siobhan and I were from two completely different worlds in a way. We were both from working-class backgrounds and had lots of things in common, but musically, we were from different worlds and from different times.

Although I was only six years older, being sixteen in 1968 was way different from being sixteen in 1974. I'd already gone through certain things in my life, and she was just going into them, so every now and then there would be a complete sort of disconnect: like when I'd play a Dylan album and she'd want to put on the Smiths, and we'd fight over the cassette player in the car. We were like a couple of kids. It's funny because now she loves loads of the same music I do and vice versa.

We had great times. Sam was growing and Siobhan was growing in a different way; she'd had enough of Bananarama's promotion schedule and the need to be permanently churning out pop hits. She felt she had no creative control. I suggested that she experiment with recording her own songs and to work with our friend, producer Richard Feldman, and that experiment turned into the first Shakespears Sister album.

But Siobhan still missed London, her sisters and her friends. So we went back but I didn't really want to be in the Smoke. I'd already lived there since I was seventeen. I wanted to enjoy a new adventure and lifestyle in California.

Eurythmics were on hiatus, as we didn't promote *Savage* by touring. Instead we had made a video album directed by the prolific music video director Sophie Muller. These were very strange videos, shot in various locations: from the château in France to the Sunset Marquis hotel in LA. Sophie often would make the videos without any crew support, just shooting on her own with an 8mm cine camera. I must say that is always my favorite work of Sophie's, when she shoots on her own.

My home in Encino became the meeting place for a little gang of great songwriters and musicians, and it was there in 1988 that the Traveling Wilburys formed, while George Harrison was living in my house. Their first album, *Traveling Wilburys Vol. 1*, was recorded in my back garden studio. I remember how surreal it was to look out my window and see Bob Dylan, Roy Orbison, Tom Petty, George Harrison and Jeff Lynne there, sitting on the grass under a tree, all strumming their guitars.

Again I had a friend from England visit me there once, and he had the crazy situation of being on the back porch with a gang of us, having a drink, while George and Tom were singing "Taxman" in his left ear and Bob was telling them to keep the noise down, as he was reciting a poem in his right ear. He looked cross-eyed and was whispering, *WTF!* The whole time I lived in Encino was pure inspiration. I learned so much about music and the magical art of songwriting.

Bob Dylan had told me back in 1984, way before the Wilburys, that he'd love to have a band again that felt like a real band. I said, "The only band I know like that is the Heartbreakers." Bob went on to do a world tour with Tom and the Heartbreakers.

CHAPTER:12

WE TOO ARE ONE

t was 1989, and Eurythmics were slowly unraveling. Annie, or people around her, had decided we should try working with a different producer or at least a coproducer on our next album. The reason for this was unclear to me, especially after making so many successful records—I guess Annie wanted another opinion that was neutral in the studio. I was really thrown by this at first and pondered how to proceed, as we'd rarely worked with an outside producer, and when we did, in the Tourists, we hadn't liked the process or the results.

A lightbulb went off in my head, and I suggested we should work with my old pal Jimmy Iovine, who by now was a legendary producer. Annie was unsure about this at first, as she knew Jimmy and I were best friends, but there was no denying his achievements, not only as a producer but as someone who had weathered many a complicated artist relationship to deliver great albums: from U2 to Bruce Springsteen, Tom Petty and the Heartbreakers, Stevie Nicks, John Lennon, Patti Smith, the Pretenders. The list goes on.

So it was agreed, and I invited Jimmy to Paris. Annie and I felt completely at home recording in Studio Grande Armée. We both now had homes in Paris and we both spoke French. Jimmy, however, was a complete fish out of water, but after a few days he began to love it, and we tumbled into a new and different recording process. I also had invited Charlie Wilson, from the Gap Band, to play keyboards and sing backing vocals to spice things up a bit, and he did. Charlie was a live wire to say the least—that guy would go for three days straight, then sleep for one!

The title track "We Too Are One" just tumbled out from a riff I was playing. Annie turned in a killer vocal over my chord changes—and a new classic song was born for our next tour. The song was not really about us but Annie's lyrics turned into a mantra for all we'd been through, and when we played it at concerts, I'm sure the audience saw it as a song about two survivors that they could relate to.

"When the Day Goes Down," another of the album's tracks, slowly became one of my favorites to play with just me on acoustic guitar and Annie singing. We played it on *Wogan*, a primetime UK TV show, while being interviewed by writer/comedian Ben Elton. It was nearing the end of the show when Annie and I just started performing it, right there on the sofa. Ben was visibly moved to tears and the whole audience was so quiet that you could have heard a pin drop. In the control room the producers knew we were out of time and were getting calls to go to end credits—this was live TV—but the director and cameramen were so into the performance that after they pulled all the way out for the ending, the cameras started to move back in. We continued to play and sing two or three more songs just for the studio audience and the whole place went crazy afterward. There's something very magical when the two of us play together; another energy comes into play—the goose bump factor. It's very emotional and people recognize it.

The single "Don't Ask Me Why" is also very haunting, and again Sophie Muller made a great music video using striking lighting, primary color contrast and brilliant editing. The album cover was shot by Jean-Baptiste Mondino, the legendary French photographer and video director. Mondino is responsible for many iconic shots over the years, as well as directing videos for Madonna, David Bowie and Björk, among others. The photo shoot with Jean-Baptiste fascinated me as he was using a very tricky Polaroid 35mm film, which he could instantly process and see the result—it's very delicate film that will disintegrate if not handled properly. Mondino held the film up to the light, wearing white gloves, while Annie and I marveled at the images. Annie on the front cover with a whiter-than-white face, white hair and piercing blue eyes—and me on the back cover, black with my hair and beard dyed blue black—complete opposites that make one whole, *We Too Are One*.

We did our last tour and called it the Revival Tour, after one of the song titles, and we decided to wear rags and ripped clothing and just tear up the venue like an old gospel-revival atmosphere. Ten years later Annie and I did a similar thing in a tiny, secret gig, just the two of us, at the Kit Kat Klub, a tiny place in Manhattan. We played an acoustic set to a packed audience, a crazy cast of characters from the whole cast of *The Sopranos* and actor Kevin Spacey to Wyclef Jean and Prince. Arista Records president Clive Davis gave a speech before we played, as Annie and I were waiting on the other side of the curtain in the dark, not knowing that his speeches can go on for a very long time!

The Revival Tour ended when Eurythmics played Rock in Rio in 1990. I was hanging out with Bob Dylan, who was also playing at the festival. Bob and I went AWOL and ended up in a recording studio in the middle of nowhere, inside somebody's house. In the house they had these little folk art figurines called spiritual cowboys, similar to the Day of the Dead figurines—all representing different aspects of spirit. I liked the sound of it, and I liked the clash of those two words together: spiritual and cowboys. Two complete, conflicting words.

I said to myself, "Spiritual Cowboys? That's very interesting." It made me think of a band that's traveling constantly. A band led by a loner who sang personal, spiritual songs. I started to think, *That's a good band name*. I wanted to be as far as possible from any Eurythmics-sounding thing. I could have made some sort of electronic music and been Dave Stewart "the record producer" making a kind of Electro record, but I just really wanted to go back to playing bluesy guitar and writing new songs. I wanted to have fun in a band. I wasn't intending it to be another global brand, launching another world of Eurythmics. It was more just a matter of how I could have the most fun possible in the simplest way.

The concert in Rio was massive. Annie and I knew we needed to stop at some point, and this was it. We had rehearsed a samba band and beautiful female carnival dancers in full costume. The show was incredible and the crowd of more than one hundred thousand was going crazy and singing along. Annie and I looked at each other onstage with this massive collection of players and dancers and a gigantic audience singing our songs. We had overcome so many obstacles and been through so much emotional turmoil, it was almost as if we were dying in slow motion. Sophie Muller captured this moment perfectly on film, and you can see the emotion mixed with exhaustion and exhilaration on both our faces as we left the stage, not to be seen again for another decade.

CHAPTER:13

ON MY OWN AGAIN

n 1989 I began making my first solo album, the first Dave Stewart and the Spiritual Cowboys album. I had my house on Balboa Avenue in Encino built to my specifications so it had everything I needed, including a great recording studio I called the Chapel, as it had an overdub room in the shape of a small chapel with stained glass windows. It also had an SSL desk and was perfect to work in.

With Annie and me, on any Eurythmics tracks, we always hit the nail on the head with this dynamic of despair and hope at the same time. It would be really dark, and then boom, it would transform musically and lyrically in every way. And those two things together made a magic kind of sound and vibe.

When I started Spiritual Cowboys, it couldn't be anything like Eurythmics, because our whole sound was built around Annie's voice. It's really weird, actually, to put all of your lifetime effort (at your peak) into something built around somebody else's voice. You never figure, "Well, hang on. If this stops, where will I be?" So I did my best to make the new stuff sound nothing like Eurythmics.

I asked Chris Thomas to produce the album, and I pulled a great band together and again recorded in the back garden of the Balboa Avenue house. I was in awe of Chris as a producer as he had made some of my favorite albums—*For Your Pleasure*, Roxy Music; the Pretenders' first album; the Sex Pistols' *Never Mind the Bollocks*— Chris also worked on *The Beatles (The White Album)*.

On the first day I was a little timid and just put down a couple of ideas. The first song was called "Suicidal Sid" and it was pretty strange, but Chris loved it and was very encouraging. In fact, after that first day, he told the band that I reminded him of the way John Lennon worked, so I grew more confident as the days went on and soon got used to the fact I was singing or mumbling my lyrics and having fun again. I had everything I needed, including a great studio. All I wanted to do was play the guitar and write great songs.

The live band consisted of Chris Bostock on bass, John Turnbull on guitar, Jonathan Perkins on keyboards, Nan Vernon on guitar and two drummers: my old mate Olle Romo and later Martin Chambers, the original drummer for the Pretenders. The whole band could sing harmonies, so we could re-create whatever was on the recordings live. That was the plan: to record in houses and then just play in France. And at first, that's what we did: we just played around France. I wanted to go into the little different areas of France and investigate. I sing about it in "The Gypsy Girl and Me" from one of my later albums, *The Blackbird Diaries*, recorded in Nashville:

Oh, we were playing in the Roman ruins
in the town of Arles.
She said, "Parlez-vous français?"
I said, "Oui, je parle."
She asked me for some cigarettes.
I gave her my per diem.
Then she bought a pack of Gauloises
and we headed to the Coliseum.

So there we were in the square, as the song said, and it had this great feeling. To be just playing around France like a troubadour and having time to soak in the culture to sit there at the café where Renoir and Van Gogh would sit. Eurythmics tours were always like a whirlwind of press and promotion, as well as concerts and flying everywhere. Now I took my time and smelled the roses, traveling to my shows in a psychedelic Rolls-Royce with a picnic basket in the trunk.

My whole idea of the Spiritual Cowboys was to create a kind of Gypsy touring band, and that spirit filled the songs.

After being ensconced in a world of competitive pop music—with constant album campaigns, TV performances and award shows all over the world—I was happy to be in one country and playing with a new kind of imagery. I was inventing characters and then creating the world to go around it. I was doing that in a small way, as a relief from the immensity of Eurythmics. Annie and I had become so huge, and everything we did was a ginormous effort. If we put on a show, it would involve about sixty people and require a caravan of trucks.

I took a break from touring to record a second album, *Honest*, in my home in France. Now I was hardly ever in the UK because my home in France had everything—a studio that overlooked the Bay of Cannes on a large plot of land, with a massive vegetable garden and a public forest in front of me. The views were spectacular, and it was an inspiring place to write and record.

In addition to the music I was making, I had this whole world created around the band. There were clothes designed by my great friend John Richmond, a British clothing designer. We created that world to extend to the stage; our shows would start lit only by a few candles burning instead of lights, lighting more and more until the whole room lit up—probably a huge fire risk looking back. Before we played, we would have the roadies walk around the venue, swinging metal thuribles full of frankincense, like they do in the Catholic Church.

I wanted to make something new and unexpected so that people would get a shock when they saw it.

I had to make it something that already existed. I couldn't spend ten years creating my new identity or I wouldn't have ever played live again. At a Spiritual Cowboys concert it had to seem that you were walking into another world. It was the world of the characters I had always admired and now had in my life: the Tom Pettys and the Bob Dylans, the sound of the jangling twelve-string electric Rickenbackers and a strong Gypsyesque feeling. I liked that feeling, like a traveling medicine show, slightly ramshackle with the freedom to change the songs around and jam; it was interesting, and it worked and we had a lot of fun.

Then I began to realize that I had a whole band with members who would be partly reliant on me to keep doing stuff, whereas I didn't want anything to tie me down. I wanted to experiment. I wanted the great escape. All the players in the band were great people and wonderful musicians. I loved all of them. We did the most amazing, crazy, quick turnaround of tours, making albums, and garnering a good following. But at the same time, it wasn't *all* I wanted to do. After all, I'd just come off a conveyor belt of making records and touring for ten years straight.

I was going back and forth between France and an apartment in Covent Garden in London. I was becoming very intrigued by the art scene there. This was when I started working with my executive assistant, Anthony Fawcett.

Anthony was formerly John and Yoko's assistant. He was there when John and Yoko met, when John climbed the ladder at Yoko's exhibition and saw the word "Yes." Anthony became their assistant that night. At the time he was the youngest art critic for the London *Times*. They befriended him and he has incredible stories of his time spent with them. He also wrote a book about John Lennon called *One Day at a Time*. He used to live with John and Yoko in the house in Henley. When he started to work with me, he said, "Oh, working with you feels exactly like when I was working with John. You think the same way. You have an idea in the morning, and within a few hours, you've written a song. You want to record it that day and get it out tomorrow—like the way John did with 'Instant Karma!'" During the recording of "Instant Karma!" John was in such a hurry that Anthony had to go around on a double-decker bus collecting kids from the street to sing on the record.

Anthony became fascinated by my world and the way my mind was working. At the same time, I was very interested in the world he inhabited. He was introducing me to new British artists—like Damien Hirst, Tracey Emin, Sarah Lucas, and the Wilson sisters. He brought the American artist Jeff Koons to my apartment, along with many other fascinating characters. I was absorbed by it all, and I also was thinking that in order for me to fulfill my crazy polymath mind, I couldn't be stuck in this Spiritual Cowboys box. I wanted to do music, but also photography and film. I wanted to dive into the art world and visit all the exhibitions of new artists. It was starting to feel like the two worlds of the Cowboys and France didn't fit together with the new exciting scene that was happening in London.

However, if I'd kept the Spiritual Cowboys going, just for France, today we'd probably be one of their most beloved bands, as French audiences are very loyal. We had already garnered gold albums there and played to sold-out venues. But everybody else in the band couldn't be sitting around while I was going off doing all these different things. It was tough, knowing I had to break up the band, but I had to come to grips with the decision. To do this I completely altered my look—clothes, appearance, everything—while we were in Switzerland doing the final gig of the Spiritual Cowboys last tour.

I spent two days—not with the band—staying in a different hotel. When I arrived in the dressing room, looking entirely different for that last gig, they knew something was up. But they didn't know exactly what. I'd been to a tailor and had a different suit and I had different boots. Then they all realized, "Oh, hang on. This must be sort of the end of something."

So it was obvious to the band it was over, and I told them my reasoning, but it was a sad thing to me, as I enjoyed being in that Gypsy band world.

I didn't know where I would go next, but I did have plenty of options. At this point, without fully realizing it, I had studios all over the world. I now owned the Church Studios in London outright, as I had bought Annie's share. I had my home in France with a studio, a home in Los Angeles with a studio, and a penthouse apartment in London with a studio. I also owned an apartment in Paris.

My home buying was "rock star out of control" and confused Siobhan as to where we actually lived. I had personally chosen all these homes, so I suggested to Siobhan that she choose a house, which only made matters worse, as she picked one called Neptune, only fifteen minutes away from my other estate in the south of France, although this was a gem of a house on the sea between Cannes and Saint-Tropez.

Siobhan would ask, "How could we ever be in all these places? And at the same time, how could we keep the family together?" Somehow we did. Every time we went anywhere, there was an entourage of assistants and nannies, and I usually invited Siobhan's sisters and their husbands and their children too, so it was like a traveling circus. In some ways it was a lot of fun, especially for the kids, who were never bored.

I agreed to go back and live in London, but then I built this place in France and I wanted to live there now. Siobhan tried that, but she didn't want to live there either. She wanted to live back where she was in the first place, London; that was her world and scene. So we became a bit disconnected.

I had formed the Spiritual Cowboys because I wanted to play the guitar and write songs, but while I was engrossed in recording my album, Siobhan was at home pregnant and writing songs for her next album, and we were drifting apart. Meanwhile, we did fly around and stay in all these different places. I would often call my home in France or LA, and someone would answer, saying, "Dave's not here." I could hear the clinking of wineglasses and a mini party going on in the background. In fact, I once told my friends Ian La Frenais and Dick Clement, the great British TV comedy writers, when they were wandering up to play tennis on my court, "Hey, you should come around to play anytime you want."

They said, "Thanks, yeah. We've been coming a couple of years now."

I hadn't even noticed!

Los Angeles helped Siobhan create and mold a new career in a relaxed place, away from the hectic demands she was used to. Just like I say to other collaborators, to remove all angst from songwriting and recording, "Don't think that you're making a record; it's just experimenting."

She'd been used to the record label dictating the studio and the producer, and setting deadlines that hung over the creative process like a noose. Siobhan was in a good place creatively in LA. She was collaborating with Richard Feldman, just experimenting and writing songs a bit. Then he introduced her to his ex-girlfriend, who played guitar and sang. Her name was Marcy Levy, though Siobhan later came up with the name Marcella Detroit for her. She was an excellent guitarist and singer and had cowritten "Lay Down Sally" with Eric Clapton.

Siobhan's first album was kind of Siobhan on her own, called *Sacred Heart* by Shakespears Sister. Siobhan named the band after a song by the Smiths but spelled it her own way. Marcy played on the album and sang. Then on the second album, it became Siobhan and Marcy together, like a duo. They did the second record together, but the record deal was with Siobhan from the beginning.

Most days I have crazy ideas that I get very excited about. The song "Stay," which I wrote with Siobhan and Marcy, was born out of one of those crazy ideas. I wanted to buy the rights to the movie *Cat-Women of the Moon*, a 1953 3-D science fiction film directed by Arthur Hilton, with an original score composed by Elmer Bernstein.

The film was just so camp; it has this futuristic setting juxtaposed with these caveman attitudes toward gender and politics.

It was the perfect fodder to mess around with and turn on its head! The idea was to change it into a musical, by replacing certain dialogue with lyrics. Once I secured the rights to the film, Siobhan and Marcy were going to shoot extra vignettes, with satirical songs about male-female relationships that would be edited seamlessly into the movie. Siobhan is a gifted lyricist. She was really into this idea, but alas, her record label was not.

Many of the songs on the Shakespears Sister album *Hormonally Yours* were written with this concept in mind, including "Stay," as well as "Moonchild," "Catwoman," "Hello (Turn Your Radio On)," and "Goodbye Cruel World," so you can see that this theme was well developed. I personally think it would have transferred to the theater as a black comedy/musical, had we been allowed to develop it.

"Stay" was another of those songs that was conceived in ten minutes. I went with Siobhan to Marcy's house, where she had a small studio, and I had been thinking about the arrangement of their voices. I suggested that Marcy sing the verses of the song and that they both sing the chorus, "Stay with me," in harmony. The twist would be Siobhan singing a different section sounding much heavier, kind of demonic, to give the song an edge that's different from most pop ballads.

Chris Thomas, the great producer who worked on the Spiritual Cowboys albums, was staying at our house, and when he heard the demo of "Stay," he thought it was great and agreed to produce it.

As the coup de grâce, Sophie Muller delivered a killer video, which was partially based on the *Cat-Women* movie! In a way Sophie was the third, unseen member of Shakespears Sister.

From the beginning Siobhan and Marcy were an odd pairing—Siobhan being an Irish girl hitting London in her teens at the height of punk in 1976, and Marcy from Detroit, who'd toured with Leon Russell before joining Eric Clapton's band in 1974. You could not have put together two people from such opposite ends of the spectrum, both culturally and musically. Yet here they were as Shakespears Sister!

In 1993, Shakespears Sister was nominated for five BRIT Awards, including Best British Group, Best British Album, Best British Video, Best British Single and Best British Female Solo Artist for Siobhan. "Stay" climbed to number one in the UK, where it stayed for eight weeks. The song is one of the longest-running number ones in chart history.

At the same time, I was encouraging Siobhan to play live. Bananarama had not managed to go on tour at that point. Siobhan had some early live experience singing backup with her friend's group the Tea Set, supporting Iggy Pop at the Rainbow. Bananarama did some early support gigs with the Jam at the Sobell Centre, and then they were shipped around the world singing to track, but were not, at that time, singing to a live audience. They were more like a band in Motown times, where you have three girls, and they sing on a track. Siobhan was the main writer of all the lyrics.

I met Boris Grebenshikov in Richard Feldman's garage in Encino. Boris turned out to be one of the "founding fathers" of Russian rock music and is often considered the "Bob Dylan of Russia." I produced his album, and we were going to Russia to play live together with Michael Apted, who had been directing a movie on Boris's journey as the first artist out of Russia since glasnost.

I told Siobhan, "Look, I'm doing this thing in Russia with Boris Grebenshikov. Why don't you come and be the support act?" Siobhan agreed and did the show. She played her first gig in front of fifteen thousand people, and it was great. She played her song "Heroine," which we'd written in France, and two other numbers. When she came offstage, she was ecstatic. It was the first time she had stepped out. The band really kicked it, they were so in the pocket, and she was singing and she delivered. I went, "Wow, you are really good onstage," because before then, she didn't know if she could sing lead in front of a rock band. I was insisting she should tour. I said, "You can do it. You should tour with Shakespears Sister."

Siobhan, by now, had gotten used to a pretty crazy life. She was thrown in with all these colorful characters in my orbit, like Harry Dean Stanton, Tom Petty, Gypsy flamenco guitarists, and a stream of musicians constantly coming in and going out of our home. She wasn't from that particular world, and a lot of people were quite a few years older than she was.

In 1989, Siobhan was there when Joni Mitchell was at our house during the making of *We Too Are One*, talking for hours about making the album *Blue*. She idolized Joni, but she was too shy to meet her. I think she felt this was all over-the-top. All these characters—Bob Dylan, George Harrison, Eric Idle, Robin Williams—would just drop in, and it was hard for her because she's naturally a shy person, though you would never imagine that if you saw her on the dance floor or onstage.

We recorded part of Siobhan's second album, *Hormonally Yours*, in George Harrison's wonderful home, Friar Park, in Henley-on-Thames, England. We lived there while George stayed in our Balboa House in Encino. Siobhan was not a big Beatles fan, whereas Alan Moulder, who was engineering, was flipping out. Suddenly, there were all of George's guitars and Ringo's drums in the studio! Siobhan was crazy for Marvin Gaye and people like that, more oriented around black music, soul music and dance music, even though she was making pure pop herself.

After I convinced Siobhan to start playing live, they got a band together, but I also had a new band and I was still mostly based in France. So by now, we were in completely different worlds. The Spiritual Cowboys were touring France and Germany while Siobhan went on the road with her outfit. All the same we took our son, Sam, with us everywhere; he was even in Siobhan's first videos for "You're History" and "Heroine."

But the more we were separated, the more distant we became. By that time, Siobhan became pregnant with our second child, Django, and we were both terrified because things were going wrong between us, and now we were going to have another baby. It was a nightmare time, because we were so disconnected, and everything was changing.

I was in the middle of playing live, touring Europe, when Siobhan was taken into the hospital to have the baby. I was trying frantically to get back from Norway to be there, which involved a small flight, a ferryboat and then another flight. I arrived just after Django was born, and I felt awful, stressed and exhausted. So I checked myself into the hospital with the flu. I'm sure Siobhan was really hurt.

Django was born, and he became another incredible child, a hilarious character who made us laugh our way back together. He was the life and soul of the party, and we had a lot of parties. Sam used to howl laughing at his antics. It was Sam who named him and he was only four years old. He was so funny and cheeky, an amazing dancer like his mum and an incredible mimic, an absolute joy. Django brought the family back together for a while, and Nida was in heaven.

Siobhan and I had lots of times when we would say, "We should make this work. We have fantastic kids. We have a fantastic life." But there was still always something wrong. It didn't feel like we were naturally connected. But I decided I was going to make this work, even though there was something off-kilter. But the longer you try to stay together when it's not right, the more it unravels, because small things can become big issues. You just want to be somewhere else, but you can't be somewhere else, and it becomes really difficult. So we went through a stressful period of knowing that it was not working, and knowing that it might end up all going horribly wrong.

When you're in that kind of situation, instead of looking inward at your relationship, you're looking outward. Anything or anybody you meet seems to like you or love you more than this person you're with. When you're with a person who tells you all the time about the things that are not right with you, and then another person is telling you that they love all those same things about you, then that's a recipe for disaster. This was happening to both of us and so it crashed.

We even went so far as to try couples therapy together. We also had a very alternative version of therapy one night when we were in the Covent Garden apartment, feeling low, just the two of us talking about breaking up. There was a loud beep from the video-intercom buzzer. We looked at the screen and there were Robin Williams and Eric Idle, their faces peering in the fish-eye lens. "Can we come up?" Even the sight of them made us laugh, but after two hours of nonstop improvised comedy about us breaking up, the apartment decor and the history of Covent Garden, we were begging them to stop, as we were experiencing actual physical pain from laughing so much.

By that time I'd bought even more homes, and I decided to move into my apartment in Covent Garden, while Siobhan lived in a house in Hampstead not far away. This made it easy for Sam and Django to be at either place, but when a married couple with children breaks up, as many of us know, nothing is easy. By this time Django was already about five years old and Sam was nearly nine. That was really tough, because I would have the boys for part of the week, and then Siobhan would have them. We'd try to be civil and talk to each other, but the stress of it all made tempers fray, and for a while, it was an awful situation.

Poor Nida was caught in the middle, going backward and forward. I thought at least she was the one constant for the boys. She would take them to Siobhan and she'd stay there for a few days, and then she would come to stay with me. So they always had Nida in the middle, and she provided a valuable anchor. Five years before I even met Siobhan, Nida was my housekeeper, cook, friend and constant presence, just the two of us really. Then it was Nida and Siobhan and me, and then Nida, Siobhan, Sam and me. And then came Django. Later in my life it would be Nida, Anoushka, Kaya, Indya, Sam and Django. This wonderful lady from Thailand has been a constant through all of my children and relationships.

During my personal drama separating from Siobhan while trying to be there for our children, I had started working with Terry Hall from the Specials. Ironically Siobhan's first Top Ten hit with Bananarama,

"It Ain't What You Do (It's the Way That You Do It)," was with Terry Hall's band Fun Boy Three. Terry and I had been talking and just writing odd songs for a while. Now these demos were kind of coming together into a crazy album. We were experimenting with electronic and dub music, and we decided to call ourselves Vegas. We called ourselves that as a joke, because we were nothing like Vegas. We used to call the experiments electrodub music at first.

We were really doing this, and we made the album using my record deal with RCA as my last album to deliver. It was released in 1992. Terry and I set about recording, but we also got up to the most insane antics—when I look back I must admit they were mostly instigated by me. We were in the south of France, and a mate of mine managed to get us the use of an abandoned casino. The record company had given us a small budget to film a documentary about the making of the album.

But instead of doing that, Terry and I kept trying to re-create *The Shining*. The location was immense and empty, like the haunted hotel. Terry would be on a desk, typing: "All work and no play makes Jack a dull boy." I borrowed a shopping trolley from a local supermarket, tied a camera to the front and sat inside and kept being pushed toward Terry like the tracking shot in *The Shining*.

In fact we did all manner of mad things. I went to the streets in Cannes and invited all these people there to audition to be in our band. We taught them completely wrong versions of the songs, and then filmed the auditions. We judged them like *American Idol* and filmed it. Of course they would all fail terribly trying to play these songs. There was one guy who auditioned with an arcane instrument that had about a hundred strings on it—he played one of our songs quite well actually. We even filmed us driving home back to my house in an electric storm with the car breaking down and having to call a breakdown service. We have all this footage totally unrelated to our album, but I bet it's fascinating to watch even unedited.

Terry would laugh all the time and hang his head. He must have thought, "This is great fun but it's the most bonkers way to make a record." Terry and I have a very similar dry sense of humor, very English. We also had Olle Romo and Manu Guiot in the band: Olle as programmer and drummer and Manu Guiot as mixer and playing bass. (I stole Manu's surname to create Jean Guiot as one of my pseudonyms for writing songs with other people.)

We went to Paris and filmed a music video for our version of the song "She," which was originally written (and made famous) by the legendary French chanson star Charles Aznavour, who is considered to be one of the greatest singer-songwriters of all time. He enjoyed major success in the UK, where he had four weeks at number one in June 1974 with the same song.

The director Tim Pope approached Charles Aznavour on our behalf to appear in our video. The song starts, and the scene is set around a fountain in a small Parisian park on a beautiful evening. Lit by the fountain, Charles appears reflecting on a lost romance. Then you see Terry hiding in the bushes just staring in disbelief. I suddenly appear having a stroll with a poodle on a leash. Terry beckons me over and drags me into the bushes with the dog yelping, and then we both just stare at Aznavour singing by the fountain. That was the music video, and it was total British comedy, but the music wasn't comedy at all. It was that juxtaposition that I always love. We were dying laughing while we were doing it, never taking anything to do with success seriously. It wasn't about getting in the charts. It was about having as much fun as possible—musically and visually.

Sophie Muller also directed another crazy video with us for our song "Possessed," which was the first single. It has me and Terry as an odd couple doing housework, looking after two kids in a humdrum life—then boom, we are parading around as catwalk models in ankle-length pink-and–lime green faux-fur coats with an orchestra behind us, and now Terry is the one clutching a poodle. The song "Walk into the Wind" is a very poignant song, and we had great trouble making the video, as Siobhan and I were literally breaking up in the middle of the shooting. In the end we had to reshoot it up in my hometown of Sunderland with just me, Terry and Siobhan in it, and it captured all the sadness and emptiness we were feeling.

I'm very proud of the work Terry and I did, and I really enjoyed his company. I think about him a lot. I miss him now that I live six thousand miles away, but those days remain crystal clear in my mind. I love that *Vegas* album.

CHAPTER:14

CLAM CHOWDER

decided to make a real solo album without a band and really express everything that was happening in my life, good and bad. I called it *Greetings from the Gutter*. I think the title aptly expressed how I was feeling at the time.

In the spring of 1994, I took up residence in the legendary Electric Lady Studios at 52 West Eighth Street in New York. It was the studio that Hendrix built. I'd always wanted to record in New York City and investigate Greenwich Village, which I'd heard so much about. I'd written a number of strange songs and chosen an even stranger crew of musicians to make the album.

For a start I had Bootsy Collins, Bernie Worrell and Jerome "Big-foot" Brailey—all P-Funk stars and three of the funkiest guys on the planet. I also had the great engineer and legendary mixer Bob Rosa. I was definitely going to be "Experienced" by the time these sessions were over.

Before I left England, David Bowie came up to my apartment and listened to some of my demos, including "Greetings from the Gutter," which was a humbling experience and a bit of an omen for how the album would sound.

Rolling Stone magazine noticed the effect in their album review:

> On "Chelsea Lovers," a stately ballad on his fine new album, *Greetings from the Gutter*, Dave Stewart creates an image of "stardust lovers in a Ziggy cartoon." It's a whimsical play on words and a telling one. As a singer, though, this musician's musician seems most influenced by Ziggy Stardust's creator. Stewart's chalky baritone and sly, sometimes ominous delivery evoke David Bowie so strongly at points that it's almost uncanny. The dreamy textures and often trippy lyrics on *Greetings* betray a nostalgia for the era in which Bowie first breathed life into his ill-fated leper messiah.

I felt like the man who fell to Earth.

Lou Reed lived within walking distance of Electric Lady, so we would hang out all the time. Lou was excited to show me around the Village, and we had breakfast at various interesting places and met up for dinner at some of his favorite restaurants. Lou and Laurie Anderson and I would often go out at night to eat, drink red wine and talk for hours. Lou ended up playing a great solo on the song "You Talk a Lot" and Laurie did a spoken duet with me on "Kinky Sweetheart."

Siobhan came to visit, and I took her to brunch in the Village and to meet Lou Reed for the first time. Just before brunch we'd had a small disagreement and Siobhan was a big fan and extremely shy, so she was a little hesitant about going, but she came along. Later she laughed and told me that when I went to the bathroom, Lou said to her, "Isn't Dave just the easiest guy to get along with?" We both laughed at the irony of it all.

I had several amazing guests on this album. Lady Miss Kier from Deee-lite sang backing vocals on all of the tracks. On the title track,

"Greetings from the Gutter," she sang an amazing ad-lib during the middle sequence, which goes through a lot of strange chord changes. Teese Gohl wrote incredible orchestral arrangements for the album and did a brilliant job on this song. It's the opening of the album and the lyrics begin:

> Greetings from the gutter
> I've been here since yesterday
> Sweet Dreams in the gutter
> All the skeletons come out to play

And they did. I used every song as a cathartic release from the tension that had been building.

The album sessions became a happening, with people dropping in all the time. David Sanborn came by and played saxophone on "Oh No, Not You Again"; he had also played sax on Bowie's album *Young Americans* back in 1975. Mick Jagger sang some backing vocals on the track "Jealousy."

I was having the best time and loving every minute of it. It's strange because while I was having such a good time, I was singing these very dark songs about death and depression. It was probably because I was singing about it that it made me feel much better.

It was like I'd flipped into that other sort of zone that Bowie inhabited, that juncture of British rock with New York soul. My music wasn't like his music particularly, but I did tip my hat to him on the title song. I realized, while recording it, that it was a sound quite close to *Young Americans*. At the end of the song "Oh No, Not You Again," I got Sanborn to play a long solo and then recorded him and Carly Simon having a huge argument, like a couple splitting up, over the top of a very complex jazz arrangement—like the score to my own life at the time.

Lots of people, I recall, upon hearing the album would say, "Wow, that's—like a David Bowie record." Ha. I wish. Truth is, when I sing in a certain way, it can sound insanely like Bowie. Although he's an incredible singer and I'm not—it's only in my lower tones. My son Sam, when he was fifteen, put together a whole track exactly like Bowie's "Heroes." He played every instrument on it, real drums, guitars and keyboards. I sang the lead, and, yes, it sounds exactly like Bowie.

Greetings from the Gutter was the first album I did that doesn't feature a band. It's just me. Not Dave Stewart and the Spiritual Cowboys. Not Eurythmics. Not the Tourists. So *Greetings from the Gutter* was actually my first real *solo* album. I wanted to do whatever I wanted to, experimentally. On that album there are tracks—like on "Kinky Sweetheart"—where there is a conversation between Laurie Anderson and me against a weirdly angular sound track.

Staying at home
Plugging it in
Kissing the screen
Being a god
I thought about it in the Galleria
Liquid crystal like a Man Ray tear
A shiny surface, velveteen queer
Bailey contrast, a Lucas idea
I've seen your setup and it's perfect in form
Let's call somebody to connect both our arms
You bring the orange I'll bring the clock
We'll pay the dream police to circle the block

"Kinky Sweetheart" is very trippy, and I encouraged the band to play free-form. Bernie Worrell is just on fire all over the Hammond organ. It's a strange and cool experimental track.

When we recorded the track for "St. Valentine's Day," I wouldn't tell the band the chords and then they had to follow me. They made some mistakes, and instead of fixing them, I had the mistakes orchestrated by composer-arranger Teese Gohl—with a full orchestra playing all the errors the band had made. I had never heard of anybody really doing that before. It's quite a startling and interesting effect, this dissonance that is so wrong, compared to normal pop music, yet so beautiful.

I played this very strange song to Damon Albarn and Alex James from Blur in my apartment one night, after stumbling around the streets of Soho with them. They were already huge in the UK, and their album *Parklife* was number one at the time. They both listened very intently until the end; then Damon slowly turned and said, "It's good but not as good as Blur." Then we went marching back out into the streets again, with Terry Hall joining us, to another private club for a drinkfest. I couldn't keep up, as Damon and Alex were as high as kites and looking at the stars while I was still in the gutter.

Every experiment I ever really wanted to do, sonically and musically, I tried at that moment. I just said, "Fuck it. I'm going to do it."

I wanted to make a real disco-type song, so I wrote "Heart of Stone," which I fleshed out with harmonies from backing vocalists from Harlem and Lady Miss Kier. The whole album was a kind of party. It was really great fun because it was just my decision to create something and have the ability to record it with amazing players, and if I didn't like it, I could just throw it away. I went deeply into the crazy experiments, and if they didn't work out, I would try something else. Though for me making this album seemed like the most luxurious time, in actuality I was only there for two weeks. The whole album was done in that short space of time.

Before I left London to make *Greetings from the Gutter,* I became great friends with Damien Hirst, the now world-renowned artist. I asked Damien if he would create my album artwork. He agreed and would come by the studio while I was recording for inspiration. Damien has the most brilliant mind of anyone I have ever met, and it's hard to believe he actually created my album artwork.

The designer Laurence Stevens and I would visit Damien at work, where he was creating a whole art installation called *Greetings from the Gutter* as well as individual art pieces for each song. It was like watching a modern-day alchemist at work. The images he was creating were so simple, and yet they made you have an instant reaction. "Jealousy," for instance, is a shelled hard-boiled egg with sewing needles and black thread stuck in it. He had it photographed so sharply, in such ultrahigh quality, that it looks like you could touch it. The work he put into it was extraordinary. Everything he did was out of this world, and he is such a perfectionist.

I remember a very drunk and heated discussion among myself, Lou Reed and Laurie Anderson one night, trying to persuade Damien not to have his hands surgically removed from his arms, then sewn back on for an art piece.

At the time of making *Greetings*, I was under the influence of the whole British art movement, and I filmed and photographed constantly in a Warholian style. So much so that one night, walking home from dinner behind Lou and Laurie, I was filming their silhouettes lit by the streetlight glow, and Lou turned around and said, "Hurry up, Andy. You are lagging behind!"

The album artwork became so valuable that years later it was worth the same amount as having an album sell almost as many copies as *Sweet Dreams*. Who would have known? Er . . . me.

After recording *Greetings from the Gutter*, I went on the David Letterman show. Lou Reed came along to play rhythm guitar, with Bootsy Collins on bass, Bernie Worrell on keyboards—my crazy, mixed-up band of all-star friends.

The day before Letterman, I was getting ready in my hotel room in New York. The ever-present Tony Quinn, my personal assistant then, was in the room next door as usual. Tony had become irreplaceable, as he was so good at everything, and boy, did I throw every kind of situation his way.

Just the day before, I'd said to Tony, "Look, I want to set up a camera and take a picture of everybody walking down West Eighth Street, in New York City's Greenwich Village." Tony said, "Um, okay."

I had a flash outside, tied to the street lamppost on a delay setting, and I was using black-and-white PolaGraph film, which I could develop myself back at Electric Lady Studios. It was very complicated, because there were a lot of dodgy characters on the street, and I remember it being one of the first times I'd seen Tony get really stressed out.

Ultimately, we gave up and went back to the hotel. You know, when you're in a hotel and you decide, "I think I'll order room service," and then you go, "Oh, I'll have a quick shower before they deliver it." They always ring the bell just as you are getting in the shower, and even though they usually say that it will take forty minutes, for some reason, when you take a shower, it only takes fifteen minutes.

I looked at the room service menu, and for some reason I ordered Manhattan clam chowder, which I'd never had before. I went in the shower, and of course, ding-dong. The guy's there at the door with a table ready to wheel in. It's a round table with leaves that they put up. I was standing there, wet, with my towel on, signing the bill. I was starving, so I sat right down on the edge of the bed and pulled the table toward me. The towel was a bit tight, so I undid it. After all, there was nobody around.

I went to put my spoon in the soup, and the leaf of the table fell down, and the boiling hot, sticky clam chowder fell on my balls and my penis. The whole bowl. You can imagine. Clam chowder is the stickiest thing you can possibly order and it was like steaming-hot glue.

This is where Tony Quinn becomes even more heroic. I was trying to sort of claw the chowder off because it's so hot it felt like ice, and in the worst possible place. I was thinking, *Shit, this is really danger-ous, like third-degree burns.* So I dove to get the phone, and I rang Tony's room in a panic.

He said, "What is it, Dave? What's wrong?"

I'm yelling, "Ah! Fucking hell! Come to my room quick!"

So he came to the door, and by then I had a towel on, but he could see my face was all red and exploding. I lay down on the bed and said, "Get my Polaroid camera!" I pulled my towel off and said, "Quick, take pictures of my penis and everything now!"

Poor Tony!

Can you imagine any job description that would include that? Taking photos of the boss's genitalia after he was scalded with chowder. Tony took photos of the whole area, still covered in clam chowder, and all red and burned. I was in such intense pain, I didn't care. He stood back on the bed, taking pictures in close-up. I was thinking, *Oh my God, what has it come to?* I had the photos taken just in case we ever had to sue the hotel, so we would have proof.

Of course I didn't sue the hotel. I just got the hotel body lotion and applied it after soaking in a cold bath to calm down. I had to play Letterman the next day, and I could hardly walk. I told Lou, and even though he was sympathetic, he couldn't help bursting out into spontaneous fits of laughter.

After that, on the way back to England, Tony put the Polaroid evidence into his passport for safekeeping. I was in the passport queue behind him at the airport when Tony handed over his passport. All the Polaroids of chowder-covered-burned sex organs fell out. I've never seen a look on a guy's face so confused and worried as on the face of that immigration officer. Tony turned bright red. I was wetting myself, trying to not laugh at Tony, who was glowering at me. I felt so bad, I had to turn away while the officer was looking at my penis and balls, all bright red, with clam chowder all over them. He must have thought, *What the hell is this guy doing? What kind of pervert is this?*

It's another one of life's great lessons. I was feeling on top of the world. I'd made a great album, *Greetings from the Gutter*. I'm about to go on Letterman. Lou Reed's going to play rhythm guitar, Bootsy Collins is on bass, it's a crazy great band, and God is telling me again, just like he did with the flying plum, "Don't get too excited. Here comes the clam chowder."

CHAPTER:15

TRAVEL SCHOOL

At the end of my time with Siobhan, I took the boys to France with me for a long summer holiday, along with their friends and cousins. Later, I joined them in Jamaica. I had been to visit St. Barts, but I didn't like it at all, way too trendy and jet-set for me. So I flew back to Jamaica, and Siobhan was there at Round Hill with the boys, and I took a separate room. Of course the boys were saying: "Hang on. You're in this room, but Mom's over there?"

Sam figured it out first and said, "Oh, you know what, though, Dad?"

I said, "What?"

He said, "If you and Mom don't stay together, I'll be the saddest boy in the world." I was devastated and tried to explain. "Not really, because you see, it's like you still have this family and I'll always be there. Mom is there. Nida will be there and it's just that we're going to make a slightly different way of working." I thought I'd better do something drastic to deflect their angst, so I went to my boys and asked, "Who's your favorite teacher at school?" They were both at the same school in Hampstead, and they replied in unison, "Mardette," a young Irish teacher. So on parent-teacher day, I went in to talk about how the kids were doing. I got to Mardette, and as she began to tell me how Sam was doing in class, I jumped in and said, "Great. How would you like to go around the world for a year with Sam and Django?"

She said, "What?"

I said, "Yeah, like homeschooling, only not at home. All over the world."

She said, "Well, I have to think about that. I work at this school."

I replied, "Well, how about two years? Japan, Australia, Brazil."

She thought about it for a few moments and responded, "Yes." She was single, and she loved the idea.

So first we went to Japan, where I was supporting Bob Dylan with Vegas, my project with Terry Hall. We then proceeded to travel all over the world. Nida, of course, came along and took care of the boys while Mardette taught them every day. What a school it was, a global classroom! We went down the Amazon on a huge boat. We went to Australia, Japan and all over the USA. The boys wrote amazing journals about every place we went on these trips, and kept all their thoughts about what they'd experienced. To make them think it was still a real school, I called it Travel School, and I had badges and shirts made with TRAVEL SCHOOL, and everything had the same logo on it. Django actually thought this must have been an official school.

Travel School went back to Jamaica when I was producing Imogen Heap's first album. The boys would be learning about the country, just as they did everywhere we went. It was very good for them, actually, because after they did that, they were light-years ahead of kids their age. They would say, "Oh, yeah, I've been there and this is how it was." While in Australia they both worked at Greenpeace offices.

Then they would go back to be with Siobhan, and she joined in too and took them all over Ireland and showed them their Irish roots. Mardette would always be either with me or with Siobhan, and then Siobhan would go to stay in Jamaica with her new boyfriend or in the house in France for a holiday, and I'd be fine with it. Slowly it all became manageable.

Later I bought a van in London that had aircraft seats, and a bed in the back, so Django and Sam could always have any of their friends come down to the country and play. By now I also had a lovely farm in the English countryside, and they'd come down on a Friday night with all their friends and play football in the backyard. Nida, of course, was there with us, making Thai food and curry. So when we went back to London, I tried to make it as much the same for the kids as I possibly could. What I wanted to do was give them memories that were powerful, like being in Brazil or Japan, or learning about lizards in Jamaica, memories packed with incident and information. I hoped that they would feel, when looking back at it all, "Yeah, Mum and Dad breaking up was bit wonky, but Travel School was amazing."

Knowing that my family was thriving allowed me to continue experimenting, collaborating and touring with the kind of all-in frenzied energy I'd been used to. I'd been really good friends with George Harrison since the mid-eighties, and through him, I met Paul and Ringo. George once invited me to come and see this guy talking in a church in London. His name was Deepak Chopra, and he was relatively unknown then. He was an incredibly compelling speaker who could hold forth on any topic, from astrophysics to the nature of time.

So there he was speaking and we were fascinated, and George said, "Well, come on. We're going to go out to eat something with Deepak afterward." We all went to a Chinese restaurant, and Deepak and I started talking and we got on really well. We became almost instant friends, and he would frequently visit my apartment. One time he came round and he had Demi Moore with him. And she saw pictures I had taken and said, "Did you take these photos?"

And I said, "Yes."

And she said, "Oh, we should do some photos together."

I said, "Okay." And this led us to doing thousands of photos. We flew to India, and I photographed her over ten days in Mumbai and Goa. We were flown by Indian army helicopters to Goa because she's so famous there too. The movie *Ghost*, in which she starred, was huge in India—I suppose because the movie-going population related to an afterlife story. They put posters and billboards of her everywhere. Everywhere we went, people would go crazy when they saw her. They just couldn't believe it was Demi Moore. So everywhere we went, there was a mini army of people, including the real Indian army.

During this period, I was really getting into photography. The way I started taking photographs in the first place was when I took some snaps of Carla Bruni with a cheap 35mm camera and they turned out really well. She was one of the most famous models in the world at the time, and was also fascinated with songwriting. She released her first solo album, which went to number one on the French charts. She later married Nicolas Sarkozy when he became the President of France. I started to take photographs of other people I knew, like Tom Petty. I was taking pictures of people constantly, instead of writing songs or playing music. For a while, everybody would say, "Bloody hell, Dave's decided to be a photographer instead of a musician." This went on for a few years. I would have exhibitions, and I enjoyed just being a photographer.

On one really bizarre occasion an interesting pairing occurred when I met Jon Bon Jovi. I arranged to bring contact sheets and some prints to Demi Moore down in the English countryside, where she was staying with Bruce Willis and their three daughters. I drove down with Siobhan and the boys to help her choose her favorite photographs. We arrived at her place and Bruce was in good spirits. He had a whole afternoon of outdoor games arranged for our kids, so they had fun while we went through all the photographs.

After a while Sarah Ferguson, the Duchess of York, and Prince Andrew came around with their kids, and then Jon Bon Jovi and his wife, Dorothea, arrived with theirs. It sounds like a strange mixture and it was, but after a good dinner and buckets of good wine, we all loosened up a bit.

The evening ended with the kids and adults swimming around in the dark in this freezing outdoor pool. When we got out, everyone squeezed into this tiny sauna next to the pool to get warm. It was a bit like "How many people can you fit in a Mini Cooper?"

In the middle of it all, there were a couple of guitars and a harmonica. Jon and I were playing guitar, Bruce was playing harmonica and we were talking about how surreal the evening was. I asked Jon what he was doing in the middle of the English countryside anyway, and he said, "I've just come over to get away from everything and everyone, to think straight and write some new songs."

Jon came around to my flat in London a few days later to experiment with an interesting idea we had come up with during our jam session. I asked him where he was staying in London, and he told me he'd rented a basement apartment in Chelsea. When I asked, "Well, what's your experience alone down there in the basement?" he said, "Well, I'm getting an interesting perspective on London, looking up and seeing all these different people walking by day and night." Then the lines just came tumbling out, and that started the song "Midnight in Chelsea," which was released in 1997.

It was interesting because it was from the perspective of a basement dweller and his strange view of the world. He was describing these different characters going by and trying to work out who they were and what their stories were. Jon was loving the fact that nobody knew where he was and nobody was bothering him. He liked being able to get about and do different things and not always be "Bon Jovi." In London he could wear a cap, keep his head down and get lost in the crowd. He was really having a great time.

I am, I admit, and surely you know it by now, rather eccentric. At first I had the idea of recording the song just driving around in a London taxi. We did actually film and record some stuff in a London black cab. I even have film of Jon singing "Supercalifragilisticexpialidocious" in the backseat. We sped it up and used it in my Internet TV show, *The Sly Fi Network*. (Believe it or not, I had sort of invented my own version of a YouTube/MySpace concept in 1996 with *Sly Fi*, except only about fifty people could see it, as these were full-on TV-quality shows and hardly anyone in the general public had fast enough connections to see it online.)

Jon and I decided to record the song properly and went through various stages, recording some at the Church and some in New York. Through the process, the music was sounding less and less like Bon Jovi and more like a strange hybrid of me, Jon and early seventies David Bowie. But as soon as Jon opened his mouth, that voice was unmistakable. The song came out, and it went to number four in Britain its first week. I performed "Midnight in Chelsea" with Jon Bon Jovi on *Top of the Pops* in Britain and at a live show for MTV in this big theater in London.

It was an odd combination: me from northeast England and Jon from New Jersey, and we seem to have completely different backgrounds. Yet we got on really well. Jon is a really smart, intelligent guy to work with. It's funny—I'm always in these situations, writing with people from completely different backgrounds. Again, not because we've set up a writing arrangement or I've been hired as a songwriter. It's just we've met under these very strange, random circumstances. From that comes a brand-new song that seems to have come out of nowhere.

Talking about something coming out of nowhere, Paul Verhoeven was in preproduction of his movie *Showgirls*. I remember I got a phone call out of the blue. "I've got Paul Verhoeven for you." I knew he was the film director who directed *Robocop* and other films. He's a Dutch chap. I got on the phone, and he said, "I need you to do the music for my movie called *Showgirls*. I've got all of the cast and the dancers in Lake Tahoe rehearsing. And Prince pulled out his music; he agreed to do the score, and then we never got the damn music."

And I was like "Well, okay. What's it about?"

He said, "I'm going to fly over tomorrow and give you two hundred and fifty thousand dollars if you can sort it out in three days."

I said, "Blimey, I'm not sure. I haven't even seen the script." But he arrived the next day. He must have gone to the airport after the phone call, gotten on a plane and flown straight from LA to London.

Upstairs in my little Covent Garden flat, he proceeded to try to explain the whole movie and all the dance moves of twenty-four young girl dancers, but he was a Dutch guy in his fifties who couldn't dance. Because of his Dutch accent, it was hard to understand him, and he never stopped shouting.

I said, "Well, the best thing is, if I know the tempos that they want to dance to, then I can make a temp track that they can work with."

He said, "Phew," and seemed very relieved.

I explained, "But I'd have to sort of understand what happens in the scene to do it right." So I ended up flying out to rehearsals in Lake Tahoe. I remember walking into this room, and there was a multitude of semiclad beautiful girls, all dancing. I was like "Wow. Now, this is an interesting job." Then, from above me, a girl slid down on a rope upside down in S&M gear. There was a lovely upside-down face smiling at me that said, "Who are you?" That girl was Gina Gershon, and we've been great friends ever since. She played opposite the other lead in the movie. Gina was the dark side.

In the middle of trying to cope with that film, it became more and more complicated. Paul Verhoeven was very hot tempered. I remember one time he came in the studio when we were back in London. We had an orchestra of about sixty and, by then, I knew a bit about orchestration.

He came in and said, "How many people are in the orchestra?"

And we told him sixty-two.

He said, "I never work without the hundred-piece orchestra."

I was like "What?"

I told him, "That means thirty-eight of them would be sitting there with a blank piece of paper."

He was furious and said, "I'm going to ring my producers in Hollywood about this."

I said, "Okay." Which is really the only response you can have to a Dutchman who has just gone mental.

So, while he was on the phone to Hollywood, I went out to a little nearby shop on the street and bought a dress and a wig and put stuffing under my shirt as if I were a girl, and went back. When he was through ranting, I could see him in the control room. I burst in and grabbed hold of him and started dancing with him to the music while dressed as a woman. He was very confused for about two minutes. He said, "What the hell is this?" And then he slowly realized it was me. He just fell on his knees, laughing, as he realized he was being crazy and unreasonable. It calmed everything down, if you know what I mean. When in doubt, dress up and dance—it seems to work every time.

I started working with another great British artist, Bryan Ferry, producing him in my house in the south of France, where he was staying with me. He is such an icon to me and to most people from England. In the early seventies, his band Roxy Music came out with these incredible, mind-blowing records that didn't sound like anything you'd ever heard before. Songs like "Virginia Plain," "In Every Dream Home a Heartache" and "Do the Strand" seemed to come from a parallel Roxy universe.

When we were in the Tourists, one of the highlights was being the support band on Roxy Music's Manifesto Tour in Britain. This was back in 1979. I used to watch Bryan perform every night and was mesmerized by the way he delivered every line. It was like watching elegance in slow motion where all the songs were so sophisticated and otherworldly.

Bryan was born no more than ten miles from where I was born, so when we first got together, it was quite relaxed, as we shared many things in common, including our sense of humor. We started to write songs together and I loved the experience. We've written quite a lot, much of which people haven't heard. We experimented quite a bit, so we have loads of unfinished sketches and songs that were either put to the side or just didn't fit with the project. We'll talk years later about an unfinished track and then get the recording out and play it. It's as if time has not passed and we are right back to that moment when we first put it down.

It was just the two of us and Bryan had writer's block, so every now and then he'd just say, "Oh, let's not do anything. Let's go to Monaco. You know, let's go on an adventure."

So we were going around, hanging out, just us two guys from the northeast of England doing the Riveria. I had separated from my wife, Siobhan, and Brian was also going through a tough marital time. One night, Bryan said, "Let's go to dinner. We've been invited to dinner by the Duchess of Seville in Saint-Tropez." So we went. Who wouldn't?

Actually I didn't really want to go. I was saying, "Oh, bloody hell, Saint-Tropez is gonna take us forever, with all the traffic. You know, it's like getting from Pasadena to Santa Monica at rush hour in the height of the summer."

I suggested we go on my boat. We went down to the ocean from my house, but somebody had left a light on in the boat, and the battery was flat. I was happy about that, thinking, *Oh, good, now we don't have to go.* But Bryan persisted and we ended up—the two of us—driving. It took two hours. Bryan drove and I said, "Okay, I'm going to film the first person who opens the door when we get there." I had a film camera with me as usual.

We rang the doorbell, and a young woman with the irresistible name Anoushka opened the door. I was looking through the camera and said, "Wow—you look amazing, just like Greta Garbo." She must have thought, *Who is this strange person?* I asked her if she'd mind standing near a lamp to get a half-lit effect. I had no idea she herself was a photographer, but she agreed and the result was breathtaking. She is a very beautiful woman. I knew nobody there, not even the hostess, nor did Anoushka, who lived and worked in the south of France but rarely ventured out. The dinner table had place cards, and I will be forever grateful to the person who arranged to seat Anoushka next to me because at dinner I was seated right next to my future bride. I didn't know who she was and she didn't really know who I was, but we started talking about photography and we realized we both had photo exhibitions happening, right next to each other. Mine was up the hill near the Picasso Museum and hers was in a famous gallery in Monte Carlo. We sparked immediately.

There was a huge electrical storm—the kind they have frequently in the south of France. We sat outside in the rain. Eventually, the duchess came out and said, "Don't you know it's pouring rain on you?" We hadn't even noticed.

Bryan and I had been invited to spend the night and given a bedroom with twin beds in it. He had been a bit fed up since we'd gotten there, as he'd driven all this way, so he claimed that bedroom for himself and locked the room with my gear in it. I thought, *Well, that's fucking great. I'm not driving hours and hours back on my own.*

Anoushka said, "You can have my bed, and I'll sleep in the kids' room." But we went to her room and lay down next to each other with all of our clothes on—talking for another two hours—and then she went to sleep in the kids' room.

The next morning, I woke up, and it was quite a funny thing. I went outside and Bryan announced that everyone was planning to go skinny-dipping off the cliff. I'm not one to turn down an adventure, so I walked down the path with Bryan and the hostess. And they said, "You first, Dave." I took off my clothes and jumped. Then they decided not to do it! So I was swimming around naked with everyone watching me. (By this time my scorched balls had healed.)

I climbed out of the sea, found a towel and went back into the house. Anoushka was making some breakfast. So we started talking again. I said to her, "Well, if you're having a photo exhibition within the next few days, you should come visit me at my house," and she did. When she arrived, Bryan Ferry and I were playing tennis against Tony Blair, who was soon to become the prime minister of England, and this British comedian called Rory Bremner, who did a famous impression of Tony Blair. So he was doing that on the tennis court, and he also looked a bit like Tony. Anoushka was really confused, watching me and Bryan Ferry playing against two Tony Blairs.

It was during this period that Bryan and I wrote the song "Goddess of Love," which was rather apt for me, but it took us quite a long time to finish. It's funny: lyrically the song epitomizes the kind of thing Bryan is so brilliant at romanticizing about—something so dark and beautiful but just out of reach, a feeling that there could be a place where everything is sensual and perfect, but when you get there everyone has left and only their ghosts linger on.

"Goddess of Love" has so much glamour attached to it and has all of the Bryan Ferry nuances. The opening line's a classic: "Marilyn says, 'I've got nothing to wear tonight, only a pair of diamond earrings that catch the light.'" Immediately you are drawn into the paradox of temptation in the lyric, but there is such sadness in its delivery of the melody. Another song we wrote called "San Simeon" does this so well. It's aristocratic but melancholy and bleak.

I shot a great piece of film of Bryan in the back of a Rolls-Royce. We were being driven to Monte Carlo, along the coast of the south of France. We're playing back these tracks we'd been recording, and we were laughing. Bryan was smiling as the sun was going down. It captures everything about his inherent style, his intellect, his demons and his warmth. Every move he makes, every word he writes and every melody he sings are totally unique. There's nobody like him, really; they definitely broke the mold.

Anoushka and I got on really well, hung out with each other, but we didn't really "go out" at first because I'd said, "Look, I've just come out of a marriage literally six weeks ago, and I just can't be involved with anybody. And I'll tell you what. I'm a lot older than you, and I advise you to go out with somebody else. Steer clear of me. I'm going to America, anyway, to work."

CHAPTER:16

PICCADILLY PICNIC

n 1998, the Internet had just started to become sort of a buzzword. I'd already heard about it years before, but now it was becoming real.

A few years earlier in 1994—during the middle of *Greetings from the Gutter*—I had created a movie story about the record industry going crazy, all triggered by the Japanese giant Sony buying CBS back in 1987. Jack Nicholson was interested in playing the lead character, and renowned Japanese film director Juzo Itami, who won the Cannes Palme d'Or for his Japanese film *Tampopo*, wanted to write and direct. It was through this film concept that I met Paul Allen, cofounder of Microsoft along with Bill Gates. Juzo had flown over for a dinner meeting in New York City to discuss the project.

Paul Allen was at the dinner, but Paul was much more interested in talking about *Greetings from the Gutter* because we were recording at Jimi Hendrix's Electric Lady Studios and he loved anything to do with Hendrix. He was just jaw-dropped, fascinated, and wanted to know if he could come by and see the studio. I said, "Of course," not really comprehending who Paul was at the time. I was trying to talk to this Japanese chap about this story, because it meant a lot to me. The movie was about what's happened to the music industry. It was important to me to show the perspective of an indie label in light of what was going on with corporations taking over record companies.

Paul came to Electric Lady Studios. He loved it and was astounded, saying, "This is where Hendrix actually lived and recorded?" Then he asked if he could come back the next day as well. Paul was watching the recording going down and was totally fascinated with the process; he was soaking it all in. He joined in playing on an electric guitar, and he played really well. Halfway through the session, Paul left the studio. He said he was going to go look at some paintings. I thought he meant in an art gallery but actually it was in a brownstone building; men with white gloves were carrying out paintings, and he'd just nod if he wanted it. He purchased two paintings by Monet, each worth millions.

I was explaining to Paul how much I loved Jamaica and that I was completely bonkers about that country. I said to him, "You should come to Jamaica. You'll love it—Jamaican music and all that stuff." So he did. He came to Jamaica, and we went up on the coast and stayed in a twenty-dollar-a-night place where you sleep on the floor and there were cockroaches in the grill. What I didn't know at the time was that his company, Vulcan, was freaking out. He was the third-richest man in the world, and for the first time, they'd lost tabs on where he'd gone. Meanwhile Paul was enjoying himself, jamming on acoustic guitars on the beach, alongside me and my good friend Brian Jobson.

Anyway, we had a great time, and we got on really well. Paul then invited me to his place in Seattle, and it was then that I really understood. I saw this immense world that he had, and his enormous brain, which soaks up like a sponge everything to do with science fiction, medicine, music, and much more. We became best friends and have been through all sorts of stuff together. Our conversations are never-ending and about anything from how the human mind works to how Jimi Hendrix played.

One day Paul and I were sitting in my penthouse apartment at Seven Dials in Covent Garden when I pointed out the derelict hospital straight down the street on the corner of Endell Street. Paul and I had been talking about doing something together, and I suggested we go have a look at it, as it could be a creative meeting place like a Warhol Factory, right there in the center of London.

Paul had been talking about a "Wired World" ever since I'd met him, and I was visualizing the creative discussions that could happen in a place like that, between many different kinds of creatives, manifesting into lots of new music, films and plays, from the interaction of different disciplines. I stole the idea from Mahler's wife, who hosted dinners in Vienna, inviting selected composers, architects and writers.

Paul and I took a look at the old empty building; everything had been left abandoned—operating tables, medical instruments and lots of scary jars with human remains. It was so strange. We walked across wobbly beams, looking at this complete mess; then we looked at each other and said, "Yes!"

Both being hypochondriacs, we were quite alarmed when construction started, and we saw the photos of workers wearing nuclear protective clothing and headgear, going in to decontaminate the place. It took about five years to get all the permits and designs to turn this very toxic, dilapidated building into a beautifully renovated members' club for the creative community, the Hospital Club.

Now it's been open for ten years, and it is a literal hive of activity. Inside this seven-story building, we have an award-winning TV and music studio, a gallery, a restaurant and bars, a screening room, and a live performance space named the Oak Room. We also just opened a floor of hotel rooms and suites. It's my home away from home.

The Hospital Club is where Radiohead made their magnificent album *In Rainbows*, and we host exhibitions such as Warhol vs. Banksy, an exhibition that explored the relationship between their creations. It really is a unique club in the heart of Covent Garden for members of the creative industries.

A few months ago Paul and I sat next to each other watching a band of four musical sisters from Colorado—called Shel—play an amazing set. I had them as the artists-in-residence for a week. Afterwards, Paul and I were marveling at the space, compared to when we were climbing over upturned gurneys and balancing on beams, looking down at derelict hospital wards, thinking we were crazy! Paul and his team at Vulcan did an incredible job at making sure it was the best renovation possible, and they had to jump through many hoops to just get the project going, which, at the beginning, nearly made us all feel like giving up.

I remember one dinner at the Ivy when we were feeling frustrated by all the red tape. Michael Stipe from R.E.M. leaned over and told me that we mustn't forget to pour milk down all the drains and that we must do other ritualistic things to cleanse the fact so many people had died there. I went back to my apartment with my head spinning at the colossal task we had taken on, and now I had to climb up on the roof and find the hundreds of drains to pour gallons of milk down. I went to sleep with my head swimming. In milk.

Paul has a beautiful farm in Idaho with a very old log cabin. Back in the winter of 1994, Paul invited me and the family there for a winter holiday.

Paul gave Siobhan and me a laptop computer each—the very first time I'd ever seen one. I remember that Christmas Day when Paul was explaining to us what it was and what you could do on it. I was just completely befuddled, amazed, because I recognized it meant infinite possibilities. Paul was going, "Yep, that's right." It was as if you were alive in caveman times, and somebody gave you a perfect spherical ball. I knew the laptop would allow a million possibilities to happen. So I decided back then that I was going to make the first-ever record released only on the Internet.

I built a house in Jamaica with my good friend the great reggae bass player Brian Jobson. It's in the little hills above St. Anne's Bay, and is called the Ice House. We named it that because it used to be where the Spanish would go to get the coldest water they could. They had a big tunnel leading to an artesian well that they dug. Later, this was where all the hotels used to get water for making ice. So if worse comes to worst, we've got water. Brian's family had the land over generations, so I paid to build the house and then we would share it. And we got people from the local village to do it, as I wanted to give them the work instead of the monies always going to Americans or Brits. I then invited the local kids to come in and play around with us but gave them the responsibility of keeping the river clean, so they became the river police and I had special shirts made for them, making them official.

This was the beginning of a lot of things colliding. I invited Anoushka to come to the Ice House. She already had an exhibition where she took photographs of tiny cactuses and plants, but shot them like Hollywood movie stars. Anoushka had served an apprenticeship with Plichta, the Hollywood portrait photographer of post–World War II years, and she applied his technique to strange plant life, using dramatic lighting in black and white so you couldn't tell what they were.

The exhibition was called Alien Sex Mother, held at the Galerie Pierre Nouvion in Monaco. The exhibition was a huge success with famous art collectors Philip and Stavros Niarchos buying most of her prints.

I said, "Well, my back garden in Jamaica is basically a jungle with incredible flora, tropical plants, a strange-looking world with a river running through it. You can come and take pictures there if you want." Though we had met and hung out, this was before Anoushka and I were actually dating. I was still keeping her at arm's length for her own good, or so I thought.

I'd decided to release the first album on the Internet, and I'd decided to make it in the middle of the jungle in my house, in Jamaica, where the electricity was on and off constantly. Everything about doing it there was insanely complicated, which was just the way I liked it. Andy Wright came as a programmer and to coproduce. I don't often produce myself, as I need a perspective other than my own. For this album, *Sly-Fi*, I spent most of the time in a swinging basket chair on the back porch looking out at the jungle.

I had invited a few different people to Jamaica for this recording extravaganza: my friend Gina Gershon and two other actresses named Georgina Cates and Rhona Mitra. So this was a very laid-back scene with people lounging around in . . . well, not much actually, and Anoushka arrived in the midst of all that and was a little thrown. What I loved about Anoushka was the fact she was very serious about her work ethic and came fully prepared with her cameras and tripods, et cetera, but she also had this old-world charm about her like she was from the forties, dressed with a large-brimmed hat, a cotton blouse and baggy shorts, like Meryl Streep in *Out of Africa.*

A few days into the recording it was Easter Sunday, and somehow Brian's wife, Suzanne, had managed to rent me a full-on Easter Bunny outfit with the big head and everything, but it was boiling hot in Jamaica, so it was like an oven in there. We went to Chris Blackwell's house on the beach. And in the Jamaican tradition, I was giving out Easter Bunny cookies to lots of little local kids, but inside that outfit, I was sweltering hot. I decided to have a rest and join my gang from the Ice House and Chris, who was talking to Tom Waits.

I was a huge fan, and I remember telling him how much I loved his work. Tom looked around at these four beautiful women I'd arrived with and me dressed like a rabbit with a big box of cookies and said, "Wow, maybe I should try one of these cookies." Chris burst out laughing, and so did I, as I realized the situation was ludicrous!

That was Anoushka's first introduction to my style of life, and I was convinced she would go back to England thinking, *What a nutcase*, and she would have been right. I'd already planned to leave for America, and promised myself that I wasn't going to get involved with anybody for at least a year, because I had my two sons to think about and I'd just come out of a marriage. I wanted to see what it's like to be on my own, and not to have to think about anything apart from Sam and Django and making music.

In Jamaica we were like a little commune, having midnight bonfires and naked meditation sessions up the river sitting on huge stones, total experimental madness, and really odd songs about what was happening in my life. Weirdly enough, the album is almost all electronic apart from the odd real instrument being played by a one-armed Jamaican plastic bottle trumpet player. The songs just tumbled out about my current situation—songs like "Piccadilly Picnic" about moving into the West End with the kids and the dinner party where I met Anoushka:

> *been sprinkling the dust again*
> *danced with lady luck again*
> *broke all the rules in the book again*
> *oh yeah*
> *I gave myself a treat again*
> *told everyone in the street again*
> *but I landed on my feet again*
> *oh yeah*

(or) this one "Happy to Be Here," about surviving my early teenage years:

> *I put all my eggs in the bacon slicer*
> *but now it's turned out fine*
> *in fact it couldn't be nicer*
> *a nice Jewish girl and a bottle of cider*
> *seven days later I was a man of the world*
> *I thought*
> *I'll go and get a slice of pizza from the pizzeria*
> *oh, and a Coke*
> *has anybody got change for five quid?*
> *I'm happy to be here*
> *So happy to be here*
> *And I wish that you were here*
> *Unhappy with me.*

I wouldn't try to make sense of these lyrics; although, if you've read this far you may recognize some parts of the songs taken from real-life scenarios. I did the craziest live performance of "Happy to Be Here" on a popular British TV show called *TFI Friday*. I had the three most unlikely backing singers you could ever imagine: Sinéad O'Connor, Kylie Minogue and Natalie Imbruglia.

We didn't tell the TV producers who they were, and the girls were all dressed in disguise with wigs and Las Vegas–type gaudy dresses. We simply told the producers that the girls were called a tramp, a drunk and an unfit mother. It was funny watching the presenter Chris Evans and the audience's faces as they gradually realized who these three were!

At this point in my life I just wanted to have fun and I didn't take anything too seriously. Good things kept happening the more I let go.

After a few sun-kissed weeks recording in Jamaica, I returned to America, where I kept writing and producing Jon Bon Jovi in my Encino home. Things were still unsettled with Siobhan, and we were dealing with all of the arrangements involving our boys that needed to be made, which meant lots of intense phone calls. As most people know, divorcing with children is a nightmare for both parties, and I found it hard to concentrate on anything else.

When I got back to the UK, however, I was in full swing of launching the first album to be released on the Internet through a company called N2K.

Anoushka and I never actually went out or dated. She took my advice and went out with a couple of people, and I took off to America. I would talk to her on the phone sometimes, and we sent faxes to each other. When I came back to England, to Covent Garden, she came around to my apartment with a beautiful present, which was one of her pictures from her exhibition that I loved. It was a black-and-white picture of a very dark and beautiful rose, ripe, turning, like Annie and me on the cover of *In the Garden*, but shot like a Hollywood star portrait with an old box camera.

She was quite shy and nervous, and gave the picture to me when there were a lot of people arriving. I put it down on these seats that I used to own from the milk bar in the movie *A Clockwork Orange*. My good friend Paul Allen arrived. There were a lot of people milling around, and he was shaking lots of hands. I said to him, "Have a seat," and Paul sat down, right on top of the beautiful print Anoushka had made for me, crushing it. Anoushka burst into tears. I was thinking, *Oh, my God, what's happening?*

We went in the bedroom, the three of us, Anoushka, Paul and me. He felt terrible. Anoushka said she was crying only because she'd spent a lot of time in the darkroom getting it perfect—a beautiful handmade print, as a gift for me. I realized, *Wow, she did all that after almost a year of me telling her we couldn't see each other.* I realized then and there that she was not only an amazing artist and a very gorgeous girl, but also a beautiful person.

I was standing there in the bedroom with them: Anoushka crying, Paul feeling devastated. She was drying her tears, and I said to myself, *Wow, she's, like, amazing. Am I stupid or something? Telling her to go out with someone else?* We lived together almost from the next day onward in my apartment, and she embraced my kids, Sam and Django, even though she was young, just twenty-seven, and Django was seven and Sam was ten.

When Django first heard she was coming to the house in France, he was running around going, "Oh, my God, there's this woman called Anoushka, and she likes my dad." When she arrived, he said to her, "Have you met Anoushka yet?" She replied, "I am Anoushka." He screamed and ran off, shouting, "Anoushka's here! Anoushka's here!"

I remember when she came the next time to the south of France to stay with me. She was driving my car, and I was in the front passenger seat. It was this beautiful open-top car from the sixties, an Alpha Romeo Spider. Sam and Django were in the back, and we'd just started to get to know each other. Django tapped Anoushka on the shoulder and said, "Are you gonna sex my dad?" Anoushka went bright red, gripped the wheel tighter and stared at the road ahead. I couldn't help but laugh.

I met Anoushka's mum at her house. We had a little meal round a tiny kitchen table, just the three of us. Anoushka and I had just started to see each other then, about a year after we had met, but Anoushka hadn't exactly told her mum the situation. When she did summon up the courage, Mum's response was "Whoa, hang on. Isn't he, like, a lot older and has children and plays in a rock group?" All the things a mother doesn't want to hear. It could've been worse. I wanted to tell her I could've been Ozzy Osbourne, but I didn't.

That day in Saint-Tropez when I first walked in with a camera and met Anoushka, she had told her mum, "Oh, I think I've met somebody that is the one." Because she was just not interested in a lot of people. Her mum was reading the local newspaper when Anoushka rang to tell her, and, unfortunately the front page of the newspaper in Nice had a picture of me with Helena Christensen, the supermodel, and Bryan Ferry and another girl. And as Anoushka was telling her mum, "I think I've met this guy," her mum said, "Idiot." Anoushka asked, "What do you mean?"

Her mum said, "I have the newspaper in front of me and whoever you're talking about is on the front." It was all actually very innocent. But of course, her mum was dead against the idea of me in her daughter's life.

By the time Anoushka decided to bring me round to meet her mum, for the meal in the small kitchen, Mum was prepared for this complete player. And I came wearing the most outlandish outfit. At that point, I'd decided to wear the very worst clothing possible, on purpose. I made a decision to wear and do everything wrong. I even did it on TV and in music videos. So I got the worst possible American nylon suit with checkers all over, and I wore it with a stripy shirt. I dyed my hair white blond and wore big thick-rimmed glasses. I wanted to look not just different but entirely—well—wrong. Before then, everything was a bit stylized, during the Spiritual Cowboys time. So I just wanted to change all that and, as it's me, go to another extreme. So whomever I was talking to and whatever about, they would have to look at me and think, "Jesus, this guy's got it all wrong." But then they'd be listening just to what I was talking about and not think, *Oh, this is Dave Stewart from Eurythmics.* It was an experiment on myself.

I arrived in my new awful look at Anoushka's mum's kitchen. I had on sneakers from the sixties that had the Playboy Bunny symbol on them. Her mum was like, "Oy vey!" But we had a glass of red wine and ate homemade pasta. Anoushka told me later that halfway through the meal, her mum said, "Actually, he's a really nice guy," and "I know why you like him." Meaning, that was bad news, because you were going to probably be with him and it was going to be a roller-coaster ride that would actually never stop. Her mum had been on the roller-coaster ride with her father, Benny Fisz, a film producer whose credits include *Battle of Britain*, *Aces High* and *The Heroes of Telemark*. He was a wonderful, fascinating, interesting person, but it was always upheaval, always chaos. So she said to Anoushka, "I understand why you want to be with Dave, but you're in for a crazy trip."

Anoushka said, "I don't mind because I want to experience life. So far I've been looking for that one thing that will take me on an adventure." She was like Alice about to go through the looking glass. We decided to get a place outside of London because the flat in Covent Garden was becoming claustrophobic and Anoushka was pregnant with our first child.

We got a farm in Surrey; I put a studio in there and we settled into country life (sort of). I was doing all sorts of experiments, but after a while, I was feeling a bit cut off there at the farm. I was mostly doing stuff I liked: an experimental album with Mudbone, the singer from P-Funk. We made this great sort of series of recordings and put it out as his record *Fresh Mud*.

Like everyone else I was a huge fan of Sinéad O'Connor's voice from the first time I heard it. I was driving my car through Camden Town streets in London when "I Want Your (Hands on Me)" from her album *The Lion and the Cobra* came on the radio, and I had to pull over to sit and listen. Soon she was in every music paper and magazine, looking stunning, with her defiant eyes and shaved head. In 1990, we all went through a fascination with the brilliant single, her first in America, "Nothing Compares 2 U," written by Prince. I was following her various encounters with the press, but it wasn't until I met her alone that I realized what a brilliant mind she has as well as a voice to die for.

Sinéad picks up on everything; not even the tiniest nuance goes unnoticed, whether it's in a conversation, melody or atmosphere. She breathes it in, absorbs it, reflects upon it and stores it in her mind, all in a nanosecond. Sinéad is so finely tuned and sensitive that I know for her to get up onstage and sing the way she does is a feat in itself.

Around 1999, Brian Eno played me one of Sinéad's new songs while he was staying with me in France. We were sitting in a motionless car outside the house with Sinéad blasting out of the car stereo. I was spellbound. Not long after, she came to visit me at my apartment in London. We had loads of fun and laughed a lot that first day. We worked together on songs that went onto her album *Faith and Courage*, which was released in the summer of 2000.

We began experimenting with music and made a crazy video on the roof, and after several hours messing around, we decided to do some work together. We wrote quite a few songs in my apartment and at the Church Studios, and once again "Jealous" happened in about ten minutes. I was in the middle of working on a video installation with French artist Philippe Perrenoud for the Paris Museum of Modern Art.

We were making a fake commercial that I was acting in when Sinéad arrived. I asked the guys making the film if we could stop for a bit, and I picked up an acoustic guitar and plugged it into the PA system. Sinéad took hold of a microphone and we invented the chords and melody in real time on the spot. Everyone thought it was a song they already knew, but it wasn't. We talked deeply for a bit about relationships, and then she said, "I'll see ya tomorrow with the lyrics." And she did.

During the recording sessions at the Church Studios, various people would drop by to see Sinéad or me and it was very laid-back. John Reynolds, her ex-husband, came by to play drums, and we also had the legendary Jah Wobble play bass on "Jealous." Sinéad had the great idea of going into a reggae feel at the end breakdown of the song to the outro. I filmed Sinéad improvising over the end section, singing, "I don't deserve to be so lonely," in the most haunting way. As I looked at her through the eyepiece of the camera, one step removed, I agreed wholeheartedly with her that she does not. Every time I recorded her voice, I got goose bumps.

Sinéad is a pure soul and full of love for the real things in life. Like me, she finds great solace in reggae music, and I was so pleased to see she'd hooked up with my friends Sly and Robbie, the Jamaican producers and bass and drum legends, not so long ago. I performed "Jealous" a few times on TV with Sinéad in the UK, and again we had such a laugh making crazy videos in the dressing room. "The crack was mighty," as they say in Ireland, and I'm sure it will be with us again in the future.

I realized that through a laptop, and through the Internet, there were good and bad aspects to both. Yes, people were going to want to have music through it. But then all hell broke loose. So I started to think about the future and what was going to happen. And I could see that there was going to need to be a new arrangement in the way that artists got to work.

I started something called the Artist Network. It was all about artists helping artists. I found people like Joanne Shaw Taylor, a brilliant sixteen-year-old blues guitarist who's now one of the leading blues artists in Britain. I also wrote songs and produced an album with the great reggae legend Jimmy Cliff and started making records with different people, like the brilliant Jamaican rapper Nadirah X. I was trying to work out how a new model that involved rights management, the Internet and music streaming would work. I even had a friend help build a 3-D virtual universe with separate worlds in it that represented the world of the Rolling Stones and the Beatles. I didn't know at the time that these worlds would later be called apps; I just called them worlds.

I showed them to as many artists as possible, explaining the Internet was going to change everything, and unless we as artists got some kind of handle on it, one day all our work would be available for free and the only people making anything would be companies ruling the Web like Yahoo! or Google, who were in their infancy. I could see it coming.

I kept talking about this stuff to everyone from Quincy Jones to Mick Jagger, George Harrison and Paul McCartney, and eventually I was getting calls and visits from all sorts of people. Michael Philipp, who was on the board of Deutsche Bank, heard three different people mention my name in two days. He said, "Whenever that happens, something's going on." So Michael came down to the farm to have dinner and ended up getting Deutsche Bank to pay the cost to finish building the 3-D worlds so they could understand better what I was talking about. In fact, I ended up calling a meeting in the boardroom on the top floor of Deutsche Bank in New York City and the attendees were Quincy Jones, Stevie Wonder, Lou Reed, Jeff Rosen (Bob Dylan's manager/publisher), Dr. Dre's lawyer, and the list went on.

I explained that if we all thought that the record business was full of shady characters and foggy accounting now, things were about to get a lot worse. Stevie Wonder had brought Berry Gordy's son, Kerry Gordy, who was getting agitated, and at one point, he interrupted, saying, "Hey, at Motown we had to invest a lot before getting any returns." He said they released six singles by the Supremes before they had any success. At this point Stevie Wonder stood up, put his hand out and said, "Yeah, and I remember when Little Stevie Wonder's voice broke. Motown had a meeting saying I was over and maybe they should drop me." He said he went home and wrote "Uptight (Everything's Alright)" and it was. The room fell silent and I carried on.

Later Michael Philipp said, "When I met Dave in September of 2000, he talked for twelve hours about the impact of digitalization on the production and distribution of media. As a banker, I didn't know what the hell he was talking about—nor did anyone else. Over the next five years, we all found out."

I had become great friends with George Harrison and his wife, Olivia. Anoushka and I would go to see them in Henley quite often. One day George called me and asked if I would come down and chat to him on camera; he said it wasn't an interview, more of a conversation. So I went along with Anoushka, and I took a small video camera to film an intimate chat. When I arrived there was a film crew and soundmen, and George was in the back garden. George wanted me to ask the questions, and then they would film his answers.

I started off asking about *All Things Must Pass*, the great album from 1970, and George insisted on finding the garden gnomes and placing them at his feet, replicating the album cover. He had names for the gnomes and he was very humorous, joking around with the crew and in good spirits. I sensed something wasn't quite right, as it felt like this was about some kind of closure. We wandered off around the garden filming for an hour or two and George talked about everything from reincarnation to the early Beatles crazy adventures, all about India and his love of Indian music. He also went in depth about the highs and lows of being so insanely famous in the Beatles. As we walked around the garden George was, as usual, naming all the trees and plants—he just loved everything about the garden. We ended up filming strange stuff with my little video camera: George and Anoushka peering from behind flower blossom trees; pretty psychedelic stuff with George saying great one-liners about life, mixed with the odd quip from the Monty Python side of his brain.

It was like a long walk into the mind of a beautiful and sensitive artist. I gave Olivia my videotape, and you can see quite a bit of this footage, as well as George talking to me about all kinds of stuff, in the movie *Living in the Material World*, directed by Martin Scorsese.

George passed away a year later. The day after, a beautiful hand-crafted box arrived, with pictures and drawings on the lid, saying, *From one loving family to another*. Inside there was a beautiful string of handwritten cards signed by George, Olivia and Dhani, and a flag with a Pablo Neruda poem on it for my daughter Kaya, who was only a few months old the day we took her to meet George and do the filming.

Around 1998, Robert Altman, the legendary film director, and his wife, Kathryn, invited Anoushka and me to dinner at a Japanese restaurant near their home in Malibu. After dinner we went back to their place, and we were sitting around talking, and Robert was rolling a big joint. He had an acoustic guitar, so I started playing a bit and asked if he had a slide. Kathryn took me into the kitchen to see what they might have that could work, and I chose a thick-bottom, straight-edged whiskey glass. While I was messing around playing slow blues, using the improvised slide, Robert sat with his eyes closed, smoking his reefer.

Suddenly he jumped up and said, "That's it!" We were all startled, and he asked, "What's making that sound?" I showed him the whiskey glass, and he took it off me and went scuttling away, laughing to himself. It was late, so we said our good-byes and drove home to Encino.

Early the next morning, the phone rang. It was Robert Altman, and he said, "You have to do the music to a film I'm making called *Cookie's Fortune*, and don't worry. I've got the whiskey glass locked up in my safe at home. Yep, I've got it safe and sound!"

He had been looking for a way to make the score to his movie different, and when I was playing the blues the night before, the whole thing had dawned on him that it was the sound he was looking for.

The movie portrays small-town Southern life in Holly Springs, Mississippi, where the film was mostly made. I went to Mississippi when they were beginning to shoot. Robert had created a great scene there, having arranged somehow with the mayor of Greenville, Mississippi, to rent some of the houses right in the town square. That way, Glenn Close, Julianne Moore, Liv Tyler and the other stars in the movie could all be very close to one another, including himself and his wife. When we arrived, it was pretty strange to see these actresses, along with Patricia Neal, Charles S. Dutton and Chris O'Donnell, all strolling around the small town square, which he'd transformed into our private little village.

Altman didn't really have any money to do the score. So I said that was okay. I agreed to do it for whatever he had, which was a pittance. So what I did was go into Memphis, where I met with some street performers, and offered them money to play on bits and pieces, and made the score up out of a collage of just me on that slide guitar, playing the glass that Robert had saved in the safe, and got amazing performances from the local players. Each day I would go to watch the rushes of the film with him and the cast in an old Mississippi barn, and I'd play some of the music I was concocting. Together we created a sort of strange *Cookie's Fortune* Mississippi world.

I found a wonderful blues singer, Ruby Wilson, singing in a Memphis bar, and she did some humming and gospel-inflected vocals, and I combined her voice with cello and with a guy playing harmonium.

It turned out a really wonderful sound track. And Robert Altman was such a fantastic guy to work with. He would sit back, stroking his little goatee, smoking a big, fat, giant joint. He'd listen to what I'd played. And he would go, "Yeah, that's it." He would never make a comment like "Man, that was so cool." Or "That needs some work." He would just say, "Yeah, that's it." When I got back to London, I invited Candy Dulfer, the most beautiful and talented jazz saxophonist, over from Holland to play on three parts of the score. And we reconnected doing film music again, for the first time since we'd collaborated years before on "Lily Was Here."

Candy and I have played together many times since I first met her when she was just seventeen. In 1989, I was asked to write the score to a Dutch movie *De Kassière (Lily Was Here)*. I wanted to do a sparse and free-form instrumental title song, featuring a strong saxophone melody, and I found one of the most remarkable saxophone players I've ever heard in the shy, sweet Candy Dulfer. She surprised us all when she began blasting out wild improvisations so inventive, with melodies flying all over the place! I knew I'd met a rare talent, and we've been friends and collaborators ever since.

The title song, "Lily Was Here," is one of the most successful instrumental songs ever released. It was number one in Holland for eight weeks, and soon became a Top Ten in all European countries. And it didn't stop there. Much to everyone's surprise, it made it to the Top Ten on the U.S., Australian and Japanese *Billboard* charts as well. In fact, "Lily Was Here" is one of the top five most played instrumental songs in history and is featured on more than one hundred compilation albums. It's one of those songs that is being played even now on the radio somewhere every minute of every day.

Soon after, Candy was spotted by Prince and has played with him since on many tours over the years. She also plays with many great artists like Van Morrison and bands like Pink Floyd, to name but a few. She is a rare talent and innovative musician, and I'm proud to call her a dear friend.

Another very, very dear friend of mine was Ted Demme, a young film director, and one of my best friends who unfortunately died way too young and before his time on Sunday, January 13, 2002, at only thirty-nine years old. He was playing basketball with his friends, a close-knit group of actors he loved dearly, when he collapsed with a heart attack. Everybody loved Ted; he was one of the most adored guys I ever met. At the 2002 Golden Globe Awards show, one week following his death, Kevin Spacey wore a picture of Ted on his suit jacket. The whole film community was shattered.

I did two movie scores for him, *The Ref* with Kevin Spacey, Judy Davis and Denis Leary, and *Beautiful Girls* with Uma Thurman, Matt Dillon, Natalie Portman, Timothy Hutton and Rosie O'Donnell.

Ted first came over to London to talk about me doing the music for *The Ref* in 1994. I loved the script—it was hilarious—but I hadn't really spent any time with him. It was the first time I'd even met him and he was kind of jet-lagged. I'd also just been given these special glasses that flashed lights in your eyes very rapidly, and when Ted arrived I was wearing them. The glasses put you into a sort of semi-hypnotic, meditative state, and Ted immediately wanted to try them on. I could see he was a very humorous guy straightaway, as he was giggling away with the weird glasses on, cracking jokes and full of energy.

I said, "We can chat for a bit, but I have to go to this Anxious Records party just around the corner in about an hour." I had started an independent label called Anxious Records and Jarvis Cocker from Pulp was going to deejay the party, which was going to be packed with all the bands and artists signed to my label. I imagined Ted and the producers (who arrived with him) would be too exhausted, but Ted said, "Okay, let's go." He was up for anything: a good sign in my book.

So we went marching off along with his producer and assistant trailing behind. They didn't understand what they were walking into. The party was downstairs in a Covent Garden basement, only a few minutes' walk from my apartment. By the time we got there, all the bands were already completely drunk, and it was only seven in the evening. Everyone there was drinking from the free bar, and the cocktails were named after the bands, like Freak of Desire or the Curve, even though they were all Long Island Iced Teas (a mixture of tequila, vodka, light rum, triple sec, and gin), basically—each one was a sledgehammer that would knock you completely out.

When we arrived, no one was dancing; everyone was just staggering around. Then this kid arrived with a bagful of Ecstasy (MDMA). At that point, I hadn't taken drugs for a very long time, but Ted and I said, "Okay, what the hell?"

We each took one. It was very similar to the Daryl Hall situation, where the producer was saying, "Hey, no, I don't think you should." We chased it down with one of the cocktails, and of course they were so strong. Ted was jet-lagged, and we didn't feel this Ecstasy pill working at all, so we took another one, which was a big mistake.

What happened next was we woke up, basically lying on top of each other, on the ground of the actual bar where the party had been held. Nobody else was there, just the freaked-out producer and some people trying to help us. When we got on the street, it was freezing cold.

I passed out, and I'm sure I nearly died right there on the cold stone pavement. Ted didn't know what to do; he was freaking out. He tried to carry me to a hospital, but he kept throwing up in shop doorways, to try to get rid of the drink and the pill, to bring himself around. Anyway, we ended up in the hospital, lying on the floor of an empty ward. We slowly began to sober up, and we all ended up back at my house at about five o'clock in the morning. I was trying to show him this weird film I'd made about people who had taken Ecstasy and passed out.

I remember we were both hugging the TV at about six a.m. We looked at each other, and Ted just burst out laughing, hysterical laughter. And the producer and everybody were saying, "What? What now?" Ted said, "I can't believe it. Disney is paying for this trip." It was true; the whole trip was financed by Buena Vista, a division owned by the Walt Disney Company.

So that was the propitious start to our friendship. I went on to do the music for *The Ref*, and then I did his film *Beautiful Girls* (1996) next, which became one of my favorite scores. I built it around the acoustic slide guitar, but with a full orchestra, orchestrated by Teese Gohl, a good friend of mine from Switzerland who has worked on many scores with me.

When I was writing the score to *Beautiful Girls*, we were all staying in my house in France. Ted, along with his wife, Amanda, and I would all go down to the sea and jump in and swim about, then come back and work on some more music. I had my sons, Sam and Django, with me, and Ted would chase them all around the garden and throw them over his shoulder into the pool, while they would howl with delight. They loved Ted too. It was a great experience working with him, and I miss him terribly.

I was lying in bed in England with Anoushka in 2002, and I got a phone call in the middle of the night. It was Gina Gershon, crying and screaming, "Teddy's dying." We could hardly make out what she was saying, as she was driving frantically to the hospital where they were trying to resuscitate him. Later on, Amanda, Ted's wife, was on the phone in the hospital room in a complete state of shock, just sobbing. We were absolutely heartbroken. The next morning we went to Heathrow and got straight on a plane to Los Angeles, and less than twenty-four hours later, we were there. Everybody was around the house, all his friends crying, and no one could believe it was true. It became a huge sort of a sit-in and went on for a week. No one would leave, because he was so loved and so young.

I stood with Ted's mother at the memorial, looking down at Ted's lifeless body in the half-open casket. He was dressed in a suit and had his usual Ray-Ban shades on. The longer I looked, the more it seemed he didn't appear dead at all. He even made me smile. His positive comedic spirit was somehow still there, hovering over us. I welled up with love for him.

CHAPTER:17

PEACE

This was exactly when Eurythmics world opened up again. Annie had been coming down to visit us at the farm in Surrey regularly, and we'd started to experiment with some songs. When we came back to do *Peace* in 1999, we never intended it as any kind of Eurythmics reunion, because we hadn't broken up, but it had been ten years. So regardless of what we said or wanted, the world saw it as a reunion. It was really a continuation.

Back in the eighties, when the press said, "So is that it, then? Is that the end for Eurythmics?" Annie and I always had the same answer: "You don't know. You can never say never." The door was always open. Eurythmics never broke up. We just stopped. But we always knew there was going to be more.

When we started writing songs for *Peace*, it was almost exactly how we did it with every other album, as if we'd never stopped. One song came tumbling out after another. "Seventeen Again," "Beautiful Child," "I Saved the World Today" and "Lifted."

We thought, *Now we've got a whole thing. But how should we present it?* We knew that anything we released was going to get a lot of attention, due to the fact that so much time had passed.

We called it *Peace*, and with that name and intention, we approached both Amnesty International and Greenpeace to work with us. As always, there were so many wars raging and so many things going wrong with the planet. We could use all the impact of our reunion publicity to shine the light on Greenpeace and Amnesty.

Simon Fuller was Annie's manager then, and rather than having multiple managers, we had him manage the entire project. We talked with him about the best way to do this, to benefit these two organizations while at the same time launching our album and tour. We arranged to give both Amnesty International and Greenpeace all the profits from the tour, the DVD and the merchandise. We also gave them a space in every venue to set up a booth with their material and information, to take it directly to our fans.

We had one of the first giant backlit screens behind us onstage. Nowadays they are very common, but at the time people had never seen anything like it. We brought in a friend of mine, the great British artist Tim Head, to create artwork for the screen. We used an effect where cameras were filming us in real time and the footage was being converted into filmic sequences on the backlit screen, and it looked like you were watching two movies at the same time. For the tour we wore sort of guerrilla camouflage suits that we had made, quite a refined look with PEACE on the red star symbol of Eurythmics.

Our goal was to do this tour in a way that would actually make money for Greenpeace and Amnesty International. There was no point in promising a lot of cash and then building an immense stage production that used up the money. With many charities, especially when such a complex organization is created, lots of people and officers are hired and paid so that in the end only a small percentage of the money ever gets out the other side. We didn't want that to happen, so Simon Fuller made sure that the tour would profit even though this wasn't the biggest tour we did—but it was vast, touching down in Australia, America, Europe and Japan.

I took Sam and Django with their teacher Mardette. Annie brought her children, Lola and Tali, who sometimes joined in with Sam and Django on their Travel School. Anoushka was there too, pregnant with Kaya. So I had a big sort of posse of children, nannies and teachers. But it was a great experience, and amazing for Sam and Django, who learned lots of things, as I like to think they do when we go anywhere.

Eurythmics commemorated the start of the new millennium by doing a show at the Royal Observatory in Greenwich, London, which is where measured earthly time officially originates, and exact mean solar time is established. It was the logical and perfect place to spark the year 2000. The whole world was waiting for Greenwich Mean Time, and we were there, with an orchestra. We played "Life on Mars" by David Bowie just before midnight, December 31, 1999. And when the song was over it was 2000.

Of course, time is an artificial division in eternity, right? My stepfather, Julian, told me, "Einstein and other geniuses have shown us that time isn't a fixed thing. It's relative. It stretches and shifts, like elastic. Even so, here we are celebrating with the entire world this momentous time shift."

I always remember that my son Sam, who was twelve then, liked being on the side of the stage and helping the guitar roadies with all the guitars. He was just gradually learning to play and he was fascinated. We did a sound check in Greenwich—and there were already thousands of people out front for the show—and Sam was playing the electric guitar, and suddenly he had a go with the wah-wah pedal.

The band heard what he was doing and started to join in—bass and drums and everything. I could see the excitement in Sam as his face lit up with astonishment. When he heard the bass and drum kick in, and it was in time with what he was playing, it was a big moment—a turning point for him. Sam went on to form his own band and

We were playing in the Roman ruins / In the town of Arles.
She said, *"Parlez-vous français?"* / I said, *"Oui, je parle."*
She asked me for some cigarettes. / I gave her my per diem.
Then she bought a pack of Gauloises
And we headed to the Coliseum. / Ooh, ooh, she was a Gypsy girl.

just wanted to play guitar and tour around France so I created a whole new identity: Dave Stewart & the Spiritual Cowboys. I had no master plan but suddenly I realized it was getting serious and I felt the need to experiment in other ways (*see over*).

(L to R) 1. Damien Hirst created my album artwork for *Greetings from the Gutter*. 2. With Gilbert & George. 3. Me and Damien Hirst. 4. With Bootsy Collins in NYC. 5. Lou Reed in my notorious Seven Dials apartment. 6. Bob Dylan through the lens of my 8mm cine camera. 7. Demi Moore in Goa, India. 8. Lou Reed and Laurie Anderson in my New York City apartment

L to R) 1. Filming Dylan inside London Café. 2. Filming outside a different café.
. Tom Petty looking pensive in my garden. 4. Tom and me having a banana break while
lming the video for "Don't Come Around Here No More."

(L to R) 1. Bono and me in Miami during a lost two weeks of nonstop songwriting. 2. Sharing a joke with Nelson Mandela. 3. The moment Mandela stepped out onstage at Greenpoint Stadium wearing "46664," his prison number, on his chest. The crowd went crazy and the moment was seen by more than one billion people on TV.

(L to R) 1. Jack Nicholson giving me some advice as Eurythmics' manager. 2. Jimmy Iovine when we lived together in 1984. 3. Writing and recording with both Jimmy Cliff and Joe Strummer. 4. With Paul Allen. We never stop sharing ideas. 5. The day I met Siobhan (on the right) for the first time, on the set of Eurythmics' "Who's That Girl" video. 6. Siobhan and me at a Eurythmics party in London. 7. George Harrison jamming all day in my Seven Dials apartment.

(L to R) 1. Wearing Andy Warhol's wig and taking notes from model Angie Hill and clothing designer Pam Hogue. 2. The entrance to my Seven Dials apartment. 3. Gwen Stefani during one of our writing sessions. 4. Katy Perry at the farm in Surrey. 5. Jon Bon Jovi while we were writing "Midnight in Chelsea."

L to R) 1. Anoushka taking a self-portrait backstage. 2. Anoushka and me just married by Deepak Chopra on the beach in France with baby Kaya on my knee. 3. Mick, Elton, Bono and our kids dancing at the wedding party. 4. Anoushka and me renewing our vows in Tahiti with John and Martina McBride. 5. Annie and Anoushka at the farm.

(L to R) 1. Me, Tony Blair, Bryan Ferry and Rory Bremner at my home in France. 2. Me and Bryan Ferry at the Hospital Club. 3. Filming Terry Hall in a French casino for no reason. 4. Kaya bringing the newspaper post-9/11 at Michael Philipp's house in New York. 5. About to perform "Happy to Be Here" on a popular British TV show called *TFI Friday* with my "backing singers" Natalie Imbruglia, Kylie Minogue and Sinéad O'Connor.

(L to R) 1. Superheavy in the studio. 2. Mick and I can't stop laughing during a photo shoot in 011. 3. Me and Mick in the south of France in 1991. 4. Martini moment. 5. Being tickled by ick and Joss.

(L to R) 1. Me and Stevie Nicks in 1983. 2. Me and Stevie 2010. 3. With Stevie filming "For What It's Worth." 4. The "shroom survivors": me and Daryl Hall. 5. My best pal, Ted Demme. 6. My other best pal, Brian Jobson, at the Ice House testing our pure Jamaican water.

(L to R) 1. Yes, I do take naps! 2. Dave Stewart's "Va Voom" a Rock 'n' Roll Circus (with a brave young Kaya riding the elephant). 3. Ringo and me writing a musical, *Hole in the Fence*. 4. Joss Stone and me in the studio, having a blast as always.

(L to R) 1. My wife, Anoushka, and the luckiest guy in the world! 2. My son Django James. 3. A young Django on Stevie Wonder's knee. 4. My children, Samuel, Kaya, Indya and Django—always an inspiration to me. 5. Kaya, age fifteen.

_ to R) 1. Indya Love. 2. Nida, my heroine. 3. Daddy and Indya. 4. Samuel Joseph Hurricane tewart. 5. Django James Lawless Stewart. 6. Kaya and Daddy jamming. 7. Kaya and Indya. . Django midflight in Travel School. 9. Sam and Daddy jamming. (Bottom Row:) Ned, my mazing music partner; Tony Quinn, family protector; and Allison J. Bond aka my Moneypenny.

became a fine musician and guitarist. This was the start. Soon he was constantly in the garage with friends, jamming, trying to learn Nirvana songs and making a great noise.

The Peace Tour was really interesting because unlike other shows, when we would do meet-and-greets with record label kind of guests, this was our chance to meet great activists who worked with both Amnesty and Greenpeace. We met people who had been political prisoners around the world, from China, Tibet or Russia, who were released because of Amnesty International. It was inspiring every night.

Anoushka was pregnant but managed to see every show on the Peace Tour. Eventually our first child, Kaya, a baby girl, was born on February 28, 2000.

This is a day I'll never forget. As I had been with my son Sam, I was very nervous about being present at the birth, and now I'd found out that Annie and our good friend Gina Gershon were both going to be present. I was starting to feel overwhelmed. I remember Anoushka being in labor for quite a long time, and I was downloading e-mails by her bedside. There was one particular e-mail from Carrie Fisher that just said, "Wish you were here." I thought it was going to be a holiday photo, so I started to download it but it appeared to be a very large file that would take a long time.

I decided to go downstairs in the hospital to rest for a little bit. What happened next is probably the most embarrassing moment of my life. I went back in the elevator to check on Anoushka, and when the doors opened, I was met with a very large, irate Jamaican midwife, who previously had been the sweetest person ever. She glared at me. I was in shock and didn't know what had happened.

I ran to the room, and Anoushka was staring at me. She pointed to the laptop. The lid was shut. I said, "What?" Then she explained that when the file downloaded, it was a movie that burst into action with loud gasping and screaming sounds. The laptop was facing away from her, so she didn't know what it was but the midwife could and it was the most extreme pornography that Carrie had sent as a joke. To Anoushka and the midwife, this was far from funny. Fortunately there were another twelve hours to go before Anoushka went into real labor. By that time I'd been forgiven, Annie and Gina had arrived, and I became the useless guy again watching another miracle.

With our little one in tow, we settled in back at the farm in Surrey, which again became a meeting place for all kinds of artists. We would have everybody from Liam Gallagher and Quincy Jones to Joe Strummer and the sisters Natalie and Nicole Appleton from the band All Saints, who had become great friends since I'd directed them in a feature film called *Honest*, a caper, a black comedy set in swinging London, in the late sixties, written with my good friends Ian La Frenais and Dick Clement. This may have been the only film that started getting bad reviews before we had even finished filming! My friend Lou Reed said a funny thing about all of the negative reviews: "Dave, the British press, first they want to fuck you up the arse, *but then* they want to piss in your face." That made me laugh at least enough to attend the premiere. Lou sat by me all the way through, and afterward we went for a stiff drink. I got completely slammed and felt shaken. A small reprieve came the next morning however, when *The Sunday Times* gave the film four stars and called it a "Cult Classic."

It was also at the farm where a young Katy Perry came to visit. She was writing songs for an album, and her producer Glen Ballard—who had produced *Jagged Little Pill* with Alanis Morissette—suggested she write songs with me for a week. During this time Katy stayed with us in the barn in Surrey, and we talked about many aspects of songwriting. I advised her to write down all the things she was going through to draw from her personal experiences, good or bad. Katy later revealed in an interview on UK TV that her career was kick-started as a result of our chat. Not long after that session, Katy wrote her first big hit, "I Kissed a Girl." I think she felt a bit freed after that.

Watching her grow from that week in Surrey into the global megastar she is today, pouring out her life story through her lyrics and eccentric videos, has been a wonder to watch. We wrote many songs together. One of them called "I'm Still Breathing," which is on her album *One of the Boys,* has the most beautiful chorus; it's a twisted song about a dead relationship, but with the beautiful melody and its juxtaposed lyrics, it reminds me of Eurythmics. Of course, one of the other songs we wrote together, "All I'm Selling Is Sex," didn't make the record but somehow it's all over the Internet.

Anoushka and I were married in August 2001. It was a secret wedding, and the most wonderful one you can imagine. Everybody who was there still talks about it; they had never seen anything like it.

Our friends suggested a beach café in the south of France, Mooréa Beach. And we held our wedding there. Tony Quinn organized the wedding with Annie's assistant, Tara Goldschmidt, in this extremely strict, high-security way, almost like a presidential event, so as to stop the paparazzi from coming to the wedding. We needed real security, because our guests would include Elton John, U2, Liam Gallagher and Nicole Appleton, Mick Jagger, Liam Howlett and Natalie Appleton, Dennis Hopper, Eric Idle and many others.

It was a beautiful wedding on the beach, with everybody glowing as the sun set. We stood on a small platform above the sea covered in leaves and flowers. Deepak Chopra performed the ceremony, and our vows were written especially for us by Neale Walsch, the author of *Conversations with God.* Paul Allen was my best man and gave a hilarious speech. We served a drink that Bono, the Edge and I used to drink a lot when we hung out at Mooréa Beach: a rum base with South American organic hallucinogenic drug properties in it. So everybody at the wedding drank this drink, and it is a very up drink, sort of like organic Ecstasy.

Suddenly everyone was dancing and singing and loving each moment. We had an amazing band playing, and we all jammed. Bono and Mick Jagger both got up to sing, and I remember Mick doing an amazing version of "Little Red Rooster." Bono actually wrote a twenty-minute song, on the spot, dedicated to me and Anoushka, with me and the Edge backing him on guitar. The whole song was based around something the Irish poet Brendan Behan said: "Friendship is higher than love." Bono's performance was an amazing finale to our wedding, with all of our friends, from all over the world, joining in and singing along with the chorus he had come up with.

CHAPTER:18

JIMMY

After our long history together, when Jimmy Iovine calls to see if I will work on something, I'm always game. Sixteen years after first meeting Tom Petty, Stevie Nicks and many others through his introductions, I was still getting Jimmy's calls. In 2001, I'd been living in London on and off for the previous ten years, when he called to say No Doubt was in town and they wanted to come around and see me. I was intrigued because Sophie Muller, the genius video director who made Eurythmics' *Savage* video album and many others, also directed No Doubt videos, including the Grammy Award–winning one for "Don't Speak." I remember seeing it for the first time and thinking the band would be huge.

I had also seen them not long before that call from Jimmy, and I distinctly remember Tony Kanal and Gwen Stefani sneaking into our sound check and watching Annie and me perform as a duo at the opening of Paul Allen's Experience Music Project in Seattle. It struck me for some reason that they were almost like a mirror image—I knew that they must have been one of the few couples in the world who had experienced anything like what Annie and I had been through—being a couple, breaking up, then becoming huge as a music group, going through that roller coaster times ten because of the emotional situation. "Don't Speak" is such a great song melodically, and when it came out, the lyrics resonated so strongly with my own situation at the time.

My penthouse apartment in Covent Garden had become kind of infamous. Every day there would be constant beeps on the video intercom that also appeared on thirty-two screens arranged as sculptures on the walls inside. Most of the time I never knew who was going to come up on the screen and now I wish I'd always had an instant photo taken to remember. It could be members of the band Blur, Joe Strummer or Sam Mendes, who was artistic director of the Donmar Warehouse round the corner at the time. The artists Tracey Emin and Sarah Lucas or the late Angus Fairhurst would be shooting an art piece on the roof garden at the same time George Harrison was teaching me "This Guitar (Can't Keep from Crying)" in the circular tower.

The doorman Sean McDermott from the Ivy Restaurant around the corner would very kindly bring guests to see me. He was always ringing the bell, saying, "Mr. Helmut Newton to see you," or "Jerry Hall and Marie Helvin here, sir." It's impossible to explain, but there are a few photographs in this book that give you a glimpse. So you can see how strange it must have been for Tony, Gwen and their bandmate Tom Dumont to walk into this world.

When they arrived, it took them a while to get used to the surroundings, and it probably didn't help that I was obsessed with the Internet and was ranting about how we as artists would create worlds (the pre-apps). I was showing them all this 3-D virtual-world stuff and being a bit manic; then I noticed two hours had passed and I hadn't shut up. So we went upstairs to the studio, where my engineer Ned Douglas had programmed an idea I had created earlier with a reggae groove; as always Ned was there, ready and waiting for the madness to begin.

I sensed it would be difficult to just start writing something en masse, so I suggested Gwen and I go down to the kitchen with an acoustic guitar just to start something. I always find it easier to write with just one instrument and a singer rather than a whole band or masses of equipment. It was a little awkward at first because I was thinking she thought I was a nutcase, like Willy Wonka on acid or something. She was so used to writing with Tony or the band. Within minutes, though, the ice was broken, and I don't really remember what happened or how it happened, but in about fifteen minutes, we went back upstairs, saying, "We've finished it!" "Underneath It All" was born.

I must say Tony was very cool and open to this new collaborative situation, and he started laying down his bass (he's a great bass player—so precise yet with a great feel). The guitar player Tom Dumont seemed quite shy but he started experimenting, and the track was beginning to sound great. My son Django, who was eight at the time, started doing his saxophone lesson downstairs with his teacher, and we could hear it. I thought this would sound good because it would be slightly wonky, so I shouted down for them to come up and play on it, and you can hear Django on the record tooting away! We must have stopped around seven p.m., and we had the whole blueprint of the song, with all the verses, bridge and choruses and Gwen's guide vocal sounding really good.

It turns out I have another thing in common with No Doubt, which is we are all crazy about Jamaica. So it was like six degrees of separation when No Doubt then decided to record "Underneath It All" and most of the album *Rock Steady* there. Brian Jobson and his brother, Wayne, helped put their Jamaican experience together. Sly and Robbie (who I'd met through Jimmy Cliff) produced the song with No Doubt and used bits of the original demo along with their amazing production. Brian and Wayne were given executive production credits, so it was a bit like a family affair.

Now, years ago, I'd heard a virtually unknown female dance hall artist called Lady Saw and was so impressed with her that even though I was leaving Jamaica that day, I arranged to meet her in Kingston at the airport, as I wanted to sign her to my indie label Anxious Records. So I was overjoyed to hear she had laid down a vocal in the breakdown section of "Underneath It All."

When I heard the finished mix, I was ecstatic. The song became a huge hit in the USA, and I traveled with No Doubt in the limo to the Grammys when the song won Best Group with a Vocal. They also won the Video Music Award for best video and MTV's Viewers' Choice Award and Teen Choice Award for best single.

No Doubt is an amazing band live. Watching Adrian Young play drums is a whole experience in itself. They were riding high with that album and the live rendition of "Underneath It All" on the DVD of the Rock Steady Tour is brilliant.

Since then Gwen and I have written a couple of other songs together. One song called "Sparkle" again works great onstage with a stripped-down arrangement. Gwen really has great melodic sensibility and uses her subconscious to express herself lyrically. She sings free-form stream-of-consciousness at first, but there are always words that appear to be coming from an emotional place. She then quickly understands what she wants to say and it all falls into place.

"Underneath It All" was an example of this, and I saw it happen in real time right there in my Covent Garden kitchen. I could see what was going through her mind, and she nailed it in the song there and then. When we spontaneously wrote the song "Sparkle," she was crying while singing it, as it was so emotional. I always imagined it with just acoustic guitar, her voice and an orchestra. One day perhaps.

CHAPTER:19

THE CALL

Not long after Kaya was born, Anoushka and I were in the south of France looking at the home of the artist Marc Chagall as a possible residence for us. We were walking around this beautiful home, and I realized that I couldn't walk up the stairs. I told my wife there was something wrong with me, and they got a car to take me back to the little hotel where we were staying.

Poor Anoushka. Kaya was a new baby then, and now here I was, lying on the bed, in trouble. She felt there was something really wrong with me because I wasn't mentally awake. I remember none of this, but she remembers it clearly, as it was terrifying for her. I was talking but making no sense, drenched in sweat, like the worst fever.

She rang the hotel, and because she is French and can speak the language, they helped us quickly. It was a Sunday, and normally getting a doctor on a Sunday is impossible. I went to the bathroom to pee and it was all blood. She called my doctor in London to describe what was happening, and he told her to get me on a medi-jet immediately and fly back to London, because, as he said, "There's something drastically wrong. You can't admit him to a French hospital that doesn't have any of his records." He said, "Get the strongest antibiotics from the doctor there, have him take them and get him on the next plane."

So there I was, on a stretcher in the medi-jet, on my way back to England, with Anoushka, Kaya and all these paramedics on the plane, just in case something went wrong. I was falling in and out of consciousness, peeing blood, with a high fever. It wasn't good. On the plane the doctor kept me on some kind of drip during the flight, testing me every half hour or whatever. As soon as the plane landed, I was rushed into the hospital, where I stayed for five days, being administered the strongest antibiotics known to man. At one point I noticed Annie was there. She might have been there for a few hours. I'm not sure, as I was drifting in and out of sleep and consciousness. I felt Annie there, but I could have been dreaming that she massaged my feet. That had a very calming effect, because when you're in that state, you are incredibly tense with all of these antibiotics and drugs going through your system. The massage allowed me to go to sleep.

Then, in 2002, while I was till shaky from the illness, I was approached to help Nelson Mandela do something about the AIDS crisis in Africa. "AIDS is no longer a disease," he said. "It's a human rights issue."

I knew I had to come up with something innovative to get people's attention, so I flew there with Roger Taylor and Brian May from Queen for preliminary meetings with Mr. Mandela's people. At first everyone was talking about putting on a concert, but on a call with Mr. Mandela, I suggested using his prison number, 46664, as a telephone number with a prefix that people could dial in to hear him talk, and also hear songs especially written and recorded by famous artists. These would be songs that you could not hear anywhere else, and while you were listening, you were automatically donating to the cause.

Mr. Mandela liked the idea, and when we got back to the UK, I immediately set about doing it. But unfortunately when I was in South Africa, I had caught a respiratory infection, mycoplasma pneumonia.

I had been in a shantytown where the poorest people were residing, in the suburbs of the suburbs of Cape Town. There was a lot of illness, like AIDS and diphtheria. I was in a place with sick and orphaned children. It wasn't a hospital, really, just a big room with some medicine. I hadn't taken any of the proper shots you're meant to take before going to Africa.

When I got back to England, I kept feeling worse, more tired every day, with no energy at all. I knew something was obviously, drastically wrong. I went to the hospital, and they found that I had an infection of the lungs. I couldn't do anything for months. It was like having the flu times a hundred. Slowly I built up just enough strength to get back to work on the 46664 telephone idea.

The first person I called to write lyrics for the title song "46664" was Joe Strummer, but not long after he sent them to me, he unexpectedly passed away. I had them handwritten on paper by Joe and the words leapt off the page.

When Freedom rises from the killing floor
No lock of iron or rivet can restrain the door
And no kind of army can hope to win a war
It's like trying to stop the rain or steal the lion's roar
It's like trying to stop the whirlwind scattering seeds and spores
Like trying to stop the tin cans rattling jailhouse semaphore
Like they know when these hands are manacled it's your spirit that
  gets raw
It's not the small patch of sky you see but the spirit as it soars

U2 loved the Clash, so I flew to Dublin and went in the studio with Bono and the Edge to finish the song. We were talking about Joe and playing the backing track I'd made when I handed Joe's handwritten words to Bono. The Edge was playing guitar, and Bono started singing as if he were channeling Joe. It was an incredible moment. I filmed some of this recording session, and the next day back in the UK, I went to see Richard Branson at his house along with Roger and Brian. I explained the telephone idea, and Richard was fantastic. Not only did he come on board immediately with Virgin Mobile, but he offered to donate Virgin airline planes to fly performers to the concert.

With this great news, I started to write and record other songs, one with Paul McCartney and another one with Brian May, Roger Taylor and Anastacia. Not long after I got back from Ireland, I received a call in the middle of the night from Bono that led to one of the craziest songwriting experiences of my life. He was very excited and talking in a mixed flow of poetry and stream of consciousness about African history; about Ghana and the role of Indian Prime Minister Nehru; about Mandela and his incarceration at Robben Island. All of this was sparking in his mind lines like "Let's not kick out the darkness. Let's make the light brighter."

He was also talking about how the sea separates us but also joins us together through lines like "This is the ground that keeps our feet from getting wet." It was impossible for me to take it all in, so I told him to stop while my wife found something to record what we were doing. Bono was singing into the speakerphone, with me on the other end playing acoustic guitar. I wanted a way to remember the great lines and what I was playing.

Anoushka came back five minutes later, and all she could find was a video camera, so I have exactly nineteen minutes and eleven seconds of videotape of my knee, the telephone, and a corner of an acoustic guitar, but at least we have it on tape. Bono and I decided to meet in Los Angeles the next day, and when we hung up, I realized it already was the next day. After a few hours' sleep, I was on my way to Heathrow Airport, and at around eight p.m., I was at the Chateau Marmont on Sunset Boulevard, so exhausted I passed out.

First thing the next morning, Bono called to say he'd be at my room around two p.m. I had a great little four-track recorder, so before Bono arrived, I made a backing track with a drum machine, acoustic guitar and cheap organ sound that I thought would work for our song.

Here was where it got complicated. Bono knocked on the door and within seconds we were carrying on the same conversation we'd had on the phone. I played him the demo, and he liked the atmosphere and chord changes, so I recorded him singing the song sketch onto the remaining fourth track. The words, chords and melody sounded like an anthem, and this was the basis for "American Prayer." It was very subtle and got under your skin. Bono was crafting the words in a way that would make people think about the fact that America as a concept, the bedrock of equality, was a truly great idea. Yet with this great idea something had gotten lost along the way; something had gone awry. Bono said in an interview not long after we started composing the song that he was writing it as "a person who has rediscovered the poetry of the Declaration of Independence and the taut truth in the Constitution."

That evening we went to visit Dr. Dre at his studio in the Valley and an amazing new song got started that at the time was called "Treason." We ended up recording it with the Gateway Ambassador singers, a group of young musicians from Ghana. These talented kids were all orphans and about to go on the road with Bono for the Heartland of America Tour, generating support in the fight against AIDS.

The next morning we were blasting out "American Prayer" and "Treason" at full volume in Bono's suite on top of the Chateau Marmont, with Bobby Shriver and two activists from Bono's ONE organization. We eventually got down to writing and practically finished the song then and there. We decided that Bono and I should fly that night to Miami and ask Bruce Springsteen to help work on our song and sing it.

We arrived in Miami a bit the worse for wear around nine a.m. and headed for the hotel. We met up with Chris Blackwell around four p.m. and drove to Bruce's sound check at the American Airlines Arena where he was playing that night. When we arrived, Bruce was onstage rehearsing, so we hung around until he came off, then went into his dressing room and started telling him our idea. We played him the song sketch acoustically, but he was distracted, as he was getting ready to do a show.

We ended up playing with him onstage, doing "Because the Night," which he had written with Patti Smith. It was a great experience, except I forgot about the key change in the middle section, and that was the exact point Bruce nodded for me to take a guitar solo. . . . Panic! But I pulled it off. With zero sleep for the last three days.

We booked a studio in Miami and finished the song with Bono singing a rough lead vocal. Then Aaron Lewis from Staind, who was next door, came in to listen and sang a harmony as I added more guitar.

"American Prayer" was starting to sound like a record, and this was when we kicked it into overdrive. The next thing I remember is Bono and me laughing hysterically in the elevator at the Hit Factory in New York, because we couldn't believe we'd invited all of these people! We had Beyoncé, Pharrell Williams and the Edge all there; every floor had someone working on the song or making a different version of the song. We kept going up and down, and whenever the elevator stopped, we quickly pressed a button to close the door, laughing too much to get out.

Suddenly I was in one room with Beyoncé as she was listening and taking notes, and I was on acoustic guitar, showing Pharrell Williams the chords so the Neptunes could do a different version. Then Pharrell went to work out a new way of doing the song with Beyoncé. Meanwhile, Jimmy Iovine and U2's manager, Paul McGuinness, were meeting with the heads of the NFL to discuss the idea of doing the song at the Super Bowl halftime show. Oprah and her whole film crew were filming everything, and J-Lo and other stars coming in just to see what was going on.

That was an amazing day. This was all happening because of one song and its journey!

Sadly, Luther Vandross died the day after he sang on that song. It was the last note on the song, and the last thing he ever sang, the words "Remember me." We tried to get the NFL to agree to let us perform this song for the halftime show, but the last thing they wanted was something so radically progressive and political. They attempt always to avoid anything potentially divisive. But Bono is so brilliant and persuasive that they sat there and listened. And then Oprah Winfrey said she was all for it, and all of those guys love Oprah.

There ultimately was a big concert on November 29, 2003, called 46664, the Mandela Concert. It was an amazing event at the giant Green Point Stadium in Cape Town, South Africa, which holds about sixty-five thousand people. At the concert Peter Gabriel performed his moving song "Biko" for the first time in Africa. We played our song that night and called it "African Prayer." I did it with Edge, both of us on acoustic guitars, Bono and Beyoncé on vocals. Oprah Winfrey flew in for that as well. That song was also used in the Obama presidential campaign, and when election results were coming in on TV, showing his victory, the song was playing.

Africa—and the Mandela experience—changed Annie's life. She is one of those people who is an absolutely brilliant singer, brilliant songwriter and brilliant musician. As the world knows, she is a genius in many respects, but she can also be quite insecure and troubled. But on the morning after the concert in Cape Town, she came to see me and Anoushka over breakfast and she was ecstatic, radiant, and said, "I found my whole meaning and purpose. I've actually found it." Which was ironic, because she was one of the first people asked to come and she said no. She wasn't going to come at first, but she changed her mind and it changed her life.

CHAPTER:20

PHEOCHROMOCYTOMA

I n the early 2000s, I'd started working more consistently in America. It had begun to become too much going back and forth. I had bought a house on Kings Road in Los Angeles, just off the Sunset Strip, and had been writing songs there and doing film music scores. We made a family decision to leave England and move to America.

Unfortunately, as we were about to do the move, I became very ill again and was going downhill fast. I knew that I needed to have some kind of operation and was unsure whether to get to the USA and have it or delay our move and stay in the UK. As I got sicker and sicker, it got urgent. Paul Allen made some calls to specialists in Los Angeles to get their opinions, then offered to take me there in his plane, and my doctor agreed to come with me.

We got to the USA, with me getting worse on the plane, and went home to rest before seeing Gary Gitnick, the head of the digestive department of UCLA Hospital at nine a.m. the next morning. I arrived with my suitcase packed and was ready to check into the hospital when Gary said, "Hang on. We don't know what's wrong with you yet!"

So my English doctor came and stayed for two days to make sure that he passed over every single piece of medical history, because I was moving there, not just visiting.

Dr. Gitnick was intensely busy, but he talked to me for about ninety minutes nonstop, asking what seemed to me the most bizarre questions—questions that seemed disconnected to me. I trusted he knew what he was doing, and I went through the whole thing.

Gary sent me for a whole battery of tests, blood tests, scans, everything. Then he said, "Right, tell you what. Here's what it is. You've got diverticulitis and you need to have an operation, because this condition could result in your blood being poisoned. Diverticulitis is the thinning of the intestinal wall, and something that's not digestible, like a seed, can get caught in it and irritate it. Then it can actually poke a hole through the intestine, which results in an infection that goes into the bloodstream, leading to peritonitis and blood poisoning, from which you can die.

"But," he added, "loads of people have it, and it's an easy operation, so I wouldn't worry about it. There's one other thing. In all this list of questions that you've answered, I've noticed there's a little pattern here. You have panic attacks. So I want you to see Dr. Pejman Cohan. He's an endocrinologist, and I want him to do this other series of tests."

It was true. For about five years, before going to Africa, I would have panic attacks. They came at random times, not while I was even doing something that panic-worthy. I could be lying in bed, reading a book, and my heart would suddenly start beating superfast. I'd go to the doctor and the hospital, but they couldn't find anything wrong.

Now I was thinking, *Oh, my God, more tests?* I started thinking I'd gone bonkers and was paranoid. On the other hand, I knew there was something wrong with me. So Dr. Cohan gave me all these weird tests. At the same time, Dr. Gitnick had put me on the strongest oral antibiotics you can take so I would be strong enough for the operation. It made me feel ill taking them.

So here I was, having just arrived in America, and I was on all these medications. I had Sam and Django coming to see me, and I wanted to take them to Hawaii for a holiday. All the antibiotics kept me stable, so I asked Dr. Gitnick if I could go on this holiday. He said, "It's not really advisable, but I do know the head guy in the Hawaii hospital. He's my counterpart there, and I'm going to tell him you're coming. If you feel ill, you can just go straight in there."

So I went to Hawaii with Anoushka and my sons, and it wasn't easy. I'd be trying to take the boys surfing, but I had no energy and couldn't surf myself. I was just watching, and trying to be a regular parent, but feeling a bit pear-shaped. On Christmas Eve I got a phone call from Dr. Cohan. "Hey, we found out something. The operation you're going to have for diverticulitis—you can't have that yet. First we have to do these other two major tests."

I said, "God, why?"

He replied, "Well, we found that you've got a growth on your adrenal gland."

I was in the car with the kids, trying to whisper, "A growth? On my adrenal gland? That doesn't sound good."

They determined I had pheochromocytoma, a rare disease caused by a growth on the adrenal gland. Dr. Cohan said, "It could be the reason you're having panic attacks. The adrenal gland stores adrenaline— also known as epinephrine—and due to the growth, it can be shooting this through your body, which is how you can have a stroke. You have to get straight on these beta-blocker tablets of the strongest variety. If your gland shoots epinephrine, they will stop you having a heart attack."

I was floored. So now I was on antibiotics and these beta-blockers and I was in Hawaii. I could hardly move.

Somehow we got through Christmas and went back to UCLA, where I had to go through another whole series of tests. The doctors needed to remove the growth on my adrenal gland. This is not a straightforward operation, because again, if anything goes wrong, you can have a stroke.

"Well, okay!"

"So," Dr. Cohan went on, "we need this particular surgeon and this particular anesthesiologist, and they are always busy because there's only a few of them that will do this kind of operation."

I said, "Wow. So, hang on. I have to have that operation first?"

He said, "Yeah, because we don't want to do the main operation for diverticulitis and risk the chance that you will have a stroke due to the growth. It's too dangerous."

I said, "Well, how about I have both operations at the same time and just start with that one and then do the other one? To recover from an operation and then be ready to go have another operation is going to be a bit tough on me."

The doctors all discussed it and said, "Okay, we think we can do that. Because we're going to do what they call endoscopic surgery, where rather than cut you open, we insert a scope. So it won't be too invasive, compared to normal surgery."

The day of my surgery arrived. On the morning when you're going to have an operation, you feel partly calm and partly panicked, because you know this is going to be something—but I had no idea how heavy it was going to be. Normally they give you drugs to put you into a premed dreamy state, like when you're getting your tooth pulled. I was waiting for those when they said, "We're coming to get you now, but first we have to shave around the area."

I said, "Hey, am I going to get one of those premed drugs?" I was getting quite anxious.

They said, "Yes, don't worry."

Then they injected something in my neck, and said, "Count backward from ten." I think I got to nine. Whatever they gave me, it knocked me so far out I didn't wake up for sixteen hours. They had told my wife, Anoushka, that this operation was going to be maybe four hours. Seven hours into it, she was still ringing the hospital and was told, "He's still in surgery."

What happened was, the first part of the surgery, the most dangerous part, went all right. But the second part was a nightmare, where they inserted a scope, this intrusive piece of metal, up my butt. Instead of stitching intestines in the old-fashioned way, nowadays they cut it with the scope, and then they insert a rivet to seal it up. When I came to, it felt like I'd been run over by a truck.

Dr. Cohan said, "Do you want to know the good news or the bad news?"

"The good news."

"Well, the good news is that the surgery was a success and the operation went perfectly. The bad news, though, is that your anus is sixteen millimeters wide and this metal disc we tried to put up there is eighteen millimeters, and we just spent two hours trying to get it up there. So I'm afraid you're going to be in some pain."

Ouch! That was an understatement. When the drugs wore off, it was hell. I'd never felt anything like that and hope I never do again. In retrospect, I can see how all things are connected, but at the time it was all a bit of a mystery, trust me, to have some random, obscure thing called a pheochromocytoma. I still can't say the word properly but very thankful they discovered it. I kept saying I was ill, but when you're a bit of a hypochondriac, no one believes you—I felt like copying the epitaph that Spike Milligan had had carved onto his gravestone: I TOLD YOU I WAS ILL.

During this time I had been going backward and forward to America, working on this project with the great singer and songwriter Kara DioGuardi—a project that had turned into the faux band Platinum Weird. We had actually made the album and finished it. We filmed five black-and-white videos of us, in rehearsal, the last day before I had to have the operation.

Kara came to see me four days after the operation, when I was in a rehab facility. She came in and said, "What the fuck?" I had a video-editing suite in my room. I was editing what we filmed five days before I had the operation. She said, "I can't believe it. Like, how can you even think straight?" Of course I probably couldn't. Then they let me out of hospital, and my friend Glen Ballard very sweetly offered me this little house on the beach in Malibu that he had owned for years.

By this time, Anoushka had moved with Kaya and our newborn daughter, Indya, into my house on Kings Road just off the Sunset Strip. Indya was such a sharp, bright toddler that she could adapt to anything but my recovery was so intense that I couldn't adapt to being there at all. Having two small children and people coming and going with furniture was too much for me. Everything was chaotic. It wasn't like coming back to the home you'd lived in for years. We were basically moving into a new place. Also, you couldn't walk on the street—it was a typical LA street with no sidewalk.

But at Glen's beach house, I could step outside and walk along the beach, which was the best possible thing for me; the sea air and walking in the sand helped me get my strength back. I could measure my progress in how far I could walk, adding a little more each day. On about the fifth day, I walked all the way to Bono and Ali's house and had a cup of tea with Ali, and then walked all the way back. Each day, I got to feel slightly better.

Ali suggested I go see U2 perform in town to get my mind off things, so Kara and I rented a limousine to celebrate me feeling better and set off for the gig. We went straight in the back to where the members of U2 park their cars at the concert. We said hello to the band backstage, and they were very sweet and concerned about my recovery (I looked about half my usual weight). Then Kara and I went on the side of the stage, in a kind of special enclosure.

Of course, U2 started a full-on rock show in front of thousands of people. I'd just been wrapped in cotton wool in the hospital and then in this tiny little beach house. I started to sort of faint from exhaustion. Anybody who's reading this who's had major surgery realizes that you don't understand how exhausted and how much energy you've lost after an operation.

So I turned around to Kara and I went, "Uh-oh."

She went, "Oh no, you're gonna faint, aren't you?"

I remember she was shouting at this security guy to get his help, but he thought she was just a fan. And she's going, "No, look, Dave, my friend, he's not well."

They couldn't hear a thing because the sound of the Edge's guitar was like jet engines. Eventually the security guy realized what had happened, and we went backstage. Within ten minutes of U2's opening song, there I was, backstage with an oxygen mask and all the paramedics at the gig. It took me a while to get used to the fact that I couldn't just go and do normal things. It took literally a full year to recover from the surgery.

I also stayed for about a week at a little old-fashioned hotel on the beach in Santa Monica. Paul Allen would come every day and take a walk with me. Of course, walking just a few yards was exhausting, but he was really sweet, because he'd been through recovering from cancer and Hodgkin's disease and he'd had a few operations. Paul knew what it was like, trying to readjust back into normal activities. What we think are normal activities, when you're ill, you realize, *Jesus—you need a lot of energy to do that.*

My first week back at home, Imogen Heap came to visit me with her manager, and was really sweet. As I mentioned, I produced her first album in Jamaica. She's an amazing singer-songwriter. They were chatting about whether to do a record deal for their new project. I remember nearly fainting, just chatting. Anything that was too over-stimulating, any kind of serious brainwork, was as tiring as anything physical.

Needless to say, it was a really bad year. It was really hard for Anoushka too. Moving to a new country, into a new house with small children, and getting one of them into a preschool were exhausting and stressful. That year slowly ended, and it brought on a really great change in our lives when we found a new house in Toluca Lake. I started to feel better. I began, at last, to feel energized.

This was now 2008. I was thinking about what was next. Glen

Ballard had a little recording studio on Hollywood Boulevard, and I rented the space next door. We had an adjoining door.

As I fully recovered, I think Glen realized, "Oh my God, Dave's got so much energy and so many things going on!" I started to work again and write songs with people, and I started a company and called it Weapons of Mass Entertainment, and chaos, happily, would reign again.

CHAPTER:21

PLATINUM WEIRD

All my experience working with Annie in the trenches, writing and producing such a vast amount of songs and records, put me in a great place to work with other artists. I came to them with the same joy with which Annie and I worked—a fearless sense of adventure that always led to new songs and new records. It was a good spirit to share with so many of my peers—people like Stevie Nicks and Mick Jagger—who were accustomed to writing only within their bands and with a lot of pressure. As Mick said, I took all the angst out of the process and reminded everyone that songwriting—and playing music—is about fun. When you connect with that fun, it goes a long way. And so I have found myself in the very lucky position of making music with many of the great musicians of our time.

Much of that journey began because of my friendship with Jimmy Iovine, who in turn led me to some of my favorite people and now best friends.

I'm not really a hired gun as a songwriter, as many people are. I never set out to be a record producer or a songwriter, but I just seem to be in situations where I meet someone and then we're playing guitars and a song starts. This has happened to me on so many occasions, and I want to take you through some songwriting stories—adventures in films, musicals, TV, theater and forming bands.

On one such occasion I wrote a song called "Taking Chances" with Kara DioGuardi. It became the center of Céline Dion's first release, in 2007, after her five-year stint at Caesars Palace in Las Vegas. It is the title of her album, her first single from that album and the name of her world tour. All of this was unplanned, and I would never have thought in my wildest imagination that it would happen! Kara and I wrote the song in the most bizarre circumstances.

I first met Kara in 2004, and guess who was to blame. Yep, Jimmy Iovine up to his old tricks again. I was in my Surrey farmhouse when Jimmy called and asked me to look at something on the Web called the Pussycat Dolls, an alternative burlesque cabaret-type show that had special appearances by artists such as Christina Aguilera and Gwen Stefani. Jimmy was going to buy this concept to make it much bigger and wanted to send over two or three of the girls to figure out what the show could be musically. I found the prospect quite interesting, as I'd just written the music for a German musical in Vienna, a very erotic and surrealistic version of *Barbarella*.

The next day, two very jet-lagged girls, Nicole Scherzinger and Kaya Jones, arrived. Here I was thinking in very old Berlin cabaret theatrical terms as reference; little was I to know it was going to morph into a sex show with a hip-hop beat.

After a couple of days, Jimmy called to say he was sending a "spitfire" writer for the Pussycat Dolls, and she arrived in the name of Kara DioGuardi. We recorded in the newly finished studio in the Hospital Club in Covent Garden.

Kara and I were two opposites, like chalk and cheese. I have no idea why, but we hit it off straightaway and after a couple of hours walked down the street to Coco de Mer (a very high-end erotic emporium that I was creatively involved with and co-owned with the

Roddick family). Kara and I bought some leather handcuffs and re-mained handcuffed together the rest of the day. It was bloody difficult at our Nobu dinner, eating sushi, drinking miso soup and swallowing cups of sake. By the end of the meal, we were laughing hysterically and were a little worse for wear. Lucian Grainge, head of Universal UK, seemed most intrigued by us.

The next day a strange thing happened. Kara and I wrote a song in three minutes, all in one take, called "Be Somebody to Love." Throughout the song we were looking at each other and knew some-thing was happening that had nothing to do with the Pussycat Dolls.

This was two people from completely different worlds and back-grounds speaking the same hybrid language. That spark of a song was enough for me to know there was going to be an adventure here, a future history, and boy, was I right in more ways than one.

Kara and I decided to get together in Los Angeles to mess around with some ideas for the Pussycat Dolls, since Kara was feeling guilty that Jimmy's Interscope label had paid for her trip to Europe. We'd meet in the basement of my small house off Sunset and just talk. When-ever we tried to write anything, it always turned out to be a hybrid of her and me, and nothing like a Pussycat song. We just couldn't help it; we were writing furiously and practically had a whole album of "our" songs in ten days. Jimmy wanted to see what we were up to, and Kara was a little nervous, to say the least, as he was coming to hear songs for the Dolls.

By then we had decided in our heads we were really a band or a duo. I wasn't worried at all because I knew we had written great songs and that the demos sounded great, as I was working with Ned Douglas, my trusted engineer and programmer, who is amazing and the fastest I've ever worked with. Jimmy arrived, sat and listened to a couple of the songs with Kara looking nervously on, and he kept saying, "Play me another," then another, and after about seven songs, he said, "Wow, you two are a band!" He didn't even mention the Pussycat Dolls!

Kara asked Jimmy if he was sure we didn't sound too weird, and

Jimmy said, "Yeah, Platinum Weird." Kara and I were relieved, and the next thing we knew, we were signed to Interscope and in the studio with John Shanks making the album. John is an amazing producer and his studio is "guitar heaven." We made the whole album in four weeks and on the last day shot seven live videos on a soundstage, which is what I was editing in my room while recovering from my major surgery, much to Kara's astonishment.

Nobody has ever heard our album . . . yet! People have seen our black-and-white films on YouTube and a VH1 documentary on my early seventies original Platinum Weird and how it links Kara and me, who were destined to meet, but no one's heard the music. The documentary features Mick Jagger, Elton John, Christina Aguilera, Bob Geldof, Dhani Harrison, Stevie Nicks, Ringo Starr, even Lindsay Lohan and Paris Hilton! They all talk about Platinum Weird's influence on music and fashion. It seems totally authentic but is a complete fabrication written by Ian La Frenais. There is even a limited edition of a seventies demo album floating around that Interscope released, and bootleg cassette recordings, fan sites of the original Platinum Weird with old reviews from *NME* and old ticket stubs, all parts of the fake backstory, but to this day our "real album" has never been released. I still have mischievous plans afoot for the feature film using our music and the story based around Erin Grace, the original singer who "disappeared" in the seventies.

"Taking Chances" started out as a Platinum Weird song that Kara and I wrote in ten minutes one crazy afternoon at her house. Kara is very speedy and loud (we joke about this, as I'm so soft-spoken). She is also very funny, and we laugh a lot when we are together. Once, I was lying on the sofa, watching her direct a whole load of furniture being delivered to her new home in Los Angeles. She'd say, "No, not over there," or "Hey, watch the staircase," as these burly guys struggled with sofas and beds. Meanwhile, I could hear some wind chimes just outside the open window where I was lying, so I picked up an acoustic guitar and was trying to play the same random pattern the chimes were making.

Kara is a genius with melody and with multitasking, so while she's shouting to the movers, she starts singing, "Don't know much about your life," much to the confusion of the guys carrying the furniture. It was like a scene from a musical. As the furniture was piling in, she was singing, "What do you say to taking chances? What do you say to jumping off the edge?" We were swapping lyrics, melodies and chords in real time while all this chaos was around us. The song was written about ourselves trusting each other and baring our souls, about committing to making something special even though we knew we were this odd couple who had no other reason to do it other than we loved it. The whole song was virtually completed in front of these guys moving furniture around, almost like a slow-motion dance routine.

After we recorded the song with John Shanks, he played it to Céline Dion and her husband, René, and they told me that from the minute they heard the song, they wanted to record it as a single. And not only that, but they wanted to use it as the new album title and the name of her world tour, her first in years since her appearances at Caesars Palace in Vegas. All this was a bit of a surprise, but even more of a surprise was having René call me as I was walking down Hollywood Boulevard to my studio. He said, "Hey, Dave, we love the song, and we are shooting a video. Here, I have Céline for you."

Céline was gracious and complimentary of the song, saying how much she loved it and that they wanted me to be in the video. By the time I got upstairs to my office, the video script had already arrived. The video was to be directed by Paul Boyd, a marvelous Scottish filmmaker with whom I have made many films. I saw how it could work, with me appearing as this mysterious man at the beginning and the end of the video, so I agreed to do it. Little did I know I was going to have a motorcycle driving straight at me at seventy miles per hour, then skidding to a halt three feet away.

It took at least twenty takes, and I mumbled something about insurance, but it was too late. We were in the middle of the desert, and it was about 105 degrees. Céline had to wear a PVC catsuit, so after every take, we'd both jump back into a car with the AC on full blast. The shoot went on into the night, and when I was finished, I went to Céline's penthouse suite at Caesars. René and I were talking on the roof garden overlooking all the lights of Vegas, and as I turned to leave, I heard Céline singing, "Never knowing if there's solid ground below. Or a hand to hold or hell to pay. What do you say?" As I made my way back through the wall of tourists, drifters and obsessive gamblers searching for some Lady Luck among a sea of numbers, slot machines and neon promises, those last words ringing in my ears seemed even more poignant.

The other extreme from Vegas, I think, would be the first time I met Paul McCartney. It was in Jamaica around Christmas 2002, when he invited Siobhan, Sam and Django and me for a New Year's Eve party at his house on a hill outside of Montego Bay. He seemed completely relaxed and content. When we arrived we realized we were the only guests and there was nothing to do, really, so we all got stoned and it turned into the best time. We ended up all in the bedroom and Paul had an electric piano there and he was singing "Maybe I'm Amazed" and many other McCartney classics. Everyone was in a good mood. Paul was just singing for fun, and he was so chill and relaxed. The only thing was, we all got so sleepy after a while and we just couldn't keep our eyes open long enough to see the New Year in!

Paul is a musical genius, as the world well knows, and not long after I met him in Jamaica, we became friends. Like everyone my age, I loved the Beatles. So it was also very interesting to be around another one of those scallywags from Liverpool.

One afternoon Paul invited me down to his country home. I asked if I could bring my mate Paul Allen with me. Paul McCartney was so gracious, and he pulled out all sorts of instruments that he played on the Beatles records. He got the actual mellotron, an odd instrument with the original tape loops inside that they used for a lot of their sounds in quite a few songs. He played the string part from "Straw-berry Fields" for us.

He then took us into a room and showed off Linda's photos, all these beautiful black-and-white pictures on the wall. We went into the studio and he played us some new tracks by the Fireman, a duo he created with Martin Glover of Youth. After that, Paul came by my studio in my crazy flat in Covent Garden. And we had a jam. Just for fun, we started to do this song. We didn't know what it was then; we were just jamming about. But it had a really great feel to it. It was almost like Wings, with acoustic guitar and strumming, and a great bass line locked in with the drums, all around this killer guitar riff we were playing. It had this weird sort of Indian music section in it as well.

Sitting there with Paul McCartney writing a song in my apartment was a little surreal but great fun, because he's so quick and so instantly tuned in to the music. He's got music dripping out of his fingers. So whether he is singing, playing the bass, playing the piano, playing the guitar, it's all there, all the time. It is remarkable to witness it. The only other person I know like that is Stevie Wonder. He's sitting at the piano and you're going, "How come the piano keys are the same for every-body, but when Stevie Wonder puts his fingers on them, it only sounds like Stevie Wonder?" It's a miracle.

I've since met Paul on many occasions, and we remain good pals. I remember a very funny dinner not long ago, where it was Ringo, Paul and me sitting with our wives between us. But then we moved, just the three men. Me in the middle of two Beatles. And it was funny, because I was listening to Paul and Ringo talking about these old Beatles songs and the recording of them. They were talking as if they were twenty-one years old—not arguing, but sort of contradicting each other about the songs on *Sgt. Pepper* and *Abbey Road* in their strong Liverpudlian accents.

Paul said, "No, no, you didn't do it like that. You did it like this."

And Ringo said, "Yeah, well, how would you know how I fucking played it?" and "Yeah, can you still sing that in the same key now?" It really was like sitting with two boys in a band who were in their early twenties. And that band was the Beatles!

When Paul made that first solo album, *McCartney*, he experimented the Do It Yourself way Annie and I made our *Sweet Dreams* album. Paul told me he loved recording like that—banging on books for drums and playing all the instruments. It reminded me of my approach on our eight-track tape recorder. He still loves that recording process, and so do I.

I first met Ringo at a dinner at George Harrison's house, Friar Park, in Henley-on-Thames. His hometown, Liverpool, and mine, Sunderland, are not too dissimilar; both are famous for shipbuilding and the grit and humor of the working class. Within moments of my meeting Ringo, he had me in stitches; he has such a wicked dry wit. I, for one, rolled about on the floor, because I got every quip he made. Ringo is very underrated as a songwriter and drummer, because he isn't all about flash technique and speed drumming or fifty tom-tom surround, like massive drum kits.

Ringo is all about the song, and that's why he was perfect for the Beatles. All he cared about was the song. He just wanted to know what they were singing, whoever was doing it, John or Paul or George, and what it was all about and how he could enable that song to transcend across many arrangement changes.

If you go into the world of "A Day in the Life" or in "Within You Without You" or most of the Beatles songs from *Rubber Soul* onward, they're a lot more complex than you think. The drums were always played by Ringo in an orchestral way. He'd know, *Okay, this is going to be an epic moment, so I'm not going to just play right all the way through. I'm going to drop out and do something with my floor tom.* His playing was so musical and subtle.

Think of "Come Together." Ringo's drum pattern, connected to McCartney's famous bass line, ties the whole thing together. Ringo also plays left-handed, but he would never actually change the drum

kit around to a left-handed kit. So on a lot of the unusual patterns—
like on "Come Together"—he was playing the tom-tom from right to
left and ending up on the high hat—the reverse of how every other
drummer would think about playing it.

So when I actually got to know Ringo really well, he would come
to our house with his wife, Barbara, and just chat. I realized quickly
that nearly everything that fell out of his mouth was, or could be, a
great song title or a great line from a song. He just couldn't help it.

Ringo spent a lot of time in the hospital when he was a kid. He
never really had a chance to study or play alongside the rest of the
kids. He told me it was only because a woman came into the hospital
one day with some percussion instruments, and handed out tambou-
rines and shakers to the kids on the hospital ward, that he discovered
his path in life. He told me he had a great stepfather, who'd played
him old jazz records with great drummers on them. They would listen
together intently and he just got nuts, obsessed, about playing the
drums and working out how to play on biscuit tins and tin cans. He
plays with a really lovely light touch, like those jazz players, but can
create a huge sound for rock and roll when he wants to. (Believe me,
I know. I've been in a very small room while he's playing!)

He's such a funny character. He'd always say the funniest things
and I would say, "Oh, my God, that's a great line. You should write
that down." And he'd say, "I already forgot it."

He has his own way he wants to live his life and he sticks religiously
to it, and I really respect him for that. Ringo, as we all know, went
wild in certain periods of his life. But he's really good at understanding what's good for him. He's very smart in lots of ways. You can tell
he's learned from years and years of being famous—like when people
shake your hand, you're bound to get the flu or cold or something.
Unlike normal people, who shake hands about twice a day, when
you're a Beatle, a thousand people a day want you to shake hands, so
giving people the peace sign is not just a positive message—it's also a
great way not to catch the flu!

Ringo isn't a great fan of my driving, though. I remember I was driving us from Santa Monica to the Sunset Strip. He noticed that I was a bit erratic. I was putting on my music, and talking my head off, laughing and joking, and we were weaving through heavy traffic, and he kept going, "Fucking let me out, let me out, let me out! I'm getting out! You're a lunatic! We're all going to die!" He shouted like this all the way home to his house, giving a constant running commentary of all the things I was doing wrong in the car. But I couldn't stop laughing, because he said it in such a funny way. We've gotten to know each other really well because we've been not only writing songs together but spending time writing a musical together.

It all started when we were together at his home in the south of France, and we went onto his small terrace and talked about our childhoods and about how we both really made friends with other kids by climbing over a railway station wall or over some railings or through a hole in the fence. Then we started singing songs about it, just making them up, as we do, for fun. He was banging on the table and we both were singing, "Break it down! Smash it up!" because we were singing about when we were kids and the things we'd do when we got on the other side of the fence. We'd throw stones and climb up inside derelict buildings, and were basically really naughty boys. And then you'd meet another boy there and ask, "Who are you?" And he'd be from the garden across the road or from over the railway line.

Ringo and I both had this same challenge when we were kids: how to meet other musicians so we could play in a band or get a band together. How do people come together to be friends and make music? So we recognized this was a great subject for a movie or a musical, and we called it *The Hole in the Fence*. It's a place away from grownups where another world opens up, the world of imagination and fantasy inside their heads. It might be an abandoned building, but to you it's a pirate ship.

So we started talking about that. A couple of days later we went to a public beach in the south of France, and it was packed. Ringo and I were on two towels, lying among everybody, and we were still working on this musical concept. We got obsessed with it. We were busy writing down words, and singing bits of songs into a tape recorder. I think a lot of people around us were slowly going, "Hang on a minute. Isn't that Ringo Starr and Dave Stewart? I think they are writing a song!" Then we had to roll up our towels and move pretty sharpish.

Later we met up in LA, and we started to record some more songs and began to flesh out the story and write it down. Ringo and I told the story to the film producer Laura Ziskin, whom I greatly admired and had been working with on Stand Up to Cancer. On September 10, 2010, along with Laura, Rusty Egan, Pam Williams and the whole Stand Up to Cancer organization, I helped pull together a group of artists to perform on a roadblock telecast on all four networks (ABC, CBS, FOX, NBC) plus sixteen cable outlets, and reaching more than one hundred seventy countries. The telecast featured an extraordinary lineup of more than a hundred actors, musicians and athletes, and I ended up jamming again with Stevie Wonder. As the TV broadcast ended, we kept on playing so people would carry on donating on the Web. Together, the 2008 and 2010 telecasts raised more than one hundred eighty million dollars for cancer research.

Ringo and I made a film deal with Paramount and then started to work on a script with my friend Dave Harris, based on Ringo's and my original story. But as is typical in Hollywood, everything just stopped. Laura sadly passed away in 2011 and Paramount seemed to become completely disinterested.

It has taken us nearly four years to get the film rights back, so now we're in the process of getting it made elsewhere and as a musical for the theater. I hope it does get made, as we love it so much.

Ringo and I have always made a good team and manage to have quite a lot of fun together. At one point, quite a few years ago, he asked me to help him finish some songs for an album. And we wrote a new song called "Liverpool 8" together. He was invited to Liverpool to open the European Capital of Culture celebrations in 2008. (The

European Union picks cities every year as culture capitals, and they're packed with events the whole twelve months.) Ringo invited me to join him, and I put together a little band for this performance. We were to perform on the top of St. George's Hall, a huge church tower, hanging in a kind of swinging basket, like the kind of gantry window washers use. It was right up in the air. And it held the whole band.

It was a cold night, and the basket was swinging a bit. We looked down on a massive crowd of about five hundred thousand people and they looked like tiny little dots. We were so high up, it was dizzying. Ringo and I looked at each other, saying, "Um . . . well, good luck, mate. Hope we don't fall!" It was the most extreme, mad performance I've ever done.

So we've done a lot of funny things together, but we always end up laughing at the end of the day. Ringo always jokes about his life being as calm as it is, considering the way it was in the Beatles heyday and his personal seventies and eighties madness. He made it through, and he's with Barbara, the love of his life. He really is happy to be here, happy to still be playing live. He's still just as nuts about playing the drums as he ever was. And that's an amazing thing, to be so excited about music and playing your instrument when you're a young teenager and still be crazy about it when you're in your seventies.

Something about being an artist must keep your mind sharp. I'm sure it helps your memory as well as keeping you young at heart. Dylan doesn't miss a thing. I remember I arrived at his house in Malibu once with my son Django, who was about three. Bob said, "Hi. How's it going?" He has these big dogs, which came running out, and Django got a bit scared. So Bob swept Django up off the ground, put him on his shoulders and said, "Come on, Django. Let's go milk a cow." Suddenly Bob Dylan was under his cow with Django. My son had no idea who Bob Dylan was; he was just a funny guy with curly hair. Bob picked up an acoustic guitar and started singing Django a song. Cut to six months ago. Dylan came to my office in Hollywood. Django, who is twenty-three and grown-up now, was sitting there.

I said, "Hey, Bob, this is Django, my son."

He said, "Yeah, Django, I remember. You came to my house and you were on my shoulder and you were scared of the dogs and we milked the cow." The man has a fucking sharp memory. All those years later, and he remembered all of it.

One time he came round to my house and was in the basement, where I had my studio, and there was a little drum machine. He said, "Oh, what are you doing with that thing?" I felt it would be too alien to him, but I showed him how you could make a beat with it. He said, "I like that thing. It's like a metronome." And he got entranced by it, and spent about an hour and a half with the same drum machine going. I was upstairs in the kitchen cooking. He was just playing this blues riff over and over, and he liked the idea of getting it locked in with the beat. He was open to change, and was in fact inventing a great new blues riff.

It was funny to me that Bob saw it like a metronome, something you would have on top of your piano. Because in the studio he would never do that, never play to a drum machine like that or a click track. In the studio, there's a load of people there and he wants to get in and out. But in the house or anywhere else, he'll spend ages just playing.

In Maida Vale, west London, where I used to live, there's a lovely old canal area called Little Venice. I had a houseboat back then, a long boat I'd steer through those old canals. It was about sixty feet long and narrow. Bob came on the boat once, I remember, and loved it. My mum was there making soup, and he hung out with her while she cooked, singing, playing and writing. We recorded stuff on the boat, and you can hear him singing with my mom clattering pots and pans in the background.

He really liked talking about old Dickensian London and he knew the whole history of the canals. One day I took Bob to Speakers'

Corner in Hyde Park, where people stand on boxes and rant about whatever they want. Bob wore his jacket hood up so no one could recognize him, and he enjoyed being in the crowd, listening to the different speakers, even joining in, asking questions. He wrote a song about it when he got back to the hotel. It's called "T.V. Talkin' Song":

One time in London I'd gone out for a walk
Past a place called Hyde Park where people talk
'Bout all kinds of different gods, they have their point of view
To anyone passing by, that's who they're talking to
There was someone on a platform talking to the folks
About the T.V. god and all the pain that it invokes
"It's too bright a light," he said, "for anybody's eyes
If you've never seen one it's a blessing in disguise"
I moved in closer, got up on my toes
Two men in front of me were coming to blows
The man was saying something 'bout children when they're young
Being sacrificed to it while lullabies are being sung

Bob loves English folk culture and the history of cities. He told me once he wanted to make a whole film about Paris and its sewage system, and have people playing the different characters like the poet Rimbaud and the artist Toulouse-Lautrec. Bob is fascinated by history and how it affects everything: personal history and global history. He can tell stories and take you to places you've never seen or heard of, and by the time the song is finished, you feel like you almost lived there.

Oh, the streets of Rome are filled with rubble
Ancient footprints are everywhere
You can almost think that you're seein' double
On a cold, dark night on the Spanish Stairs
Got to hurry on back to my hotel room
Where I've got me a date with Botticelli's niece

She promised that she'd be right there with me
When I paint my masterpiece

I must say I am blessed to have spent so much time in Bob's company, and the more I get to know him, the more respect I have for him as a true artist and a beautiful, sensitive soul.

love working with one of my best friends, Glen Ballard, as I said earlier. We used to have studios and offices in the same building in Hollywood, and it's a madhouse, like a train station with a dream arriving every five minutes. He's most famous for cowriting Michael Jackson's enormous hit "Man in the Mirror" with Siedah Garrett, and cowriting and producing Alanis Morissette's first albums, but he has written so many more great songs. Glen stood by Katy Perry for years, telling everyone that girl would be a massive star, and of course when she became a star, many people said, "Oh, yes, we knew that all along," but believe me, they didn't. I think only a certain kind of person can tell when someone "has it," and Glen is one of them. We love writing songs, and we also love writing songs for films, as it is a different process and forces you to use both sides of the brain. The left side of the brain is trying to deal with the needs of the director, the producers and the film company, while the right side is trying to dream up a meaningful piece of music and a poetic way to express what the movie is calling out for.

Writers need to be able to drift off and experiment, and sometimes we find beautiful mistakes that may become the center of a piece. But all of this is very worrying and incomprehensible to the noncreative "money people" in the film industry. It is just a very different process.

In 2006, Glen and I were asked if we would be interested in writing a song for the movie *Charlotte's Web*. I had never seen the original version, but as a strange coincidence, I'd just bought the book for my daughter the week before.

During the first run-through of the script and the early animation, Glen had a very bad flu, so I attended alone, and halfway through the movie, I sent him a text saying the song should be called "Ordinary Miracle."

The next day Glen played me the verse he had written ending in "It's just another ordinary miracle today." It was perfect.

We started working on the song and within an hour had laid it out and recorded a demo with me singing. We both wanted Sarah McLachlan to sing the vocals, and we flew to Vancouver and spent a great day with Sarah at her home. She was so gracious and worked hard to give us a great vocal. She is great at playing piano and singing to her own internal pulse, so we jammed around for a while with me on acoustic, Glen on bass and her on piano. We decided to abandon the way we had recorded it in our studio and started to build it around Sarah's piano part. It was amazing, being in the middle of a forest with Sarah playing piano and singing our song as the sun went down behind her.

The next step was to rebuild the song around her piano and vocals, which we did in Los Angeles, using Randy Kerber's string arrangement. We ended up with a mix that was wistful and delicate yet still had a resonance that made it unwhimsical. We did put some backing vocals on the track that we were not sure of, and when we sent the mix to Sarah, she loved all of it except the backing vocals, confirming our own doubts. So we immediately erased them, and the song was ready to go over the end titles of the movie. The single ended up winning the 2006 Film Critics Society Award for Best Song! Sarah performed the song on *The Oprah Winfrey Show* as well as during the Macy's Thanksgiving Day Parade. She also performed the song during the opening ceremony of the 2010 Winter Olympics in Vancouver, in front of an estimated three billion television viewers worldwide!

Glen and I went on to collaborate with Academy Award winner Bruce Joel Rubin, who wrote *Jacob's Ladder*, one of my favorite films, as well as the amazing film *Ghost*, starring Demi Moore and Patrick Swayze. I was offered the opportunity to work with Bruce on turning the movie *Ghost* into a stage musical. First I asked to meet Bruce himself, and we immediately clicked. I then asked if my good friend Glen could be involved, and everyone agreed. We dove straight into it and started a journey that took six years. Directed by the brilliant Matthew Warchus, recipient of best director from the Tony Awards and the Laurence Oliver Awards, the musical had its world premiere at the Manchester Opera House in Manchester in March 2011. *Ghost* then had its West End premiere in summer 2011, opening on July 19. It opened on Broadway in April 2012. It is now being performed in about thirteen countries and has a touring version too.

CHAPTER:22

24 KARAT GOLD

n 2006, I was asked to host a music/interview show for HBO called *Off the Record*. Jimmy Iovine and I decided that Stevie Nicks should do the pilot, so we called her up right there and then, and she said she would love to. And so, after our history, we reconnected all those years later on the set of an HBO special that I don't think anybody's ever seen.

On the show, Stevie and I discussed her life, from being a young girl growing up to dealing with the megasuccess of Fleetwood Mac. She talked about her entry into music and getting her first guitar, how that changed her life and set her on her way. She started playing and writing songs when she was sixteen. There's a tiny bit of it in the documentary *In Your Dreams*.

At the end of the HBO show, Stevie and I played an epic eight-minute version of "Rhiannon," with me on guitar and her on piano. Afterward, Stevie said, "Oh, really, I loved the way you played that, such a great feel." I was just improvising, supporting her. But she seemed to love it. A few years after that, she called me and said she thought it would be really great if I produced a Fleetwood Mac record.

We were talking on the phone. I said, "Well, I don't know what Fleetwood Mac would think about that or even what's happening with the band right now." But it made me think about Stevie's voice, so I called her a few days later and said, "Hey, I've written a song for you. I have a chorus, chords, lyrics and melody, but I left the verse melody and lyrics empty." I had a girl sing the chorus an octave above me, and I sent it to Stevie to see if she liked the feeling of it. I called the song "Everybody Loves You."

The chorus I wrote goes, "Everybody loves you, but you're so alone/ Everybody knows your name, but you can't find your way home/But no one really knows you, I'm the only one."

So I sent it to her, but I didn't hear anything back. I didn't think anything of it, as Stevie doesn't use the Internet or text messaging or anything like that. I didn't hear anything for about three days or so.

Then she called. "Oh, my God. I've had no sleep. I've been playing that song over and over a hundred times. I've been playing it and playing it, and I think I've got something that fits on top of the verse." She sent me a recording with her singing on top of my stereo track, just singing along with it. It's this amazing sketch of a verse. And so we said we had to record it.

When she came to the studio to record, she brought with her a bag, which had two big journals in it, huge folders with poetry in them. She said, "I wanted to give you these. You may find something in there that you like."

We recorded that song and it was coming out really beautiful. Stevie kept saying, "Hey, you should keep your voice on the chorus, as well, like it was in the demo." I wasn't expecting that, but I said, "Okay." And it seemed to make a nice sort of rounded blend.

A few days later I called and told her, "Hey, so I read all your poems." And she said, "What? Nobody ever reads all my poems! Nobody ever reads all of them."

I said, "No, well, I read all of them, and here are the ones that I think aren't just poems, but would make great songs." This was natural for me. This is how I worked with Annie for years. I might have a musical idea, and she would open up a journal of poetry, and somehow we put the two together.

I named twelve passages that were perfect for songs. Some of the poems went on for five pages. But that didn't matter. I said, "Why don't I come around to your house and we'll just open the books up?"

And she said, "Okay."

So I went to her house, and we started going through the books. She had a couple of guitars lying around, and she had this little recording center that Karen, her amazing assistant, operated. She had a microphone that could hang above the sofa, and it could pick up the two of us, playing and singing.

I took one of the poems and said, "Well, you see this section of words here? It could go with these chords in this rhythm, in this style." I started playing it in the style, and was sort of mumbling a bit about how I felt it should be. She was into it and said, "Oh, that's interesting."

I said, "Well, why don't you take the book and you sing it while I play?"

She replied, "But I haven't worked anything out yet."

I said, "That doesn't matter. Just sing the first thing that comes in your head."

I hadn't realized that this was alien to Stevie. I hadn't even realized that she didn't ever cowrite with anybody in the room. She'd sometimes written songs on top of a Mike Campbell track he'd send her, but never did she do a face-to-face collaboration. In Fleetwood Mac, Lindsey Buckingham would often produce her songs. But never did they write together. When she'd write with Mike, he'd give her a tape or a CD with music on it, and she'd run away for a month to write.

But this was me, right in front of her, exactly the same way as Annie and I wrote. We both sat together in the room, and I'm just piling on things as normal. Stevie had never done this but I took away all fear and said, as I do for every artist or wannabe artist, it's just for fun. And we went through about three or four songs in about two hours.

We recorded them on this single microphone, the two of us together. Afterward, Stevie was wonderstruck. She said, "Wow. There's a basis of about four songs there."

I said, "Yeah, and if you don't like any of it, we'll just throw it away, 'cause it doesn't matter." This was a huge epiphany for her, to write a song fast and for fun, and not under massive stress in a studio, with lots of people judging if her song was a hit or not.

She was so happy, she said, "Why don't you come around tomorrow and do that again?" So I came around the next day and suddenly many more songs were born. Then her team started, which was sweet. Stevie had her backing singers and other friends arrived. They would start making notes, taking bits we used and pasting them into a separate book, and this book became like the songbook for the album, all extracted from what Stevie had already written, but then somehow sort of put together in song form.

I said, "It sounds good." She said, "Hey, aren't we making an album?" I said, "Well, we are, kind of. But we haven't really started making an album yet, but we've now got what looks like a great album in songs."

She said, "I like it in my house here. I wish we could make the album here."

I said, "Well, so do I. It's nice. You can make an album anywhere."

I'd come from the world of making albums many ways—in Paris suburbs, in a château, in a shed, in a Jamaican ice house. It was easy enough to outfit her little studio with the right equipment.

I proposed bringing Glen Ballard in to concentrate on the arrangements and recording so that I could focus on Stevie and the songs.

With Glen came his great engineer, Scott Campbell, and we also brought in my longtime engineer and programmer, Ned Douglas. Seven of those songs were ones Stevie and I wrote together. So again I was being a co-songwriter and coproducer and also Stevie's confidant.

I had a method where I filmed everything I could on little Flip cameras, which are now defunct. But by doing this, I could see my fingers, which made it simple to determine what I was playing during improvisations. I had about four of these Flip cameras, which were about the size of Zippo lighters. I would stick one on, filming what I was playing and one on filming what Stevie was singing and one as a wide shot of the room, and let them shoot.

So we started to get a little video version of what we were creating. And I said, "Hey, look, why don't we film the process, and then you'll have a great documentary to go with the album?" Nowadays, it's very hard to get people's attention about albums coming out, because it's so overcrowded. But when her fans heard that we were working together, they started going crazy, writing her, wanting to know what we were doing.

Stevie decided to answer them all with a handwritten letter. The letter was scanned and then posted online. So all the fans started handwriting letters back and scanning them and posting them, and a buzz started to happen. It got Stevie and me quite excited, knowing that a lot of people out there were dying to hear her new music. At that point, she hadn't released anything in twelve years.

So we decided to bring in real cameras and some guys to film to make a real movie. And that became our film, *In Your Dreams*.

If you just use static, stationary cameras, it's going to look boring. I already had my own film company; I still do, a production company. So the boys came over, including my head of production, Paul Boyd. We also had Shane McLafferty and Chris Champeau, both very talented shooters and editors. And they were very, very subtle. As Stevie said, after a while, she forgot they were there. We didn't approach the shoot like blinding reality TV with lights everywhere. There were mostly no lights. It was just quite low-key, most of the time, which felt less intrusive.

But then Stevie got creative. She would say, "Hey, this song, why don't we film outside and do like a fantasy piece?" And as Paul Allen calls me, I'm "Mr. Permission." I give my permission to proceed on crazy, creative projects. So I said, "Yeah, why not?"

Stevie said, "Okay, just imagine a white horse in the garden . . ." And she spun a beautiful, dreamlike visual. Then the next day, she woke up and looked out her window and a big trailer was arriving with a white horse in it. She was ecstatic.

Suddenly everybody started turning into characters, influenced, no doubt, by the house and by Stevie's obsession with Edgar Allan Poe. People dressed in Edwardian costumes started turning up. Even my daughters, Kaya and Indya, were involved, dressed as spooky little characters, holding owls and walking through walls.

The place became a crazy house. Suddenly you couldn't tell if it was a film set or the interior of Stevie's mind. The film turned into a mixture of a documentary that went off into these fantasy pieces, and then back to reality again. And this became our movie, *In Your Dreams*.

Stevie got so fascinated by the film, she asked Shane to come to her house to edit it her own way. She is a true artist and loves every part of the process. She is very sharp. She remembers every guitar note and every drum break, and she has a really astute awareness of everything that's going on. People might not think that. They might think, "Oh, she's floating away with the fairies." But it's quite the opposite.

So when she joined in the editing, she put too much of me in the film. I was trying to make a documentary about her, but Stevie kept saying, "No, it's about the two of us." I understood, because we were writing songs together. But she kept putting more and more of me in it, and taking bits of her out of it.

In the end, I said, "Well, it should be, then, directed by Stevie Nicks and Dave Stewart, by both of us. I'm not going to direct the film of you and then put me in it all the way through." And that was how we did it.

We had so much fun during the day, and every night, when I had to leave, all the girls would come dancing and singing to the door, and flash their lights, making it all spooky and acting like vampires.

Anything was possible. As I always say, "Hey, there are no grown-ups here." Grown-ups being people who say, "Oh, you can't do that." There was nobody there to say that. And we were keeping it all low cost. It wasn't like "Oh, let's have a huge film crew and be all professional." It was just DIY. Stevie realized then: "Anything's possible, because if I don't like it, I can just chop it out." Then she really opened up and was telling hundreds of stories.

The film was already long: one hour and forty minutes in length. But we have fifty hours or one hundred hours; I don't even know. Her whole life came tumbling out, and this turned into *In Your Dreams*, the documentary, which coincided with *In Your Dreams*, the album.

Back in the studio we were doing some overdubs on Stevie's album. There was tension between her and Lindsey at the time, but she said at one point, "The one person who can play this would be Lindsey." I said, "Well, let's ring him up."

She said, "Oh, and only one drummer can do it like this. That's Mick." Mick Fleetwood.

I said, "Well, let's ring him up too."

She said, "What? Get Fleetwood Mac to play on my record?"

I said, "Well, they're all your pals, right? I mean, these are your people, if you want them." And they all turned up and played. It was just very sweet.

Once, in the studio, Reese Witherspoon came in. I'd already had a martini. The music was blasting out, and Reese was digging it. I told her I had to go to Nashville to record, and she said, "Oh, you should stay in my duplex there."

Stevie, quick as a flash, says, "Hmm, that'll be cheap."

Reese turned around and said, "Hey, well, what's cheaper than free?"

Stevie and I looked at each other, and we knew there was a song in there somewhere. While I was in Nashville I called Stevie and said, "Hey, where's the lyrics for 'Cheaper Than Free,' then?" She is so used to tormenting herself over lyrics for months, if necessary, which has obviously resulted in so many amazing songs. But now I was asking for lyrics on the spot! Amazingly a fax came through, and Stevie wrote, "What's cheaper than free? You and me. What's better than alone? Going home. What does money not buy? You or I." She nailed it. One hour later, I sent the whole track back from Nashville, finished.

She was amazed and liked my singing too, saying, "Oh, my God, I love this." And so on the record Stevie sang along with it all the way through. The whole thing is like two voices together. And Stevie said, "Oh, this is so great. I want it on my album too." I said, "I don't care. You can have it on your album too." So she did. I sent Reese an e-mail with the song attached and Reese said, "I love it, but hey, where's my copyright on that?"

For the very last song on her album, Stevie said, "I need something really up, like an old rock-and-roll kind of beat, almost like skiffle." We recorded something, just the two of us. And it's the title track, "In Your Dreams." But whenever we were in the studio trying to get it, we couldn't get the track right. So Waddy Wachtel, the legendary guitarist who was there, said, "Why don't you just play it like you did in the room when the two of you were there?"

We said, "Okay." We started playing and singing it, just the two of us. And Waddy started joining in on guitar. Then Mick Fleetwood came off his drum kit and came into the room and started playing with just brushes on the table, very delicately. He is a monumental drummer with this huge powerful sound, the engine of so many classic records. Yet here he was softly playing brushes on the table.

And we felt, *Yeah, that's what it was sounding like in the first place. That's great. That's how we want it.* And that's how we recorded it.

There's a great moment you can see in the film that is proof that Stevie isn't the ethereal sprite people think she is, that she is a very sharp and smart musician. I played a solo on one song just to get going, to figure it out before I did the official solo. I always record everything, just in case—because the one that I feel first is usually the one. So luckily, this engineer Scott did record it.

Stevie heard the solo that I kept playing on the track, and she said, "But that's not the one he played." She was sure. All of us thought that she was wrong and that there was no other solo. This argument went on for half an hour. Stevie was so sure, she started saying, "I'll bet you my house."

Scott, the engineer, went digging through all the files, and he said, "Was it this one?" He found it and played it, and Stevie said, "Yes, that was the one. I can remember every single note in it." It was the very first thing I ever played. She was absolutely right, and all of us had assumed she was wrong. The one she chose fit perfectly.

She loved this painless, joyous process of recording so much that she said she wanted to record another album of songs, built on lost demos, songs that her assistant Karen found on the Internet that she thought she had lost forever.

I said, "Well, there's only one way to do that, in Nashville. And we'll get it recorded really simply and quickly, because all those songs are finished." She agreed. And we went down to Nashville and did the whole recording in ten days. And she was amazed. That became her latest album, *24 Karat Gold*.

Stevie showed me boxes of beautiful Polaroids she'd taken, which she'd had under her bed for years. I said, "Well, they're so beautiful." She said, "Yeah, I took them myself and did the lighting." Amazing self-portraits. I suggested she make an exhibition out of them. I helped her. I got them taken to a special place for scanning and printing: Graham Nash's company, Nash Editions, which prints beautiful photographs for museums and galleries. We created a massive exhibition through my friends at the Morrison Hotel Gallery in New York, and made giant prints of the Polaroids. One of them became the album cover for *24 Karat Gold*.

I got Stevie to write in her distinctively florid calligraphy, her handwriting, and we made it into a font so that anything could be typed in her handwriting. So all her songs, and the album cover, and the Polaroid exhibition, all came together in a really quick manner. And then Stevie was off on this Fleetwood Mac tour that she's still on as I write these words.

In our short time together, we created about forty new songs. We recorded them all and made a film and a photo exhibition. It shows what can be done when you transcend fear with joy.

CHAPTER:23

SUPERHEAVY

Mick Jagger is very comfortable to be around. We can spend hours chatting—not about music necessarily, and if he did talk about music, it would be about Blind Willie Johnson or somebody like that; he's obsessed with old blues music and soul music. He knows just about every blues and soul song there is. But he wouldn't ever talk about a Stones song, or even bring up old Stones stories. He's very in the moment. He's also very knowledgeable about an array of subjects such as social political history, poetry, or Italian painters, and he speaks quite a few languages. If you get him on any of those subjects, he's passionate, always erudite, and can keep you fascinated in any subject because of the way he chooses and delivers his words. People may not realize it, because they think it's always Keith who comes up with the riffs, but Mick is brilliant with riffs and guitar ideas. I've heard him make up great stuff on guitar that sounds like classic Stones rock and roll. Keith is, of course, a genius riff merchant too. When I was growing up, Keith was the most exciting guitarist I'd ever seen, and when the Stones came on TV, I sat with my guitar, trying to work out what the hell he was doing, fascinated by his every move.

One of the reasons the Rolling Stones are so great is that they are empathetic with one another: Mick understands Keith's riffs, and Mick can build on those. And Mick has a brilliant instinct for fusing words and music. Whereas some other singer might be lost within the rhythm and chords of "Sympathy for the Devil," and not even be sure where the tune begins, Mick always makes it work: "Please allow me to introduce myself." And you know you're there.

I don't think Mick ever gets enough credit for being such a brilliant songwriter for the Stones. Watching him write songs and how effortlessly he does it is amazing, and you realize what a brilliant lyricist he is and how easy it is for him to make up melodies. You start to understand that there is no one on this planet who could come near him as a rock-and-roll songwriter. Of course Keith, being the epitome of rock-and-roll swagger, gives it all an edge.

I've spent quite a lot of time with Mick, and we've been writing songs together on and off since sometime in the eighties. I remember the first time we got together to write. I was playing the guitar and Mick was banging on this weight-lifting machine with metal barbells in the basement of my house in Maida Vale, London. He was dancing and singing at the top of his voice: "Brain Damage." It was so fucking loud, I think by the end of the day we were both brain damaged.

Some of our songs end up on albums but mostly we do it for fun. I have a cassette recording of Mick singing in falsetto to the sound of a taxi engine and the wet New York streets, while we were squashed with an acoustic guitar inside a yellow cab. It sounds pretty cool. We both love the Caribbean and have had lots of good times there, songwriting and sometimes just hanging out. Mick loves to dance and check out dancing moves in different locations and cultures around the world from Brazil, Trinidad, New York City—whatever is happening dance-wise in those places, he wants to check it out and join in.

One time we were in a large fitness room, and at one end Ned, my engineer, and I had a small recording setup, and while we were getting tracks ready for Mick to sing, he would literally do three hundred sit-ups or be using weights and running on the spot or skipping with a rope, as if preparing for a fight or an Olympic race, rather than singing. It's an everyday ritual for him, and as we all know, he can run around that stage, singing and dancing for three hours while we get exhausted watching! Anyway, around nine or ten in the evening after we'd eaten something, Mick says, "Hey, let's go to this great club I know." I was doubtful, as we were in the middle of nowhere on an island in the Grenadines.

Mick drove us along these windy hills, down dirt tracks and roads with huge potholes, till we got to this wooden shack. He said, "Come on, this is it. We go round the back. They have a VIP lounge." I was laughing, thinking he was joking, but we went round the back of the shack and up a tiny path, and we were met by two local guys who pulled back a curtain to reveal a door, not quite hung straight, with a small plastic sign that read VIP LOUNGE. We tumbled in.

The room was about eight foot square, with a sofa against two walls and a tiny bar in one corner. In an ornate gold plastic frame was a picture of a waterfall, which was plugged into the wall, and the waterfall looked like it was moving and gave off a glowing pink light— it was the kind of thing you'd buy in Woolworth's. Within seconds nine stunning women burst in to join Mick, Ned and I, laughing and giggling and kissing. "Hi, Mick," "Wha gwan?" "Mi miss yuh," "Weh yuh a do." Mick and the girls continued to chatter away in Jamaican patois for a while, but one beautiful and fulsome lady came up to me, and from what I understood said, "Hot inna here. Let's guh upstairs. Me show ya a Vincy Wine."

It *was* hot in there, and I did fancy a refreshment wine or whatever, so she took me by the hand up some steps and into the back of the shack. It was so dark I could barely see. I could hear lots of bass mixed with the sound of merriment, and the room was lit only by tiny Christmas tree lights strung everywhere. Anyway, my newfound friend went to the selector/DJ. Now I started to focus and could see a hefty sound system and an empty dance floor, and I was waiting for my wine to see what happened next.

Boom! A huge dance hall track nearly blew the walls off, and I was swept off my feet into the middle of the dance floor. But my partner seemed to be facing the wrong way, and she was bent down and making huge circular movements with her hips. I also noticed now we were not alone as a number of good-looking, strapping local guys stepped on the edge of the floor, looking serious and checking me out.

Not sure what to do at that point, I went slightly Isadora Duncan, remaining with my feet firmly on the ground, just using my arms, when *slam* like I'm a docking bay and the space shuttle (in the shape of her butt) connected firmly with my crotch, while her hands somehow managed to grip me tight even though I was behind her. She started to grind, and the music was deafening. The guys came real close, and it was feeling a lot hotter in there than it had been in the VIP lounge! After five minutes of this enlightening ritual, the music stopped, and the woman turned and said, "You like my Vincy Wine?" and gave me a big kiss. The guys all burst out laughing and I, feeling like Woody Allen, scampered back to the VIP lounge, which was now in full swing.

Mick was surrounded by beautiful women, and Ned looked on anxiously while leaning on the tiny bar counter. Mick knew what was going on—he must have set it up, as the minute I stepped in, he shouted, "D'ya get your wine, Dave?" and burst out laughing, along with all the girls. One of them fixed me a huge drink of overproof rum and pineapple with ice. I was so overheated and red-faced, I gulped it down. Now I can't remember much else about that night, although I did find a film of us all in the VIP lounge. I must have given one of the girls the camera; the scene looks like twelve people squashed together on a sofa, and you can hear Mick saying, "Ya gotta go out on a Saturday night," above the booming of the bass from upstairs.

On the other extreme, I have a song Mick and I recorded sitting under a hanging tree at Eddy Grant's studio in Barbados. While we were recording, Mick didn't know his wife, Jerry Hall, was being arrested at the Barbados airport. The authorities mistakenly claimed she was trying to smuggle in twenty pounds of marijuana. If you think about it, why would you need to smuggle any marijuana from one Caribbean island to another?

When I was approached to work on the music for the movie *Alfie*, I suggested to the director Charles Shyer and to Paramount that I work on the score with Mick. I wanted to create songs a bit like Simon and Garfunkel had for *The Graduate*, where the music and lyrics expressed the true identity of the characters. In some way to me, Mick kind of was Alfie, and I knew the songs would be very poignant.

Burt Berman, the president of music at Paramount at the time, was thrilled with this idea and managed to get the studio to go along with an experimental approach, but the studio still wanted a traditional score as well. We thought this was a big mistake and still to this day don't understand why they didn't let us go wild and experiment. It would have made the score that much more unique.

The theme song we wrote for the movie, "Old Habits Die Hard," won the Golden Globe for Best Original Song in a Movie in 2005. The song reflects what was happening in Mick's life, while also speaking perfectly to the way Alfie was feeling at that moment in the film. Mick wrote these lyrics in the inner voice of Alfie, but also as a reflection of himself. It was magic and just what I had hoped for.

The song has this great opening. It is very up and has a bit of the late-sixties band the Small Faces–type feel to it. The verse has such a strong melody, and as soon as the vocal comes in, it triggers this descending chord change leading to the classic line "Old habits die hard." Mick nails the vocal, and with a little falsetto jump on the word "hard," he adds a tenderness and vulnerability among a wall of drums and guitars.

We recorded the whole sound track live in Abbey Road Studio B, the famous Beatles room where they made most of their early albums. We set up with Mick in the middle of the room, me on guitar, Chris

Sharrock on drums, Mike Rowe on organ and piano, Yolanda Charles on bass and Ally McErlaine on second guitar. We had the best players and the best time. During recording, the stars of the movie, Jude Law and Sienna Miller, would come down and just lie around on the sofa, listening. It became a whole "vibe" for the film.

We shot a really cool black-and-white music video in Abbey Road for "Old Habits Die Hard." Jude Law was filming us on an 8mm camera just as we were set up when we recorded the album. You can see this footage in the video.

The sound track itself has some other great songs: "Blind Leading the Blind" and "Let's Make It Up" both sound like timeless classics to me. "Blind Leading the Blind" was recorded live in one take!

As we were sitting there at the Golden Globe Awards ceremony, it was odd because we were all just watching and having fun but for some reason we didn't really think we would ever win. When the award presenter announced we had won, neither of us had written a speech. We got onstage, and were both just sort of cracking jokes and thanking all of our kids.

It was a funny moment, but for me it was also a really great moment. Mick and I had written a lot of songs that nobody really knew about. It was cool standing there alongside him and being recognized for something we'd written together.

Every time I sit down and play the guitar and Mick starts singing, something magical happens. He has such powerful energy around him, when he's singing in a studio it's as if he's on the stage. He can't not perform! Every time we get together for a writing session or just to jam, there's always a tiny glimpse of playing onstage with "Mick Jagger." As you can imagine, it's quite mind-blowing! Fortunately, I've captured lots of it on tape.

Our friendship has led to many adventures over the years. I'll never forget the time Mick arranged to meet me on a bateau I'd hired on the river Seine for a soiree with all the artists from Anxious Records, the small indie label I'd just created. It was the twenty-third of September

1987, and I'd just been married to Siobhan for seven weeks. I was in Paris at the Studio Grande Armée again, probably just finishing mixing the album *Savage*. Anyway, bands and artists I'd signed came over from the UK and one act was from Paris. Tony Quinn, or the Mighty Quinn as we now called him, was helping organize the mayhem once more and by now he was also running the label.

It was a crazy day. By lunchtime I had already been out and bought three limited-edition Salvador Dalí bronze sculptures: *Space Elephant, Persistence of Memory* and *Woman with Drawers*. They were delivered to the studio, and we were looking at them when another delivery came to the studio: this time a boxful of pure MDMA reportedly from Alexander Shulgin's original supply (MDMA had been created before the First World War but Shulgin was the chemist who helped start to bring the drug into the mainstream in the seventies). There had not been much discussion about this drug in 1987, but I had heard about its ability to make people lose their inhibitions and cause a kind of "honesty" effect, so to break the ice among all of us, I thought this could be a good experiment. After much debate among me, the various artists, engineers, Tony Quinn and even my solicitor at the time, who was there for signing purposes, I proposed we all take it at exactly the same time and head to the bateau waiting for us on the Seine. I explained we would be safe there since the boat was not moving. We had two waiters with snacks and drinks, and we could close the hatch and just stay inside.

So everyone, including my solicitor and TQ, did exactly that, and we got to the bateau just in time. The waiters were very confused, as here was a bunch of what appeared to be very happy, drunken people, yet no one was drinking. The waiters were offering champagne, but everyone was saying, "No, thanks. Just water," drinking it, and then appearing even more drunk.

As the evening progressed, everyone was smiling and talking about how much they loved one another and even the waiters. All of a sudden there was banging on the boat and a bit of a commotion at one end. Mick Jagger appeared. I had forgotten completely that he was coming, so you can imagine these young artists, high as kites, their brains doing a somersault, as Mick bounded in, saying hi to everyone.

Within seconds Mick could tell something was wrong, or right. What happened next was magical and a moment I'm sure none of the attendees will ever forget. Because everyone had lost their inhibitions or shyness and was being totally honest, all the artists, musicians and engineers were immediately saying things like "Hey, Mick Jagger" and touching his face and smiling two inches from his nose. People were stroking Mick and asking all sorts of questions like "Wow, 'Wild Horses,' Mick. How did you even sing that?" or "Hey, Mick, 'Sympathy for the Devil,' but why?"

Mick was so sweet. He sat on a chair in the middle, and for some reason, everyone sat cross-legged on the floor like kids in kindergarten, and Mick started what was like a storytelling class.

"Well, 'I watched with glee while your kings and queens fought for ten decades for the gods they made.' What I was saying was . . ." And he would begin to explain the whole song, with the transfixed audience occasionally going "ooh" or "aaah" and "wow" or "yeah" and stroking Mick's hair or touching his face while Mick kept on talking for about an hour.

Even the waiters sat down and were in complete shock at the scene. The whole experience was unfortunately missed by one poor guitarist who decided to pee on the boat next door. He jumped, but because the boat was one that collected silt, instead of landing on a solid deck, he sank into the silt up to his chest. As we were leaving, we could hear his weary voice whimpering, "Help . . . help," and we dragged him out.

TQ, my solicitor and I went back to my Paris apartment and tried to sleep. At one point TQ climbed into my bed and was calling his girlfriend's name. I discreetly suggested he had gotten it mixed up, and he stumbled back upstairs, confused. The next morning I was meant to play live acoustic with Mick on a French TV show called

Rapido, just the two of us, and we had to meet at eleven a.m. in a hotel to get ready. Trouble was, the MDMA had not worn off. Tony crashed the car en route, and I insisted that in order to play guitar, I needed to drink a load of vegetable soup or something to make the effect of the drug wear off.

We stopped at a vegan shop, and I had to get the soup in a jam jar, as the shop workers had no takeaway cups. I arrived just in time for the show, in the same clothes I had gone to sleep in, clutching a jam jar full of soup. Mick said, "Fucking hell, do you think you can even play?" I, of course, said, "Sure!" and staggered onto the TV set, which much to my horror was designed like the hall of mirrors in a fairground. I had to not only play the song correctly but not look to the left or right, as Mick and I were changing shape and morphing into each other with giant arms, noses and hands in the bendy mirror reflections.

The Stones would never sound like the Stones without all the elements in the group. When Mick would do solo albums, he had to shoot himself in the foot every time because he tried to not make it sound like the Stones. But then all the reviewers would say, "It doesn't sound like the Stones," and he would go, "Well, I'm trying not to make it sound like the Stones." If you were to hear some of the unreleased tracks we made together (no one has yet), they do sound a lot like the Stones. Mick's singing with its twist and turns, the chord progressions and the feel is unmistakable; he can't help it. It would be like trying to get Picasso to paint like Constable.

When it comes to any great band, if you take away any element it wouldn't sound quite right—like U2 with the Edge, Bono, Larry and Adam. The Rolling Stones are made up of separate elements that come together to create that amazing sound. Mick's songwriting, his voice and his soul are such a huge part of it, and having spent hundreds of hours with just the two of us in a room jamming or writing with Mick wailing away, I can tell he has probably been responsible for most of that band's brilliant works.

People rarely discuss Bill Wyman's contributions to the band, but his playing on lots of those Stones records has bass lines that are so infectious, they become stuck in your head like glue. He was always locked in tight with Charlie Watts—the perfect gentleman, such a soulful rock, blues and jazz drummer. As anyone who understands rock and roll knows, bass and drums create the foundation of the whole sound. It is the ground floor on top of which Mick and Keith can twist and turn and do their thing. Even at the height of Stones mayhem, when they could hardly hear what the hell they were doing live, they were always locked in. It's the essence of the Stones' greatness.

The last two times I saw the Stones were both in tiny venues in Hollywood: the Echoplex and the Fonda Theatre. Each time I was blown away by Ron Wood. He is also an amazing player; I love his guitar playing. He plays blistering solos, and he shone throughout the whole show. Ron is such a great character to hang around too, full of mischief and always a wink and a nudge. Mick, being the creative genius he is, has been and continues to be a huge inspiration in my life.

So I got into the creation of the SuperHeavy band and enlisted Shepard Fairey to do artwork. I decided that we should just secretly record and not talk to a record label or anything, just go in the studio. Mick and I paid the bill, and we went in for ten days at Henson Studio in Hollywood. In the first few days, we wrote twenty-seven songs between us all. So we never really tried to write much more; we just homed in on those.

We started to be a really great-sounding band. We had Damian Marley's bass player, Shiah Coore, and his drummer, Courtney Diedrick. We brought in Mike Rowe, a great keyboard player we worked with on *Alfie*, as well as Ann Marie Calhoun on violin. I suggested we bring in the composer A. R. Rahman from India. He had a tough time, because just as he arrived, he was about to win the Academy

Award for the score for the film *Slumdog Millionaire*. So he kept getting dragged off to these press things he had to do.

We began the SuperHeavy album, and it was an amazing journey. To finish it, everybody went all over the world, and I would have to go everywhere to work with them. I was always trying to finish these recordings, but I had to go to Miami to get Damian to overdub. It was getting too chaotic, so then I thought that the one way I was going to get everybody together, away from telephones and management and everything, was on a boat.

Years earlier, I had helped Paul Allen choose the gear to put on his boat to make a little studio after he'd seen Electric Lady Studios. Now he'd built a sophisticated boat with a full-on recording studio, and I said, "All right, everybody. We're going to sea. Fly into Nice Airport in the south of France, and we'll pick you up and bring you on board."

Now, the trouble was I was on the boat with Anoushka and Paul. A. R. Rahman was going to arrive in Nice, and Mick said he'd be in Italy at the time on holiday. So we said, "That's all right. We'll pick you up on the coast of Italy." What happened was, Paul had forgotten that A.R. was arriving in Nice, so he told the captain before he went to sleep to sail to Portofino, off the coast of Italy. I woke up and asked, "Where are we?"

The captain said, "Oh, we're in Italy." I said, "Oh, no, A.R.'s arrived in France, in Nice."

So it became this jigsaw puzzle of moving this person here and that one there. Eventually, Mick got picked up on the boat in Italy. Joss Stone was already on the boat with me, and she and I had written a song called "Beautiful People" while we were waiting for the others. We nearly killed ourselves writing it, because after a few martinis we were sitting on the front of the boat in the dark, dangling our legs, and we nearly fell off a moving boat into the sea.

Eventually we all came together at sea, and we started to record. It was incredible doing vocals because nobody could get off the boat. I had captured them all. Nobody was distracted about the usual stuff.

I ended up with nearly everything recorded, and then Mick and I did some vocal overdubs, and then we mixed it back in Los Angeles with Chris Lord-Alge.

The name SuperHeavy came from Damian singing along to a beat "Yeah, we're heavy, heavy, heavy, super heavy." And I thought at the time that would be a great name.

When we had the album finished, we didn't know where we should put it out. I wanted to break all the rules, and thought, *We shouldn't try to put it out as a record. We should just go to a cell phone company and say, "Give us five million dollars, and here is this album by me, Mick Jagger, Joss Stone. . . ."* Because we would never make five million in royalties selling the album now, since everybody was downloading everything for free.

Then a great guy called Danny Socolof came into the picture. My manager, Dave Kaplan, and Danny had a really good plan to work with about three companies where we would give them all this content and cover the world. We would get all of the income up front, since everybody was going to download it for free anyway after that. You couldn't stop it. But at least it would be all over the world, seen everywhere and heard everywhere.

For some reason, one of Mick's advisers was against that. There were other complications with different managers, and in the end, it was decided to just put it out on a label. Irving Azoff said, "Look, hang on. I'll get you X amount advanced to put it on this label, Universal Republic." So we created a straightforward record, which I didn't think was a good idea. We were more than that.

In retrospect, I was right. It wasn't a good idea. It was just a normal record deal, but I wanted to do something really groundbreaking, leading toward the worlds that I'm always describing. But it came out and I love that album. The idea that I also thought of was that Super-Heavy should have been a festival and we would choose our favorite artists to play. It could have been lots of different things.

At one point, Mick realized, "Oh, God, I'm in a band again. And I've already got a complicated band." It was a great, fun period of time, and it resulted in a great album.

I love Joss Stone. Not only is she an amazing singer but she is also a great friend to have. I first met her when Mick and I invited her to sing the title track on the sound track of the movie *Alfie*. She was only about sixteen years old and she was going to sing this very complex song written by Burt Bacharach and Hal David, which goes through many chord changes and with an incredibly complex melody. We were amazed to see she learned it in about ten minutes and did it all in one take. Mick and I looked at each other and said, "Hang on a minute." We ran to the bathroom and wrote a song in ten minutes, pretending we had written it earlier. We came out and said, "Oh, we have another song we want you to sing, too. It's called 'It's Going to Be Lonely Without You.'" They sang it as a duet with amazing vocal delivery. That's also on the sound track.

I called her up one time after the SuperHeavy album was released and said, "Hey, Joss, you know, I've just had this great recording experience in Nashville and met all these wonderful players." I'd made my album *Blackbird Diaries* and had a blast doing it. I invited Joss to meet me in Nashville to make an album. I said, "You should come. It's brilliant. We'll make an album in five days. We'll just write it from scratch."

She was in Spain helping her friend paint his small dinghy boat and she was with her dogs. She said, "Well, how am I gonna do that? I'm in Spain, with a Volkswagen bus with four of my dogs. How do I get a flight from here to Nashville anyhow and who's gonna look after the dogs?"

Eventually a friend volunteered to look after her dogs, and two days later Joss managed to get to Nashville in a roundabout route. We woke up the next morning and went into the studio and made a killer album called *LP1*—which came out as Joss's first independent album on her own label, Stone'd Records, partnered with Surfdog Records, my then-manager's label. We had the most fun ever. It was such a great experience, and boy, did we laugh.

At the same time we were writing and recording about fifteen brand-new songs, we made a bunch of little comedic films, very odd British humor. There's one where we pretended we were stealing a bicycle from a girl in the park, and we filmed it from all different angles. We made poor Becky (the camera lady) the bicycle victim, and we would laugh our heads off on the way to the studio, then arrive and write another song.

Writing with Joss is a little bit like writing with Annie (for me) in that we could write a great song in literally twenty minutes. I had all these great musicians I'd already worked with playing in a circle around Joss. They loved her too. Not only did they think she was one of the greatest singers they'd ever played with, but they were like "She is so hilarious and so much fun to jam with." Joss loved these guys' playing ability too. She would do things while we were recording, like go upstairs and bake stuff in the oven for everybody. We'd be in the studio, and she'd come downstairs smiling with a whole load of cakes. All of us— Joss and me, the musicians, the engineers and assistants—became such a close-knit little family in only six days. But it does become like that, when you're all working on something together like a great little gang.

I remember when we wrote "Newborn," which became the first song on the album. We were working on the SuperHeavy album, and we wrote it right on the spot, standing in the room while Mick and Damian Marley were standing there right next to us. They didn't have their earphones on, only Joss and I did, so we could hear each other. It was just a sketch then, but when we were working on the album, we pulled it up, and that was the first song we recorded.

The song "Cry Myself to Sleep" is a very structured song that reminds me of something Dusty Springfield would sing. We put real strings on it, and the whole band was playing. It's a track that's complex, tight and structured, yet all played live, in one take.

There's a funny YouTube video of Joss and me writing the song

"Landlord," which is based around the lyric "I don't want to be your landlord anymore." It's a story where basically we're chatting about life, in general, and relationships. It was two o'clock in the morning, and we'd had way too much to drink, because we are both big fans of a well-made vodka martini. We started writing this song, a great old-fashioned blues song, like a song for Bessie Smith, and you can see it being formed live on video, and we were so into it, we finished it there and then.

Joss's friend Paul Conroy has a song he cowrote with Joss on the album, and it was his little boat she was helping him to paint. Paul is one of Joss's best friends, a famous British freelance photojournalist best known for covering combat zones around the world. While covering the 2012 Syrian uprising, he was seriously injured and had to be smuggled out of the country into Lebanon. His friend Marie Colvin, the French photojournalist, was killed in the same attack. Paul had started to write a song on the boat that they were painting. He played a little bit to Joss, and it was called "Take Good Care." It's about all of the awful atrocities that go on and that he had witnessed. I suggested that we give that song to Amnesty International, and we made a little video for them with our footage in the studio and Paul Conroy put images from the footage he'd shot himself in Syria—unbelievable, harrowing footage.

After making *LP1* together, Joss and I decided to do another album called *Homemade Jam*, which was basically the two of us having a great time jamming in her countryside cottage in Devon, in southwest England.

Just before I was about to visit, two men were caught trying to hatch an awful plot to kidnap Joss and murder her. Fortunately, it was a terrible plan, and they got caught and sentenced to prison. Right before I went over there to work with her, she called me to tell me about this. The police were in her house right then. It was terrifying.

Joss said, "I refuse to move out of my house. Nobody's going to make me move." She did not allow the plot to deter her from living in her own house. So I went there, and we recorded in her little cottage. And then she came over to my house, and in my basement we carried on these great recordings. Nobody has really heard them, because we've yet to release them.

Joss got diverted and had to make *The Soul Sessions Volume Two*, because it has been ten years since *The Soul Sessions Volume One* and she was contractually obligated to deliver the follow-up. And so the album *Homemade Jam* is still not completed. But it's got some of my favorite songs on it.

Joss has gotten a lot of stick, as we say in the UK—a lot of criticism. It all boiled down to when people thought she spoke with a slight American accent at an awards show. This is how fickle Britain is. From then on, the British press annihilated her, which is so unfair. I know her very well, from being with Joss onstage as a singer, to working in the studio with her, to being drunk under the table with her. She never falters from being an amazing, giving, shining and positive person and a true British national treasure.

CHAPTER:24

COUNTRY WINE

Country wine, life is sweet
I got my feet under the table
And all that country food to eat

've never really had a master plan all my life. I've followed little signs that point me in the direction of a road less traveled. In April 2010 an Icelandic volcanic eruption spewed an ash cloud creating the highest level of disruption to air traffic since the Second World War. Naturally, given the random nature of my life, I was stuck in London when I should have been on a plane back to Los Angeles. On the other hand I'd been given a rare time-out from the hectic pace of life at the time, and the first thing I did was to go walking in Soho, one of my favorite parts of London. I headed for Denmark Street, which is full of guitar shops and for years has been a meeting place for musicians and song pluggers. In 1963, Paul and John were browsing along this street when the Stones got out of a taxi. The two Beatles congratulated them on getting a record deal, but Mick told them they didn't have a song yet. Paul said, "We've got one," and gave them "I Wanna Be Your Man," which was their first hit record.

So here's the first weird thing: I ended up buying a vintage guitar previously owned by another Dave: Red River Dave, a country-and-western performer from the fifties. He was famously eccentric, another common bond, and once wrote fifty-two songs in twelve hours while handcuffed to a piano.

I eventually got out of London by getting on a flight to Nashville, for a twenty-four-hour stopover just with a carry-on and my Red River Dave guitar. I had an idea in my head for a television series called *Malibu Country*, so I had a meeting arranged with country legend Martina McBride. The meeting turned into dinner with Martina and her husband, John, during which we got on very well and proceeded to get blind drunk. We staggered back to Blackbird Studios, one of the city's most iconic and productive recording establishments. John proceeded to play music in all of the rooms till four in the morning and I was amazed and enamored with them and their whole setup. It was the start of a love affair with the place, the music and the people.

In the past five years, I have produced eight full albums in Blackbird Studios, as well as a TV documentary of my adventures there. I made a trilogy of my own albums, *The Blackbird Diaries*, *The Ringmaster General* and *Lucky Numbers*.

I made Joss Stone's *LP1* album there, Stevie Nicks's *24 Karat Gold*, amazing female guitarist Orianthi's album *Heaven in This Hell*, and the first solo album by Martin Longstaff, aka the Lake Poets, a boy from my hometown, Sunderland. I recorded some of my daughter Kaya's album at Blackbird Studios, and recently produced some tracks for my son Django's first solo album. I recorded all of these albums at lightning speed in three- or five-day sessions, except Stevie Nicks's, which took two five-day sessions.

John McBride has engineered all eight albums, and I must say he is the greatest engineer I have ever recorded with. John is the biggest music fan and sound enthusiast I've ever encountered; his collection of vinyl albums, vintage instruments and equipment is mind-boggling. Put it like this: John has thirty thousand Beatles albums—but they only ever released thirteen original albums!

Whenever I'm in Nashville, Martina is always in and out, listening to what we're doing, or making tasty food and sharing a martini at the end of the session. All three of Martina and John's daughters come running in and out of the sessions too, and I hired their eldest, Delaney, to run my Nashville office.

I asked John McBride to handpick not only the best players he has ever recorded, but players who would also work together as a band, and he certainly did. I must say these guys are insanely good together: Tom Bukovac on guitar, Dan Dugmore on slide, Chad Cromwell on drums, Mike Rojas on keys and Michael Rhodes on bass. Each one is a legend in his own right, but when we play together, it's like a dream come true.

When I made my first album in Nashville, I decided on the spur of the moment to book a gig at the Belcourt Theatre and play the whole album live. I think we rehearsed for about three hours and then played almost a two-hour set. There was a big buzz about my recording sessions, so a lot of Nashville artists including Lady Antebellum, Big and Rich, Jessie Baylin, and Karen Elson turned up to see what was happening. None of the artists had seen these guys play live as a band before, and with John McBride mixing out front, it sounded just like the record. The crowd loved us. We had a big party afterward, and in one night, I got accepted and initiated into Nashville's inner sanctum, and that's somewhere I'll always be working from now on. Well, it's not exactly work—it's brain sailing!

One of the reasons I love Nashville is the way the musicians are integrated with the community. It's different from LA, where a lot of the younger stars are so often inaccessible, living in gated estates, escorted by personal bodyguards, and spending evenings in clubs closeted with hangers-on in the VIP. area. I don't think I've seen a VIP area in Nashville, although I often see superstars in the Pancake Pantry with their buddies and families. On my first Nashville album, *The Blackbird Diaries*, all sorts of people would hang out in the studio and just watch, or join in, from famous Nashville songwriters to musicians recording in other studios. It was like "a happening" again. I ended up doing duets with Martina McBride, Stevie Nicks and the Secret Sisters, as well as writing and recording fifteen songs, all in five days straight.

The second record, only ten months later, called *The Ringmaster General*, featured my same band of musicians, and on this album, I had duets with Jessie Baylin, Alison Krauss and Joss Stone. Orianthi came to visit and played amazing guitar on one of my song "Girl in a Catsuit," which we then shot as a music video with Orianthi wearing a leather catsuit, just like Emma Peel from the TV series *The Avengers,* which I loved when I was a kid. Judith Hill came and sang too, along with country writing star Hillary Lindsey on "The Gypsy Girl and Me."

I'm always looking for a new inspiration and welcoming new collaborators to work with. I'll never stop seeking the creative charge that comes from a new sound, the right verse, a beautiful melody. In the past few years, I've found that inspiration and more in Nashville. And that is why I regard the place and its players with enormous affection and gratitude. When contemplating the album *Lucky Numbers*, Paul Allen said to me, "What would you like for your sixtieth birthday?" He offered me five things to choose from, and my favorite of the five was, and always is, going out on his beautiful yacht, *The Octopus.*

I decided to fly my Nashville band out to join in on the celebration. These guys were used to just going to a studio every day in Nashville, and suddenly they were on a magical mystery tour ensconced in a private jet headed to the South Pacific.

Anoushka and I were married on Moaréa Beach, in the south of France. Now that we were in the real Mooréa in French Polynesia, I wanted to re-create the wedding ceremony. Anoushka was the only person who didn't know what I was planning. Both Kaya and Indya knew. Martina McBride knew. All of the boat crew knew, as did all the musicians from Nashville. All of the arrangements were kept secret including the fact that Indya had packed Anoushka's original wedding dress.

We set it all up for eleven in the morning on the end of the boat. We made a beautiful little wedding altar with all flowers, all very South Pacific. I kept walking around, singing all those songs that my dad kept playing, back at the beginning of this book and my life, from Rodgers and Hammerstein's musical *South Pacific*. There I was in the real South Pacific, renewing my vows to the love of my life, surrounded by musicians and friends, with our daughters, Kaya and Indya.

I said that when I first saw Anoushka, she reminded me of Greta Garbo—what's extraordinary is our family home was once the house that Garbo resided in. My favorite times in this house are when the whole family is together, the girls and Sam and Django, for a meal, a chat, laughter and good wine. And sooner or later Sam will get out his guitar, Django or Kaya will start singing and Indya will dance the night away. . . .

My dad played "Oh, What a Beautiful Mornin'" by Rogers and Hammerstein nearly every day, and when I wake, that is what I feel. I am one of those blessed people whose life is their work and vice versa. I have been doing what I love most for over half a century, probably since the first time I heard my brother's blues records.

I've achieved an amazing amount of success and the rewards that go with it. There's been failure as well as fame, ridicule as well as acclaim, and grief and loss as well as laughter and lunacy. But there's been continuous joy and fun, fueled by the creative spark that can be just as potent jamming in a shed with a few friends as in some recording studio in New York, or Nashville or Paris, or even playing Wembley Stadium. It helps, of course, if the shed is in Jamaica.

I won't pretend not to like being famous; fame after all is a measure of what you've achieved. But anyone who knows me well will tell you that what drives me is experience and experiment, insatiable curiosity, mischief and, yes, a little mayhem. And a taste for the bizarre, which must have owed its DNA to the day in my childhood when a neighbor's daughter gave me an exploding eyeball as proof of her love for me.

ACKNOWLEDGMENTS

All of these adventures in freedom could not have been possible without so many helping hands. I would like to thank all of the artists I have encountered during my journey so far. In this book I have tried to give sketches, moments in time when something magical happened. The thing is, I've had so many amazing experiences with so many artists almost every day since the first time I wrote a song with someone. I was so overwhelmed when I first sat down to put pen to paper in Jamaica that I gave up and just wrote a sentence or two on sticky notes and stuck them to the wall. Then it became a whiteboard in the back garden, and eventually it was the whole wall in my office studio. So many characters were written on the wall, it was like that joke when a prisoner keeps asking a guard for a book to read, and in the end the guard throws him a telephone directory. A day later the guard quips, "How do you like that book?" and the prisoner responds, "Well, I haven't got to the plot yet, but it's a hell of a cast!" For some reason I have met and befriended so many artists—young, old, rich and poor—and still seem to be in touch with them all in one way or another. As Mick says in the foreword, my e-mail in-box is insane. But it's not only artists who have enriched my life. The army it takes to allow creativity to flow is immense, and I would like to thank all the engineers, programmers, assistant engineers, personal assistants, runners, tea boys, sandwich makers and secretaries who ever worked with me in the studios all over the world. I greatly appreciate everyone and everything that goes headfirst into the vortex of one of my recording sessions and comes out the other side, clutching a tape or hard drive, still laughing—or at least smiling.

Behind all of this madness over the years is another small army of people in management: Kenny Smith, Gary Kirfurst, Simon Fuller and Dave Kaplan, all great people. My offices and studios have always been, as my dad would say, "bedlam," and the staff members that stay for more than a few years deserve medals: "Cool Under Fire" and "Recorded Under Great Peril."

Damien Hirst named the first show he curated "Some went mad, some ran away," and that's what may have happened to some of these great friends, artists and workers I met along the way. I apologize if I instigated that! The thing that kept me going was always believing in music, and believing that somehow things would work themselves out if I kept making music. Things may crash around you: your relationships perish, you lose all your money and your girlfriend, too, but music remains. A few simple notes turn a bad time back into a good time, and if you are a songwriter, "Even the bad times are good times." I would not be in the position I'm in without Annie Lennox, and we both know what we went through to deliver our best. It wasn't easy, but I never lost sight of what a special bond we have.

Special thanks to my great friend Ian La Frenais. I hope we always have as many laughs as we did in the last few months going through this book. Special thanks, too, to Paul Zollo for his work and his obsession with songs and the songwriting process. Long may your conversations continue.

All my staff at Dave Stewart Entertainment has coped with me writing this book—searching for photos, fixing computer crashes, dealing with lost passages, et cetera. Paul Boyd, who came in and rescued the day when the book seemed to have taken over my life and I thought it would never be finished. We got there! Allison Bond, my right hand—so much so that I don't bother telling her what is happening anymore; she tells me. Ned Douglas, who for the last twenty years has programmed and engineered more than a thousand recordings and never once dropped the ball; even when recording me in the Jamaican jungle with a headdress of leaves, or down the Amazon covered in war paint, he remains calm and collected. Ed Shiers, Chris Champeau, David Jacobson, and all of Dave Stewart Entertainment's brilliant minds have helped me through this process. Thanks to Jono Hart for his boundless enthusiasm, and Hartwig Masuch and Thomas Scherer for bringing me into a whole new family and being so welcoming.

I would like to thank Anoushka, who, almost twenty years ago, gently ushered in an epoch of relative calm and stability to my life. My four children: Samuel, Django, Kaya and Indya, who have given me more joy, fun and anxiety than any other beings could. My father, mother and brother, who laid the foundation that assured my survival; even in the most treacherous of situations, I had a feeling I would come out on the sunny side of the street.

It was a pleasure and an honor to work with Jennifer Schuster at New American Library—thank you for talking me off the cliff and back onto the boat. To Kara Welsh for taking on a book by nutcase like me, and to all at Penguin Random House.

LYRIC CREDITS

PHOTOGRAPHY CREDITS

INSERT 1

Page 1: Sadie Stewart

Page 3, photo 1: Photo by Michael Putland/Getty Images

Page 5, photo 3: Photo by Caroline Greville-Morris/Redferns

Page 5, photo 4: Photo by David Corio/Redferns

Page 9: top three photos: Photo by Christa Fast

Page 12, photo 2: Photo by The LIFE Picture Collection/Getty Images

Page 12, photo 3: Photo by Popperfoto/Getty Images

Page 13, photo 1: Photo by Brian Rasic/Getty Images

Page 13, photo 2: Photo by Dave Hogan/Getty Images

INSERT 2

Page 1: Photo by Michelle Shiers

Page 4, photos 5, 7, 8, 9: Photo by Dave Stewart

Photo 5, photos 1 and 2: Photo by Ana Maria Vélez Wood

Page 5, photo 3: Photo by Dave Stewart

Page 7, photo 6: Richard Young/REX Shutterstock

Page 8, all photos: Photo by Dave Stewart

Page 9, photo 1: Photo by Anoushka Fisz

Page 10, photos 1 and 5: Photo by Anoushka Fisz

Page 10, photos 3, 4 and bottom left: Photo by Dave Stewart

Page 11, photos 1, 4, 5: Photo by Collin Stark

Page 11, photo 2: Photo by Frank Ockenfels

Page 12, photo 3: Photo by Kristin Burns

Page 13, photo 1 and 2: Photo by Michelle Shiers
Page 13, photo 4: Photo by Kristin Burns
Page 14, photo 1: Photo by Jeffrey Mayer/WireImage
Page 14, photo 2: Photo by Paul Boyd
Page 14, photo 4: Photo by Anoushka Fisz
Page 16: Photo by Michelle Shiers